Fortunate People in
a Fortunate Land

In the series *Urban Life, Landscape, and Policy,*
edited by David Stradling, Larry Bennett, and Davarian Baldwin.
Founding editor, Zane L. Miller.

A list of additional titles in this series appears at the back of this book.

Lauren E. M. Everett

Fortunate People in a Fortunate Land

At Home in Santa Monica's
Rent-Controlled Housing

TEMPLE UNIVERSITY PRESS
Philadelphia • *Rome* • *Tokyo*

TEMPLE UNIVERSITY PRESS
Philadelphia, Pennsylvania 19122
tupress.temple.edu

Library of Congress Cataloging-in-Publication Data

Names: Everett, Lauren Elizabeth Morrow, 1981– author.
Title: Fortunate people in a fortunate land : at home in Santa Monica's
    rent-controlled housing / Lauren E. M. Everett.
Other titles: Urban life, landscape, and policy.
Description: Philadelphia : Temple University Press, 2025. | Series: Urban
    life, landscape, and policy | Includes bibliographical references and
    index. | Summary: "Analyzes the experiences of tenants in
    rent-controlled housing and the implications of the author's findings
    for housing policy"— Provided by publisher.
Identifiers: LCCN 2025031072 (print) | LCCN 2025031073 (ebook) | ISBN
    9781439926284 (cloth) | ISBN 9781439926291 (paperback) | ISBN
    9781439926307 (pdf)
Subjects: LCSH: Rent control—California—Santa Monica—Case studies. |
    Apartment dwellers—California—Santa Monica—Case studies. | Housing
    policy—California—Santa Monica—Case studies.
Classification: LCC HD7288.85.U62 E94 2025 (print) | LCC HD7288.85.U62
    (ebook)
LC record available at https://lccn.loc.gov/2025031072
LC ebook record available at https://lccn.loc.gov/2025031073

The manufacturer's authorized representative in the EU for product safety is
Temple University Rome, Via di San Sebastianello, 16, 00187 Rome RM, Italy
(https://rome.temple.edu/).
tempress@temple.edu

9 8 7 6 5 4 3 2 1

Santa Monica Beach, early twentieth century. *(Albert M. Price Panoramic Photograph Collection, Library of Congress Prints and Photographic Division, Washington, DC.)*

For my mother, whose spirit inhabits this work
For my father, who at 83, still believes a better world is possible
For my hometown, populus felix in urbe felici

INITIATION SONG FROM THE FINDER'S LODGE
Please bring strong things.
Please come bringing new things.
Let very old things come into your hands.
Let what you do not know come into your eyes.
Let desert sand harden your feet.
Let the arch of your feet be the mountains.
Let the paths of your fingertips be your maps
And the ways you go be the lines on your palms.
Let there be deep snow in your inbreathing
And your outbreath be of shining ice.
May your mouth contain the shapes of strange words.
May you smell food cooking you have not eaten.
May the spring of a foreign river be your navel.
May your soul be at home where there are no houses.
Walk carefully, well loved one,
Walk mindfully, well loved one,
Walk fearlessly, well loved one.
Return with us, return to us,
Be always coming home.

—URSULA K. LE GUIN, *ALWAYS COMING HOME* (1985)

Contents

Preface

You Can't Go Home Anymore

My awareness of renters' rights as a concept started with some of my earliest memories. I was born in "The People's Republic of Santa Monica" in the summer of 1981. My parents were both nearly forty, and I was their first and only child. Both of them had been living what might be described at that time as a bohemian lifestyle, with progressive values that were often incongruent with their middle-class upbringings in Kansas City and Washington, DC. My dad was working as a lighting technician for film and television productions, and my mom was picking up work as a script supervisor and costumer. We lived right on the beach path, on the second story of a dilapidated old house surrounded by cottages inhabited by other people my parents knew from the industry. There were parties in the yard and surfboards on the fence, and a little pond with fish that our cat Mischa liked to catch and leave on our doorstep.

Shortly after moving to California in 1977, my mom started volunteering for the fledgling Santa Monicans for Renters Rights (SMRR), which was waging an aggressive campaign to pass rent control by local ballot measure. She was galvanized by an epidemic of condominium conversions that posed a threat to the city's large population of seniors, which was also the cause of my parent's eviction from their first rented beachfront home. This led my mom to testify in front of the city council in support of a moratorium on conversions, with a flower tucked behind her ear. She later became SMRR's first volunteer coordinator. As a child, I had little understanding of what

SMRR did; I mainly remember her friends, the lively parties, and the endless goodbyes at the end of the night.

My parents separated when I was almost three years old, and neither of them remarried. From that time forward, my mom and I lived in a house my parents owned in Venice, and my dad moved back to Santa Monica. After a brief tenure in a backyard cottage, he moved to a rent-controlled apartment building a few blocks from the Third Street Promenade, where he would live for over thirty years. When I started middle school, his residence in Santa Monica gave me access to public schools that were considered much higher quality than the Los Angeles Unified School District options by our Venice home. While some of my Santa Monica school friends' families owned their homes, more often they were working class and lived in rent-controlled apartments. Like my dad, some of their parents lived in their apartment homes for many decades.

Santa Monica felt boring as a teenager, though in retrospect, it was a pretty decent place to grow up. It still had a 1960s vibe, with midcentury diners, dingbat apartment buildings, and a sort of sleepy feel. At the same time, it *was* the mid-90s, and the Third Street Promenade was a wealth of record shops, vintage clothing stores, and anything else a thirteen-year-old who played guitar in a punk band could want. There were also a few classic coffee houses scattered throughout the city and one decent music venue. Overall, though, it still felt like the suburbs, and my friends and I preferred Hollywood and Downtown Los Angeles where the excitement was. Venice felt equally dead in terms of culture, and the beach generally held little interest for me as a sullen teen.

After attending film school in Brooklyn and Austin, I returned to Los Angeles in my early twenties and lived with my mom for several months while I looked for an apartment. During this time, one of the largest lockout eviction events in Los Angeles history happened just a few blocks from our home, in the Lincoln Place apartments. Almost all of the eight hundred apartments in the 1951 development were sitting empty by the time I moved back, and it was devastating for the community. Some of the former residents were still engaged in a lengthy legal battle with the owners, and I reached out to offer support. This was the beginning of my interest in tenants' rights. A few months after I moved back to Los Angeles, I found a cheap apartment in the Sunset Junction area of Silver Lake, which was still in midstage gentrification. The neighborhood was a mix of low-income immigrant families, "creatives," white-collar professionals, and longtime LGBTQIA residents, and this diversity was evident in the array of businesses on Sunset Boulevard. Almost all the residents in my sixteen-apartment 1928 building were Latino families, living in studios the same size as mine. The building was rent-stabilized (Los Angeles uses a different term), and I paid $690 when I moved in and $820 when I moved out nine years later. Over those years, I saw the neighborhood change significantly, becoming more upscale, while most of the families in my building remained.

I moved to Portland in early 2014 and have lived in my North Portland rental home since then. Shortly after moving to Oregon, I was shocked to learn how little protections tenants had compared to in the City of Los Angeles. I started volunteering with the Community Alliance of Tenants, where I worked on the renters' rights hotline and then spent the summer as the hotline supervisor. Over these two years, I talked to hundreds of renters who were deeply stressed and scared, and whose lives were in upheaval due to the lack of protective policies and resources to enforce what parts of the law *were* on their side. I later joined the Organizing Committee of the city-wide tenants union—Portland Tenants United—where I hoped to have more impact on improving conditions for the city's renters.

Just as I graduated from Portland State University, with a master's in urban studies, my mother became terminally ill, and I began splitting my time between Los Angeles and Portland. I decided to use this time as an opportunity to support local advocacy efforts to pass Proposition 10, which would have overturned a California state law called the Costa-Hawkins Rental Housing Act, allowing local jurisdictions to expand and strengthen rent control. Drawing on my background in documentary photography, I began interviewing and photographing people who lived in rent-controlled homes all over the Los Angeles area. I talked to about twenty individuals and couples of all ages, races, and ethnicities.

In doing this project, I gained a deeper understanding of the policy's strengths and limitations. I was inspired by what I learned: rent control and other tenant protections had profound positive impacts on these individuals' lives. Stable housing meant the ability to really put down roots in the community and opened up possibilities in life. I also heard about the enormous stress of potentially losing a home to which one holds not only an emotional attachment but a material and financial one as well. As I watched the debate about rent control unfold in real time around Proposition 10, it became apparent that what I was seeing on the ground was missing from academic research about the policy, which has shaped popular conceptions and misconceptions. Excited about this insight into a policy about which much ink has been spilled, but nuanced understanding is still limited, I decided to pursue doctoral studies at Portland State University using the interview project as a template for my dissertation research.

My mother passed away in early November 2018. My dad and I spent the evening before canvassing for Proposition 10, knocking on doors in Mar Vista by the house where she lived temporarily after being displaced from a Santa Monica sublet. The house where I grew up was torn down earlier that year, my beloved childhood neighborhood diner, the Cafe 50s, closed, and Venice and Santa Monica are now two of the most expensive rental markets in the Los Angeles area. I am forever priced out of my home environment, which has changed beyond recognition. It feels unbelievable that my family ever lived by the beach—now exclusively the purview of the wealthy. Today I live in a home I've made in a house I rent, in an expensive West Coast city where homeownership is no longer financially accessible for even many middle-class households. I feel mostly secure, protected by both Oregon's moderate rent control law and my neutral relationship with my property manager. But like all renters, I live with the knowledge that I could lose it all if my landlord decides they really want me out.

The housing researcher Jim Kemeny, whose ideas about *how* housing is studied are the epistemological foundation of this book, wrote that "science is not a neutral and purely cerebral exercise. It must rather be understood as a socially embedded act in which involvement and detachment interfold in complex ways."[1] This is the spirit in which I share my autobiographical history. My experience with profound environmental change, my feelings of deep attachment to different places, my many years as a renter in three U.S. cities, and my ability to form empathetic connections with others are the foundation of my approach. Participants shared many things that resonated with my experience as a renter: the risk assessment before asking for a repair, the stress of not knowing if you'll still be in your home in a year, the willingness to invest time and money in improving it anyway because it's still your home. As the first academic study to consider rent control from the vantage of the tenant's experience, my intent is to add a fresh and much-needed perspective to the debate around this policy. I hope it will be useful for academics and students who study housing policy, community development, environmental psychology, political economy, and sociology, and for policymakers. But more than anything, I hope it will be of value to my fellow renters, with whom I am united in solidarity and struggle. Together, we can control the rent.

Acknowledgments

There are so many people without whom this research and book would not exist. The first is Dr. Karen Gibson, professor emeritus at Portland State University, chair of my master's committee, and author of several important works about systemic segregation and disinvestment in Portland's Black community. I never imagined myself as the type of person that belonged in a Ph.D. program until Karen invited me to present my initial research in one of her classes, and encouraged me to pursue a doctorate. Our conversations about property capitalism—and the knowledge she shared with me about the spatialization of race, in particular—illuminated the political economy of urban spaces in a way that made the pieces fall together.

I'm deeply grateful and endlessly thrilled that Temple University Press took on the publication of this work. It is surreal to be on the same press as a classic work like *Critical Perspectives on Housing*. The editor-in-chief Aaron Javsicas and the staff have been patient and helpful with my questions, and guidance from my editor David Stradling and the peer readers have strengthened the work considerably.

The twenty Los Angeles area renters I interviewed in 2018, and the stories they shared, inspired me to pursue my doctorate, and directly informed the design of this research. Thank you for letting a stranger into your home. Similarly, this work wouldn't exist without the generosity of the participants in this study, some of whom shared difficult, painful, and personal experiences with the intention of helping maintain and improve tenant protections in Santa Monica and life in the city, more broadly. Thank you for your service; this Santa Monican salutes you.

I can't remember a time before I knew the term "renters' rights." What a gift to have been raised with the value of housing as a human right—not just in theory but in praxis. This has been fundamental to my understanding of the world, and how I want to be in it. Thank you, mom. And to my dad, for remaining a true believer in SMRR's vision and sharing his memories and knowledge with me. Thank you also to my mom's dear friend Cheryl Rhoden for graciously agreeing to check my work on the Santa Monica history, and to Cheryl, Denny Zane, and Michael Tarbet for their support throughout.

I also want to acknowledge the hundreds of Santa Monicans who fought tenaciously over the years to maintain tenant protection policies, without which my dad likely would not have been able to continue living in the city, and I would not have attended Santa Monica's excellent public schools. All those thousands of hours—copying flyers, canvassing, doing literature drops in the middle of the night—have a real material impact on people's lives, even now, forty-five years later. What a truly beautiful way to be in service to your community.

So many thinkers have inspired me, catalyzing various revelations and connections in my brain and shaping my understanding of the world. I proudly stand on their shoulders with this work: Nicholas Blomley, Anne Buttimer, Desiree Fields, Mindy Fullilove, Karen Gibson, David Harvey, Dolores Hayden, Kath Hulse, Amanda Huron, Jim Kemeny, Maria Lewicka, Lynn Manzo, David Madden, Peter Marcuse, Melinda Milligan, Allan Morris, Hal Pawson, Susan Saegert, Sharon Zukin, and many others.

My fantastic dissertation committee—Drs. Moriah McSherry McGrath, Amie Thurber and Greg Townley—shared feedback and critique that pushed me in just the right ways, bringing perspectives from their respective fields of urban studies, social work, and community psychology. My deepest gratitude to my dissertation chair, Dr. Sy Adler, for all of the above plus being a beacon of light when I was lost at sea in the turbulent waters of academia. I would not have completed the program without him taking a chance on me.

Last, to all of the tenant organizers I've met and learned from over the past ten years, I couldn't possibly have had a better education about what it means to be a renter in America than from y'all. For my comrades in Portland Tenants United, the Autonomous Tenants Union Network, the Los Angeles Tenants Union, and many other groups I've interacted with, your dedication to housing justice for your communities, friends, neighbors, and families lights the way. Thank you.

Fortunate People in
a Fortunate Land

Introduction

People, Not Housing

The observer who explores place speaks of housing, whereas the resident of that place lives the process of dwelling.

—Anne Buttimer, "Home, Reach and a Sense of Place"[1]

It's high summer, and Santa Monica's Ocean Front Walk is thronged with people of all ages, races, and ethnicities, clad in everything from bikinis to burkas. Walking the length of the path, you might hear a dozen languages spoken, as tourists and locals blend together: gliding by on bikes, rollerblades and skates, Segways, wheelchairs, and skateboards, running, walking, and, occasionally, breakdancing. From a row of immaculately restored classic cars in the parking lot—their suspensions lowered as far as they can possibly go—emits the sweet sounds of Art Laboe's golden oldies, piped through a stereo system with a serious subwoofer. The Ferris wheel spins on the pier, and perhaps you hear carousel music spilling softly out of the historic Looff Hippodrome. In the distance, the ocean shimmers, stretching endlessly to the horizon, dotted with tiny sails and the shapes of surfers in their wetsuits. Palm trees sway in the coastal breeze, their fronds making a rushing water sound like the inside of a shell, as the smell of creosote from the pier fills the air.

Two miles east, school is out for the summer at John Adams Middle School, but the pergola outside the cafeteria is buzzing with activity as people arrive for the annual Santa Monicans for Renters Rights (SMRR) convention. This year members will hear candidate speeches and arguments for and against various ballot measures before casting their votes for who will receive the organization's coveted endorsements. At stake this year are seats on the city council, the rent control board (RCB), and the school board. At the door, volunteers offer stickers and literature to support the various candidates while old friends greet each other warmly. Inside the cafeteria, a few hundred Santa Monicans sit in folding chairs, converse with each other, and cast their votes. The candidates emphasize their connections to the city: attending public schools, legacy small family businesses, length of tenure, and, above all, their loyalty to SMRR and its ideals. Longtime SMRR leaders and volunteers circulate through the crowd making sure everything is running smoothly and occasionally making announcements in front of the room. There is a general spirit of camaraderie and familiarity, and the occasional quip from the crowd provokes a wave of laughter.

SMRR cochair Denny Zane introduces a motion to endorse Proposition 10. This California ballot initiative would enable Santa Monica to return its rent control law to something closer to its original form. A motion in support from a woman named Sylvia lists the many reasons why strengthening and expanding the existing law is crucial. Jay provides a counterpoint, arguing that it will only worsen the housing affordability crisis by forcing landlords to take their properties off the market. The motion to support Proposition 10 then goes to a vote, as someone yells out "the rents are too damn high!" and the crowd cheers. Members vote "yes" or "no" by raising red cards, and Zane declares, "the 'ayes' have it, SMRR will endorse Prop 10."*

This convention has taken place every year since SMRR's take over began in 1979, with a series of dramatic electoral victories that made headlines nationwide. This tiny revolution not only brought strict rent control to the small coastal city, which was 81% renters at the time it began; it was also the catalyst for a holistic progressive vision and a new era of participatory democracy and civic engagement in the city. Over forty years later, Santa Monica is probably better known within the Los Angeles area for its expansive public beach, pier amusement park, and astronomical rents. Yet, for the thousands of Santa Monica residents who are able to remain in their homes by way of the city's tenant protections and resources, SMRR's legacy remains integral to their continued residency in the city. One of the underlying questions I address in this book is, To what extent does this vision endure more than forty years on? How do tenant protections like rent control play out "on the ground," in tenants' actual lives?

In her seminal essay, "Home, Reach and a Sense of Place," the geographer Anne Buttimer wrote, "Before one leaps into issues of planning policy it would be vital, it seems to me, to understand the fundamental life processes which are at stake and are vulnerable to changes in the physical and political identity of place." In the human-centered spirit of the distinction Buttimer articulated between the dynamic lived experience of home in all

---

* This vignette of the 2018 SMRR convention was created from several recordings and my memory of the event.

Figure I.1 Ocean Front Walk, looking westward from Bernard Way. *(Author's collection.)*

its scales (the "insider's" view) and the planner's or policymaker's focus on housing and other technical concerns (the "outsider's" view), thirty Santa Monicans' stories are the heart of this book. Interviews with these renters are supported by the historical context around property rights and tenancy in the United States, a review of the city's history of protenant policymaking, and insights into the culture of the real estate investment industry. In my analysis, I show how these external elements inform the experience of living in rent-controlled housing in Santa Monica. I also explore how these external factors impact the experience of being "at home" in rent-controlled housing.

Ramona, who is in her sixties, has lived in Santa Monica her entire life. For the past twelve years, she has shared a two-bedroom duplex in the Pico Neighborhood with the five members of her multigenerational household, where they host community events and care for a vibrant flower garden beloved by passersby. Katya grew up in a rent-controlled apartment in the Bay Area after immigrating to the United States from Eastern Europe with her family. Now in her thirties, for the past five years, she's lived by herself in a one-bedroom apartment in the Pico Neighborhood. She is highly engaged in Santa Monica's civic life, spending a great deal of her free time volunteering for various committees to improve life for the community. Dave, an artist and art professor, has lived in his home in the Pico Neighborhood for two decades. Over the years, he transformed what was once a ramshackle bungalow into a charming home with a porch, loft, and other improvements. Vanessa also used her professional skills from working in the art department field of the film and television industry to extensively renovate, over the years, her home of over four decades in Mid-City. She initially moved to Santa Monica in the late 1970s so her son could attend the highly regarded public schools. She is also active in the community. Patrick worked in the school district's custodial department for decades. He retired two years ago at age sixty and feels fortunate to be able to continue living in the city in his home of four decades.

At Home in Santa Monica's Rent-Controlled Housing

This book is a case study on the experiences of low- and middle-income households who reside in rent-controlled private market housing in Santa Monica. In its most basic definition, a case study is a type of research design that explores an issue through one or more distinct cases. It entails the triangulation of multiple sources of information, such as observations, interviews, audiovisuals, documents and reports, participant observations, and physical artifacts. Case studies are often the preferred method when "how" or "why" questions are being posed; the researcher is not attempting to control events, as in the case of an experimental design; and the topic is a contemporary phenomenon.[2]

Social scientists have studied Santa Monica as an exemplary case of a protenant government with bold progressive policy since the initial tenant coup in 1979. At the same time, deregulation legislation at the state level—

combined with speculative investment in the local real estate market—has seriously eroded the radical potential of the city's original policy, threatening its progressive community vision. Though Santa Monica continues to have tenant protections and resources far beyond those of most urban areas, and the tenant lobby held the majority power in city government for most of the past four decades, the rental housing market is also one of the most expensive in the Los Angeles area. As such, the contemporary city is one in which low- and moderate-income residents live in below-market housing alongside affluent—and often transient—millennials and zoomers working in the tech and entertainment sectors, in a community that is bifurcated along socioeconomic lines.

The city's neighborhoods are also distinctive, reflecting the economic diversity of its residents. The historically working-class Pico Neighborhood has the city's highest concentration of residents of color, along with well-preserved "old Santa Monica" establishments like McCabe's Guitar Shop, UnUrban Coffee House, and the Daily Pint. Just a few miles away, the upscale Montana Avenue with its expensive boutiques and restaurants borders the Wilmont neighborhood, and the high-end hotels and restaurants on nearby Ocean Avenue cater to wealthy tourists and locals. While the Pico Neighborhood is characterized by some of the city's more affordable multifamily housing and modest single-family homes mixed with commercial buildings, the area north of Montana is occupied exclusively by expensive single-family homes with manicured landscaping.

The primary data in this study are thirty in-depth interviews with Santa Monica renters. Participants were selected for demographic variation in race, ethnicity, and age, length of tenure (at least three years in the current home), immigrant status, household size, and income level. The maximum income threshold was set at $100,000 annually, which approximates the area median household income of $92,490. Participant recruitment was conducted on social media, through civic groups, within my personal network, by snowball sampling, targeted mailing, and posting flyers at high-traffic locations in Santa Monica in the late winter and early spring of 2021.

All interviews took place in the months of March through May 2021 on Zoom, due to the pandemic and my university's restrictions on in-person research. Though conducting the interviews remotely was less than ideal, the ubiquity of video communication platforms like Zoom, during this time period, meant that participants were generally comfortable with this method, and we were able to have substantive conversations that ranged from about forty-five minutes to two hours. I had expected to hear that some participants had experienced stress with their living situations, due to having to spend so much time at home, or difficulty paying rent, with pandemic-related income loss. Instead, several participants' connections with and appreciation for their homes, neighborhoods, and neighbors had deepened during that first year. Some found solace in aspects of their living environment that they had not noticed before, like local plant life and nearby parks. No one reported that their living situation had worsened due to the challenges of that first year.

Participants span many decades in age, from thirty to eighty-eight years old. They live in every neighborhood in Santa Monica, though the Pico Neighborhood and Wilmont are more heavily represented. Their household incomes range from under $20,000 to $100,000. The length of tenure in the home ranges from three to over forty years. The average household size is 1.7 people, and some of them live with partners and/or children, some with roommates, and others live alone. Six of the participants grew up in Santa Monica and three others are from the immediate area. Seven individuals were born outside of the United States, and five are first-generation Americans. One-third identify as Latino, while just over half are white and the remainder identify as Asian or mixed race. All names have been changed to protect participant anonymity.

These interviews are supported by additional materials that provide the context necessary for understanding the individual residential experience. These include a historical review of relevant policymaking in the study area, summaries of government resources and tenant education materials, a review of two years of the landlord industry publication, *Apartment Age*, and interviews with tenant attorneys, advocates, and City staff. These materials were reviewed and analyzed before doing the interviews, enabling me to bring a deeper understanding of Santa Monica's contemporary policy and political and sociological landscape to the process. I analyzed the interview transcripts with ATLAS.ti, a qualitative data analysis software, using social science research coding techniques to look for themes across the interviews. I used an "open coding" or "initial coding" approach, which entails line-by-line coding that considers any and all elements of interest. Other coding strategies at this phase included "descriptive coding," "emotion coding," and "values coding."[3] In the final phase of analysis, themes from all of the materials were synthesized to identify two groups of factors that impact the feeling of being at home.

As social science researchers Wayne Booth, Gregory Colomb, and Joseph Williams wrote in their seminal guide to research design, "You have no research problem until you know the cost of your incomplete knowledge or flawed understanding, a cost that you define in terms of a yet greater ignorance or misunderstanding."[4] The breadth of what we *don't* know about how rent control works is a serious obstacle to understanding its strengths and weaknesses. Answering sociologist Jim Kemeny's call for a "sociology of residence," my research draws from theoretical frameworks in environmental and community psychology, sociology, and cultural geography to explore the nuances of individuals' lived experiences. The intention is to develop an understanding of the material conditions, events, perceptions, interpretations, and subsequent behaviors of tenants living in market rental housing with rent control and other tenant protections, and how they relate to those protections. Additionally, this book provides insights into the efficacy of Santa Monica's value-driven protenant programming.

I ask two overarching questions in this book. First, I use concepts like "dwelling," "residential alienation," and "place alienation" to understand the extent to which individuals feel at home or not at home and what factors contribute to those experiences. This means examining aspects of the participant's relationship with their home environment on multiple scales (residence, building, neighborhood, and city) to understand their holistic relationship to place. Second, I explore the nexus of these experiences with Santa Monica's tenant protection policies, infrastructure, and resources,* and the extent to which they inform stability—both perceived and actual—and life decisions. I identify the importance of three additional factors that shape the residential experience: the rental/real estate market, local sociopolitical ideology about renting, and the personality and business model of the landlord or property manager. In asking these questions, I seek to understand the residential experience in this specific local context, how it relates to policy and other externalities, and how those experiences impact the lives of renter households. While case studies are not generalizable in the way that experimental research design is, this book offers insights about rent control and other protenant policies that may be applicable to other locales.

In this book, I identify some previously unexamined positive outcomes of tenant protections that benefit both the individual household and the community as a whole. I also illustrate how the policy functions in some of the more obvious material ways (e.g., longevity of tenure, less rent burden). At the same time, elements like policy loopholes and landlord behavior have the potential to critically undermine these policies' intended outcomes. Despite these challenges, these tenants have strong attachments to their home environments and deploy a repertoire of coping strategies to maintain their sense of being at home in their residences when faced with precarity and other housing-related stresses. Their tenacity and resilience is a testament to the bonds they have with their homes, neighbors, community, neighborhood, and city.

---

* Henceforth referred to as "tenant protections." These protections include rent control, "just-cause" eviction policy, anti-harassment legislation, mediation programs, tenant education resources, and support offered by various city agencies.

"Everybody Knows" or "It's Just ECON 101"

Social scientists and practitioners in the social services sector widely acknowledge the importance of safe and stable housing for mental health, physical health and general well-being. In addition to positive outcomes for individuals and households, they also believe housing stability fosters strong and vibrant communities. Harvard housing researcher Matthew Desmond writes, "Residential stability begets a kind of psychological stability, which allows people to place an emotional investment in their home, social relationships, and community and promotes subjective well-being based on empathy and reciprocity."[5] However, one-third of Americans rent their homes, and many renter households experience housing-related stress due to a range of factors. These include inequitable relationships with landlords or property managers, unregulated rents, poor housing conditions, and the threat of eviction without cause.

In light of this, it's logical to theorize that households residing in localities with *stronger* tenant protections may experience the positive outcomes of safe and stable housing, without as much precarity and other stressors that characterize the experience of renting. In the long term, these outcomes might include the ability for renter households to remain in gentrified neighborhoods they would otherwise be priced out of, increased opportunities (such as career or educational paths), deeper connections to their communities, more equitable relationships with their landlords and property managers, protection from evictions, and an overall sense of stability in their housing. At the same time, policies intended to support renters might fall short of their intended effects due to inadequate enforcement resources, unclear guidelines, and other deficiencies.

Rent control (or "rent stabilization," depending on the location) is the most well-known tenant protection policy, aside from the "implied warranty of habitability," that underpins landlord-tenant law in the United States. Santa Monica voters passed the city's rent control charter amendment in 1979, and they have amended it eight times since. The main features of the rent control law, which remain unchanged, are regulations around how much rent can be raised annually* and restrictions on the circumstances in which a household's tenancy can be terminated. These are the two universal elements of rent control. Property owners also have the right to a "fair return" on their real estate investment, as outlined in both the U.S. Constitution and the California constitution. This means owners may petition for a rent increase if they are able to establish that the rent is not covering their

---

* In Santa Monica, this is primarily based on 75% of the change in the consumer price index (CPI).

operating expenses, including capital improvements. "Pass-throughs" are also allowed for certain fees, including the annual registration fee that funds the rent control program's administration.

Rent control has existed in several different forms over the course of the nation's history. These range from the "first-generation" regulations of World War II, which were much stricter limitations than any rent control policies that exist in the United States today and included total freezes on rent increases. The "second-generation" rent control policies of the 1970s were generally viewed as more moderate, setting the amount the rent can increase annually rather than freezing increases altogether. However, some localities—including Santa Monica and nearby West Hollywood—had a stricter form of rent control. This type of rent control allowed for increases that were substantially lower than the CPI, included vacancy control—meaning landlords weren't permitted to raise rents to market rates between tenancies—and had tenant-majority rent boards to administer the law.[6]

All jurisdictions in California with local rent control laws have been required to implement vacancy *decontrol* since legislators passed the Costa-Hawkins Rental Housing Act in 1995, which has weakened the impact of local control as rents steadily climb with tenant turnover. California's Ellis Act also emerged from the conservative and centrist backlash against the second-generation rent control movement and has played an equally detrimental role in blunting the impact of local rent control laws. However, for the past ten years there has been a surge of activism and advocacy around rent control and other tenant protection policies both in the United States and internationally. For the previous several decades tenant advocacy in the United States had primarily been the purview of nonprofit organizations, but, by the mid-2010s, there had been a proliferation of grassroots organizing and tenant unions in response to rising rents, harassment, and poor housing conditions. The Crown Heights Tenant Union in Brooklyn was founded in 2013, the Los Angeles Tenants Union (LATU) was established in 2015 and now has almost fifteen locals, Portland Tenants United in Oregon was founded in 2016, the Washington, DC, group Stomp Out Slumlords emerged in 2017, and the Bay Area tenant union Tenants and Neighborhood Councils formed in 2019—to name a few. Meanwhile, nonprofit groups like California's Tenants Together, the Alliance of Californians for Community Action, and the Los Angeles–based Coalition for Economic Survival have worked in tandem with or alongside grassroots tenant unions to advocate for rent control and other tenant protections.

In 2019, Oregon became the first state in the nation to enact a moderate version of rent control at the state level, with California following shortly thereafter. That same year, the city council in Inglewood, California, unanimously approved an emergency interim rent control ordinance to address concerns about rent increases and displacement related to the football stadium that was under construction. They later made it permanent, with some adjustments. The economic inequalities laid bare in the pandemic era only fueled this third wave. According to Diane Yentel, the director of the National Low Income Housing Coalition, over 270 new tenant protections have been enacted nationwide since 2021 at the local and state levels.[7] In November 2021, voters in St. Paul, Minnesota, approved a rent control ballot measure. The proposed policy included vacancy control—limiting rent increases *between* tenancies to 3%—and didn't exclude new buildings or properties owned by mom-and-pop landlords. The original ordinance would have been the strongest rent control law in the United States, but it was later modified significantly by the city council.* In the same election, Minneapolis voters approved a ballot measure directing the city council to develop a rent control policy.† Voters in Santa Ana, California passed a rent control initiative in the fall of 2021, and the newly elected Boston Mayor Michelle Wu included rent control in her campaign platform in that same election cycle.‡ The following year, voters in Pasadena, California, approved a rent control ordinance. It was supported by only one member of the city council.

Yet despite the resurgence in popular support for rent control and other tenant protections, its proponents continue to face fierce opposition from both policymakers and the real estate investment lobby. Many of the challenges the policy's advocates face are due to the fact that the vast majority of the research about rent control is from the field of economics. This research is quantitative, uses large existing datasets ("big data") that aren't designed or collected to answer their research questions, and is situated within an economic framework in which housing is a commodity resource. The economists' bias toward free markets means that the majority of research on rent control can be used to support an argument opposing rent control. Their orientation against the policy has featured prominently in public discourse around it, with rent control's detractors stating that economists agree it doesn't work. In this scenario, opponents evoke economists' arguments as a means to bring an end to the discussion. For example, in a news release responding to President Biden's announcement that affordable

---

* The city council amended the proposed ordinance to be substantially more moderate, with an exemption for properties less than twenty years of age (more than the standard fifteen years), partial vacancy decontrol (increases of 8% plus CPI permitted between tenancies), and a process for landlords to request an exception to the 3% annual increase cap based on the right to a reasonable return on investment.

† The city council has not moved forward with referring a rent control policy to the ballot due to internal opposition, most notably from the mayor.

‡ In 2024, the mayor championed a bill in the state legislature to exempt Boston from the statewide preemption on local rent control ordinances.

housing funded by the Low-Income Housing Tax Credit (LIHTC) program will now be subject to a 10% annual cap on rent increases, Adam DeSanctis of the Mortgage Bankers Association wrote, "Now is not the time to repeat a policy widely recognized as a failure at the local, national, and global level by nearly every economist."* [8]

In this popular framing, economists are recognized as the undisputed experts on housing policy. The conclusion that rent control is an ineffective policy is presented as almost self-evident—as something "everybody knows." This kind of rhetoric is what economist John Kenneth Galbraith described as *conventional wisdom*. Conventional wisdom describes the way in which, over time, knowledge about a given subject becomes calcified to the extent that those who hold the conventional view are able to simply dismiss counterarguments without truly engaging with them. Opponents of rent control, who offer familiar concepts like the law of supply and demand, "are able to say that the challengers of conventional wisdom have not mastered their intricacies. Indeed, these ideas can only be appreciated by a stable, orthodox and patient man—in brief, by someone who closely resembles the man of conventional wisdom."[9] In this sense, debates about rent control that hinge on economic concepts and research and little else tend to contain a kind of intellectual gaslighting.

While economists make valuable contributions to our understanding of financial markets and other macrolevel market phenomena, economic inquiry alone is unable to tell us everything we need to know about housing policy. First, researchers that use large quantitative datasets in their design are unable to identify rent control's positive outcomes beyond the relationships between variables like demographics, length of tenure, and rents. To be sure, some elements of the value an individual or household derives from the place where they live *are* quantifiable—such as the percentage of their income they have left after paying rent—but, for the most part, there is simply no way to explore the complexity of the human experience with census data and complex quantitative analysis. For example, this kind of research is unable to capture the benefits of an apartment building's social network to individual households—especially low-income ones. This kind of question—qualitative in nature—complicates the economists' belief that a healthy housing market is one in which renters are mobile in response to changes in household composition and other factors. The overreliance on this approach in the housing studies field has critically limited our understanding about both what it means to actually *live* in this housing and, by extension, its positive impacts on the individual, family, and community.

---

* It's worth mentioning that the Mortgage Bankers Association's opposition to this policy change is due not to how well rent control supports tenants but rather to how it impacts the financial sector. As is typical of this discourse, that is never actually stated.

The second shortcoming of relying on the economic lens is the ideology underpinning mainstream economics and by extension, research on this topic. Arguments against rent control are often grounded in the assertion that the policy interferes with the free market. This is predicated on the belief that the relationship between supply and demand in the housing market is as simple as what students learn in high school economics (what I call the "it's just ECON 101" argument), and thus market activity for housing "units"* follows the same rules that apply to iPhones or running shoes. Proponents of this theory often cite government regulation as the primary obstacle to an equilibrium between supply and demand. They implore policymakers to allow the benevolent hand of the free market to do its work by removing "artificial" constraints, making it easier to build. In their view, this would result in everyone living in housing that suits their needs.

This logic holds both that there is only one housing market in each location and that it's a market with perfectly competitive conditions by the standards of classical economic theory. Neither of these things are true. Housing in any urban location is composed of housing submarkets that vary by price; type, size, and mix of housing; and neighborhood characteristics. An oversimplified supply and demand model that treats housing "units" like identical commodities cannot account for this complexity. That's why a two-bedroom, one thousand square foot house in one area of a city or region doesn't cost the same as a similar house in another location.[†]

Leaving that complication aside, the competitive conditions necessary for rents to respond to changes in the supply of rental housing and reach equilibrium—as may be the case with the production of widgets—do not exist. Housing scholars Richard Appelbaum and John Gilderbloom reviewed each of the seven conditions necessary for this outcome and found that rental housing markets don't meet even one. These conditions include the absence of collusion,[‡] entry into and exit from the market being free for both producers and consumers, housing being a homogeneous commodity, and both parties possessing perfect knowledge of the market to take advantage of the opportunity to increase profit or utility. The authors conclude, "In crucial respects rental housing markets are not perfectly competitive, and

---

* I only use the word "unit" to describe housing or a home when quoting or referring to someone else, as I believe it represents a dehumanizing commodity view of housing.

† Boston's Metropolitan Area Planning Council created an excellent resource for understanding housing submarkets. Available at https://housing-submarkets.mapc.org/.

‡ In 2024 there were successful lawsuits against both the National Association of Realtors, for setting standard agent commissions, and Yardi Systems Inc. and RealPage, property management software companies that have enabled property owners to set rent levels collectively. The RealPage lawsuit was initiated by the U.S. Department of Justice on the grounds that the software was violating antitrust laws.

as a consequence, rents will not respond in any straightforward manner to changes in supply." They confirm this with a quantitative analysis using census data.[10]

This commodity framing is the rhetoric of the real estate investment industry. Its logic has permeated the research around rent control, and by extension, the public debate around how it functions. Economist Lisa Sturtevant's comprehensive review of the existing research on rent control, commissioned by the National Multifamily Housing Council (a trade organization for landlords) Research Foundation, identifies several themes: targeting housing benefits, allocating units, maintenance and building quality, housing availability, rent levels, fiscal impacts, and homelessness.[11] While most of these aspects are worthy of consideration, there's a notable absence of inquiry around the psychosocial benefits of the policy to the household and community. Instead, economists are primarily interested in the distribution of housing as a commodity good, the financial and physical implications of said distribution, and whether a household is or isn't housed—a binary without nuance.

"Housing misallocation" is one of the most interesting constructs to emerge from this line of inquiry. The idea of misallocation is situated in the belief that each housing "unit" has a perfect consumer, and the Pareto optimal scenario is when the two are matched. The goal is to avoid "overconsumption" of the product. This necessarily entails households changing residences whenever life circumstances shift—for example, in the event of a marriage or birth of a child. Harvard economist Edward Glaeser summarizes this concept by explaining, "A major social cost of rent control is that without a fully operational price mechanism the 'wrong' consumers end up using the apartments." In this view, imperfect allocation means that people who "gain little utility from renting" will continue to do so, while others who "desire [the units] greatly" will not have access to them.[12] In a later work on misallocation in New York City's rent-controlled housing, Glaeser and economist Erzo Luttmer conclude that 21% of apartments "are in the wrong hands," meaning they are inhabited by households with fewer members than the number of bedrooms. This effect increases with the number of years a tenant has resided in their home, which the authors theorize may be attributed to changing family composition over time.[13]

In a similar vein, economists Morten Skak and Gintautas Bloze compare welfare effects between rent control and rent stabilization within different U.S. localities, finding housing "overallocations" and "underallocations" according to household size and square meters. In their analysis, this means that households are living in the "wrong" homes because the pairing between the number of residents and the size of the dwelling isn't optimal.[14] This narrow frame of analysis treats rental homes as interchangeable commodity goods, where the only relevant features are the number of inhabitants and size. It completely overlooks the neighborhood context, social networks, proximity to employment or school, place attachment, uses households might have for additional living space, and favorable physical characteristics like abundant natural light or historic character. While this is partially due to the limitations of quantitative research—especially that which relies on existing datasets like the census—the bigger issue is the problematic assumption about right and "wrong" consumers. It aims to reduce the complexity of the human experience and the making of a home to a mathematical equation.

This logic also ignores the fact that misallocation happens *without* the presence of rent control. In expensive rental markets, households are faced with limitations and advantages relative to the price of rents and their household incomes, combined with the high costs of moving. Meanwhile, higher-income households may be able to afford rental homes with more bedrooms than they need. Again, this is because perfectly competitive conditions do not exist. One of the strangest things about the belief that rent control introduces market distortions that otherwise wouldn't exist is that anyone who reads the news or had tried to rent or buy a home in most urban centers knows that the free market is failing to provide housing for low- and moderate-income households all over America, most of which does not have rent control. What's more, in most places, there is no penalty for a property owner leaving their property empty as long as it doesn't become a public nuisance. This is because the real estate investment market doesn't actually exist to provide housing for every American; it exists to make money for investors.

While what we know about rent control through academic research is already limited by economists' focus on the "sticks and bricks" of housing over the people who live in it, there are a few recent studies that also made bold claims about the policy while ignoring the role of important contextual factors. In Sturtevant's literature review, the "housing availability" category of research refers to the studies finding that rent control reduces housing and increases rents due to the practice of landlords converting their rent-controlled property to other uses to maximize profit. In 2018, Stanford Business School economists Rebecca Diamond, Tim McQuade, and Franklin Qian made waves with their widely publicized study about the outcomes of rent control in San Francisco.[15] Interestingly, for a study that is critical of the policy, the authors concede that rent control mitigates displacement, particularly for people of color. They also identify a 15% reduction in the rent-controlled housing stock—correctly attributing these reductions to landlord-speculators taking advantage of legal loopholes at the state and local levels, with the Ellis Act and owner move-ins, respectively—in addition to legally permitted buyout offers (which may or may not have included harassment).

Having laid out some important macrolevel data about how the policy functions, they leap to several unsupported conclusions. First, the authors argue that rent control contributed to the gentrification of San Francisco due to the 15% reduction. They further claim that rent control increased income inequality in the city due to its effect of limiting the displacement of presumably low-income minority households while attracting higher-income households who moved into the newly converted condominiums (yes, they are saying *these* condominiums are what attracted wealthy people to the city). Last, they assert that rents in the city are higher across the board due to the 15% reduction, without accounting for new housing, the constraints on development presented by the city's physical form, or all the other reasons rents increase, such as the desirability of a location. While rent control's detractors triumphantly point to this study as evidence that the policy doesn't work, the more logical conclusion is that speculator-investors' desire to maximize profits, enabled by *loopholes*, is what isn't working. Rent-seeking behavior is a given.

Media coverage of this study mostly centered on the finding that "rent control doesn't work," while ignoring the mechanisms through which the 15% reduction in rent-controlled housing was enabled, in addition to the positive findings around the prevention of displacement and preservation of diversity. Even liberal news platforms adopted this framing. Diamond was interviewed for an edition of National Public Radio's *Here & Now Anytime*, which summarized her findings as showing how, "in the long run, rent control drove up rents because it led a number of landlords to convert their housing to other uses." In her interview, Diamond suggested it's unfair to expect landlords to bear the cost of preventing displacement. Instead, taxpayers should fund more rental subsidies for low-income families. At no point in the broadcast did she use the words "Ellis Act" or offer any explanation about *how* property owners circumvent the spirit of this law.[16] The paper's impact on the public discourse led the California renters' rights organization Tenants Together to release a ten-page response. In the paper, they pointed out that one of the authors was a former Goldman Sachs asset manager and another used to work at UBS as an investment banker. They write that the paper "uses flawed assumptions and conjecture to conclude that the direct, proven benefits of rent control are somehow negated by indirect effects."[17]

In a study the following year, economist Brian J. Asquith of the W. E. Upjohn Institute explored how landlords who own property along newly established private Silicon Valley shuttle routes respond to increased rental values. Not surprisingly, he found that some property owners use the same tactics identified in Diamond et al.'s study to remove tenants. He also failed to point to the key role played by the loopholes, which policymakers have the power to close. Asquith's analysis of his findings illuminates how most economists perceive this issue. First, he concludes the policy is dysfunctional because it does not allow landlords to "respond to significant demand shocks," like the addition of the shuttle amenity, by "being able to use prices to allocate their units" (raise rents).[18] Second, he portrays tenants who desire long-term stability in their homes as problematic for healthy market dynamics: "The crux of the problem is that unlike nuisances and rent delinquents, controlled landlords lack any direct remedy for long-stayers. Tenants have indeed been repeatedly found to disproportionately have long tenures in all forms of rent control."[19] While supporters of rent control would point out that long tenures are the objective, this argument is indicative of the view that housing "units" have optimal allocation and occupants who don't conform to this are somehow deviant for remaining in their homes and neighborhoods. Furthermore, the use of words like "allocate" obscures the lived experience of residents who are struggling to remain in their *homes*, not buy expensive gadgets or designer clothing.

Quantitative analysis methods and big data *are* useful for gathering macrolevel knowledge about housing policy. But they paint an incomplete picture at best. Without a richer, more nuanced understanding of rent control's benefits, drawbacks, and weaknesses—one that considers the macro- and mesoscale as well as the nuance of the human experience—policymakers and the public cannot make an informed decision around whether to implement it.

If We Want to Know How Well Rent Control Works, We Should Ask Tenants

How knowledge is produced, and by whom, matters. Housing research—like most, if not all, research—is the product of money, power, and ideology embedded in universities and research centers. As housing researchers John Gilderbloom and Lin Ye write, housing studies is not "a neutral field of study carried out by dispassionate academics." Given that "the battle over rent control is often over which study is right and which study is wrong," the stakes of this research are high, with the potential to impact millions of lives.[20]

Sociologist Jim Kemeny's interest in different types of housing tenures and the role of cultural ideology in shaping the residential experience came from his own time as a renter in several different countries. Recognizing that our knowledge and assumptions about housing are shaped by the very same ideology that informs that lived experience, Kemeny was interested in the role of ideology and power in housing research. In a 1988 paper, he applied a "constructivist perspective" from the sociology of science to housing studies, to consider how dominant paradigms and hegemonic ideologies in the housing research field act as a barrier to deeper understanding.[21] In his seminal book, *Housing and Social Theory*, he critiqued the housing research field for its "subject-fixated approach," which he describes as having a "sterile and limited empirical focus, concentrating on analyzing the housing market and housing policy."[22] He worried that the institutionalization of power structures in the field will lead to an entrenchment of this "unreflexive empirical study in abstraction from society as a whole."[23] This points to a need to "consciously reintegrate housing into broader issues of social structure and to do so by explicitly relating housing to debates in the social sciences."[24] Reimagining housing studies requires thoughtful consideration of how this research is designed: the focus, methods, data sources, questions, and framing of the problem itself.

Furthermore, Kemeny argues that focusing exclusively on the home itself neglects locational factors that connect housing to the macro issues of the nature of social structure, which contextualize housing's fundamental place in shaping society. To address this deficiency, Kemeny called for a "sociology of residence," rather than housing. He defines residence as a concept that "directs attention to the dwelling as home, *but within its locational context*."[25] Thus the sociology of residence is a critical approach that shifts the emphasis of housing studies from the physical structure itself to conceptualize the phenomenon of "residence" as the interplay between social and spatial dimensions of the home environment on various scales. It is an interdisciplinary approach, drawing on theory found in social science fields like geography, political economy, and environmental psychology.

This book is not concerned with the economics of housing markets, optimal unit allocation, or other macrolevel analyses of this policy. Instead, I adopt the sociology of residence lens to understand tenants' lived experiences and how they relate to policy and other external factors. I follow the path illuminated by qualitative research that uses concepts like ontological security, dwelling, and "at-homeness" to understand the nexus between tenure arrangement and well-being. This rich vein of inquiry provides the conceptual tools to explore what I call the "residential experience," in its totality.

My approach also answers LATU's call to center the tenant rather than the physical housing itself. Tracy Jeanne Rosenthal of LATU summarized this orientation in *101 Notes on the LA Tenants Union (You Can't Do Politics Alone)*:

1. First of all, there is no housing crisis.
2. Housing is not in crisis.

3. Housing needs no trauma counselors.
4. Housing needs no lawyers. Housing needs no comrades or friends. Housing needs no representatives. Housing needs no organizers.
5. When we call this crisis a housing crisis, it benefits the people who design housing, who build housing, who profit from housing, not the people who live in it.
6. It encourages us to think in abstractions, in numbers, in interchangeable "units," and not about people, or about power.
7. We don't have a housing crisis. We have a tenants' rights crisis.[26]

This call for an epistemological shift demands immediate attention from housing studies researchers. I answer it in this book with a research design centering on the resident, recognizing tenants as the ultimate experts on rent control in Santa Monica. Their relationships with the apartments, buildings, neighborhoods, community, and city they call home cannot be quantified by any equation under the sun.

A Better Housing System Is Possible

This book begins with a wide view at the macroscale and gradually zooms in to the microscale of the individual tenant experience. Chapter 1 provides the sociopolitical context for the rest of the book. It offers an overview of the American cultural ideology of property ownership and how it has evolved into the supremacy of homeownership. It begins with the Enclosure Acts and their impact on emigration and land acquisition practices in the New World, leading to the emergence of our contemporary "homeowner society." This is followed by a brief history of the tenant's status in American society and how tenants have responded with rent strikes and other political organizing. Finally, it examines how the political economy of the provision of housing has changed over time, from the "welfare state" to the neoliberal ideology that persists into the present.

Chapter 2 is devoted to exploring Santa Monica's unique local context as a small city known both for its expensive rents and as a stronghold of tenants' rights. It begins with a brief introduction to the city's history, then offers a detailed historical account of the evolution of tenant protection policy over the past four decades. This historical narrative illustrates the prolonged dance between protenant advocates and the real estate investment industry, as city leaders and activists struggle to hold ground amid strong market forces. Chapter 3 expands on the history and concepts discussed in the first two chapters. It explores the contemporary ideology and rhetoric of the greater Los Angeles real estate investment industry through a review of two years of the local trade publication, *Apartment Age*, ultimately identifying five major themes in the magazine's discourse. Together, these themes communicate a perception of unfairness and persecution around rent control and other protenant policies. The chapter concludes with a snapshot of the market language used in multifamily housing listings.

Chapter 4 presents an alternative to the stereotype of renters as transient and unattached by examining the complexity of the "person-place relationship" as experienced by study participants. Drawing on theory from human geography and environmental psychology, it explores participants' thoughts and feelings about their home environment, beginning with the residence and expanding to the neighborhood and city. It considers factors that inform and detract from the experience of "dwelling," or the feeling of being at-home in one's environment. Chapter 5 explores three interrelated aspects that shape the residential experience: variations in the landlord or property manager's business model and demeanor, legal loopholes that weaken the efficacy of policy, and the pressures of the real estate market. It homes in on how these experiences inform security and insecurity and some of the coping behaviors tenants use to feel at-home in spite of these conditions, including knowledge or deployment of tenant protections. Last, it examines how these experiences and perceptions relate to behavior and decisions.

Chapter 6 synthesizes themes from the previous chapters to explain how micro-, meso-, and macrolevel elements coalesce to holistically inform dwelling for these tenants. It discusses the ways the policy supports stability and dwelling in the face of challenges like speculative investment behavior and landlord harassment as well as limitations to the policy's efficacy. It also identifies previously unexamined benefits. Finally, it considers how this form of tenure, in this place and time, can be understood in relation to other tenure types and contexts. The book's Conclusion offers policy recommendations that point toward a decommodified housing system, where an apartment or house can truly be a home and not an investment vehicle.

1

Life, Liberty, and Property

Renting in America

omeownership has been a cornerstone of the American dream for generations who were raised with visions of domestic harmony in the owner-occupied single-family home, ranging from the rugged survivalism of *Little House on the Prairie* to the idyllic postwar suburban comforts of *Leave It to Beaver*. The suburban expansion of the mid-twentieth century extended the dream of the detached single-family home to millions of American families,* promising that each hardworking man could be the master of his own castle, an embodiment of American individualism. Over time the significance of homeownership evolved as it became a means of building intergenerational wealth—arguably just as important as an investment vehicle as a place to live. Despite this, around one-third of American households rent their homes, with a disproportionate representation among Black, Latino, and Native American households. Homeownership has decreased in accessibility in recent years for all except the wealthiest households, due, in part, to the role real estate investment plays in global finance.

What does it mean to be unlanded in a country where property ownership is intrinsic to national identity and the sense of personal accomplishment?

---

* The postwar suburban dream was heavily racialized, in most cases excluding everyone except white households. This was achieved through restrictive deed covenants (encouraged by the federal government), discriminatory lending policies (also stemming from federal policy), and white residents taking direct action against residents of color. Suburban zoning also prohibited the construction of multifamily housing, siloing renters in the urban core.

If property ownership signifies a responsible, upstanding, and reliable character that supports longevity of tenure and participation in the community, long-term renters are then by extension implicitly *irresponsible*, rootless, and even deviant. The impact of this "homeowner ideology" on tenants is not only limited to lower social status and class but also to material conditions. In many cases, a housing and land market most favorable to tenants is diametrically opposed to homeowner interests because rising property values correlate with higher rents. In this zero-sum game, the homeowner's windfall of increasing equity is connected to the tenant's severe cost burden or displacement. Property ownership may even play a role in which political party one is more likely to vote for. Data analyst Aziz Sunderji used data from the American National Election Studies to examine the relationship between homeownership and political orientation. Controlling for age, income, and other variables, he found that homeowners are twice as likely as renters to identify as Republican. Homeowners started progressively shifting to the right in the 1970s, and renters began to lean more toward the left in the early 2000s.[1]

The nation's housing infrastructure and policy support homeowners and landlords with tax benefits like the mortgage interest deduction and multifamily housing depreciation deduction, respectively,* without comparable benefits for tenants. A laissez-faire approach to regulating the private rental sector (PRS) has contributed to the conditions of precarity and displacement, including for the over seven hundred and seventy thousand (a vast undercount) Americans who experience homelessness each year. Sociologist Anne Shlay argues that, while there are a number of well-intentioned policies designed to address issues produced by the housing market, "it is the overall organization of the housing market, not occasional economic aberrations or market failure" that work against the objectives of these policies. The outcome is that "U.S. housing policy continues to wreak havoc with the application of core American values such as equal opportunity, social tolerance, and beliefs in cultural pluralism."[2]

What may initially seem like a system failure—with millions of renter households facing unsustainable rents, living in housing that doesn't meet their needs, or struggling to access housing at all—is actually the system *working* for those by and for whom it was designed. Scarcity enables landlords to charge higher rents and have the upper hand in relationships with

---

* Property owners are allowed to take this deduction even if the dwelling isn't occupied, as long as it is technically available for rent. With the large amount of vacant newer apartments in many expensive urban markets, it's possible the benefits of depreciation, combined with returns on the investment over time, may outweigh the financial necessity of renting the residence for some owners.

their tenants, while real estate agents reap larger commissions from sales. Abundance is antithetical to the aims of real estate investors. Landlords large and small use a variety of strategies to extract the maximum profit from renters, who convert their labor to wages and then to rent. That this system is natural and inevitable seems unquestionable. Americans are told from a young age that the way to end or prevent the precarity and lack of control that comes from renting is to work hard and buy a house.

The American housing system was formed by ideology and power. As a sociocultural product, it is only one of many possible modes of being. For example, cultural norms in Germany, the Netherlands, and Austria favor policies that support security for tenants. Conversely, "Anglophone" societies—where English is the primary language and the dominant culture originated from Great Britain, such as Australia, the United Kingdom, and the United States—prioritize landlord/investor flexibility. Additionally, many Western European governments have invested heavily in publicly owned rental and limited-equity owner-occupied housing. While public housing in America has traditionally been the domain of the poor, 80% of Austria's population is eligible to live in social housing. In Vienna, three of five residents live in homes owned, constructed, or managed by the local government. The city also funds large nonprofit cooperatives that house almost as many people as the state-owned properties, under strict governmental regulation. In Finland, 73% of the population is eligible for social housing and the government provides financing for the development of locally owned and nonprofit housing through loans, guarantees, and interest subsidies.[3]

In the late 1970s, tenant activists in American cities from Washington, DC to Los Angeles challenged the primacy of private property rights by fighting to enact local rent control ordinances. In doing so, they seized on one of the fundamental contradictions of American ideology and identity: the tension between the freedom to own property without government interference and the democratic values of equality and prosperity for all. Their arguments and struggles echo other movements for land and housing that have taken place for hundreds of years in America and beyond.

Private Property and the American Dream

Our story has roots in the sixteenth-century British Isles, where a significant segment of society lived adjacent to common land and enjoyed various types of use rights—such as foraging and livestock grazing—that provided subsistence and independence from wage labor. According to historian J. M. Neeson, "Living off the produce of commons encouraged frugality, economy, thrift. Productive commons had always been the insurance, the reserves, the hidden wealth of commoners—they were the oldest part of the ancient economy."⁴ Over the course of more than four hundred years, much of this common land was privatized by its owners for the purpose of large-scale agriculture, in order to maximize productivity and increase financial returns. Geographer Nick Blomley argues this was the period in which "modern conceptions of real property became hegemonic," with the emergence of land laws that centered around absolute personal ownership and preempted competing claims based on historical use or relationship.⁵ Contemporaneous projects to survey and map land facilitated this transition, creating clear boundaries around parcels. While enclosure initially took place on an informal basis, it eventually shifted to the purview of the legal system and policy, with a long series of parliamentary acts that formalized the controversial project.

The economist Carl Polanyi described the enclosure process as, "a revolution of the rich against the poor," due to the total restructuring of the social order that entailed defying ancient law and custom, often by pressure and intimidation from landholders. This project was undertaken with the rationale of "improving" how the land was used, disregarding traditional uses and the role they played in the socioeconomic life of people in a diverse range of circumstances.⁶ The result was, as Neeson writes, "a memory of expropriation that informed, legitimized, and sharpened the class politics of nineteenth-century villages" in Britain and later the U.S. colonies.⁷ Using the rationale of improvement that would later drive both Indigenous dispossession and twentieth-century urban renewal in the United States, proponents of enclosure argued that commoners stood in the way of the nation's growth.⁸ Their dual objectives, of increasing agricultural productivity and creating a labor force to work the factories and large farms of the burgeoning industrial era, required the end of this traditional subsistence lifestyle. Karl Marx theorized that the enclosures precipitated the transformation of the peasant into the proletariat through a process he called "primitive accumulation."⁹ This transformed both the land and its people by making land a site of commodity production for market exchange, turning the peasant class into wage laborers.

Between 1604 and 1914 Parliament enacted over fifty-two hundred individual enclosure bills, resulting in the privatization of over a fifth of the land in England.¹⁰ Parallel processes were unfolding in Wales, Ireland, and Scotland. After the common land in their parishes was enclosed, many individuals and families were displaced to other parishes, cities, or the British colonies as either freemen or indentured servants. In this way, enclosure had multiple outcomes: it created laborers for factories and farms and colonizers and indentured servant labor for the colonies, and it enriched a growing landlord class in Britain. But perhaps the greatest impact was that it codified private property in dominium as a natural and unquestioned mode of being.

This remains the status quo in present day Britain and America, where common property (aside from that owned by the state) is viewed only as the purview of radicals and dreamers, and private property rights are often prioritized above basic human rights.

As the enclosures were taking place, the British colonies were also focused on the reordering of landownership, habitation, and use. The English legal doctrine of *vacuum domicilium* (unoccupied or unfenced land) facilitated the colonists' establishment of land allotments and townships in the New World through Indigenous dispossession. Puritan leaders justified their takings on the grounds that the "savage people ruleth over many lands without title or property; for they inclose no ground, neither have they cattell to maintayne it."[11] This "empty" land was considered free for colonial settlement, disregarding Indigenous ownership claims and traditional land uses in a similar manner to what was unfolding across the Atlantic. In a painfully ironic twist, the abundance of this "empty" land must have had a strong pull on dispossessed commoners, who had seen their entire way of life change with these powerful shifts.

Landownership continued to be an important component of social organization and the burgeoning American consciousness through the colonial period and after the Revolutionary War. With the emergence of the Industrial Revolution, people began pouring into rapidly urbanizing areas, and, despite the ongoing efforts of municipal officials and reformers, the social issues created by poverty were persistent. In housing researcher Allan David Heskin's analysis, the importance of property ownership positioned agrarian tenants in early America as peasants in a system that was beginning to resemble the feudalism and landlordism they had emigrated to escape. The class significance of being landless—even for nonindentured white men—was implicit from the beginning. In the colonial era, only freeholders (landowners whose holdings held a specified value) could vote. Tenants did not participate in the writing or ratification of the U.S. Constitution. Many tenants joined in the call for independence from the British, as taxation without representation was especially salient for them due to their disenfranchisement.[12]

In response, Jefferson and his contemporaries decided that, by opening undeveloped land in the west to new settlement, they could achieve the dual goals of converting working-class urban tenants into industrious rural property owners while expanding the U.S. territory and pushing Indigenous people further west. The centerpiece of Jefferson's vision for the fledgling democracy was the yeoman farmer: a nonslaveholding white man who worked a small plot of land with his family. This picture of rugged independence—where each man would be the master of his own domain—was the embodiment of the young country's ideological emphasis on individualism and self-sufficiency. To support this objective, Congress adopted the Land Ordinance of 1785 to survey "unsettled" western land and sell it to prospective yeoman farmers.

Articulating the role property ownership was to play in social cohesion and as a defense against political factions, Missouri Senator Thomas Hart Benton later told Congress, "Tenantry is unfavorable to freedom. It lays the foundation for separate orders in society, annihilates love of country, and weakens the spirit of independence."[13] But this proto-American dream was only accessible to white men, and, even for them, only to those who could save the substantial start-up sum and possessed farming skills and knowledge. The hope that factory workers and other unpropertied Americans would eventually become homesteaders—thereby avoiding the threat of a permanent tenant class—was shattered by the reality of the resources needed for the endeavor. The cost of the land itself was also a hurdle for the average working-class man, necessitating the use of buying on credit from the speculator owner. The Homestead Act of 1862 had similar objectives and outcomes.

Meanwhile, increased demand and speculative investment combined to undermine the feasibility of owning one's home in urban centers. According to architectural historian Gwendolyn Wright, in the decade after the revolution many artisans—members of what we would now call the middle class—were able to afford the purchase of single lots. Soon after, investors began to acquire large tracts of land, and, between 1785 and 1815, land values in Manhattan rose by more than 750%. By this time, more than half of the homes in the country's larger urban areas were occupied by renters, primarily the families of artisans and unskilled laborers.[14] Speculative investment catalyzed a spike in urban land values again in the early nineteenth century, with increases as high as 220% between 1833 and 1837, resulting in commensurate increases in rent. As a result, rental housing deteriorated, creating some of the country's first urban slums.

Early movements for tenants' rights took several ideological and rhetorical approaches. While agrarian tenants made arguments for ownership or land redistribution based on their status as both residents *and* laborers on the land they rented, urban tenant leaders generally organized around improved rights rather than abolishing landlords. They engaged with the economic framework of emerging industrial capitalism, pointing out how price gouging on rents enabled by land monopoly threatened the viability of commercial enterprises by necessitating wage increases. Advocates also adopted a consumer rights framework, including the issue of high rents with the ballooning costs of other basic goods in an 1837 protest in New York City.

In 1848, renters formed the Tenants' League of New York. Their platform included a vacant lot tax to pay for the construction of new housing, rent controls, and prohibitions on evictions without cause. The Tenants' League also called for reforms like rent controls and prohibitions on evictions without cause. The next wave of mass tenant action took place in response to the depression of 1873 when about three hundred thousand people lost their jobs, prompting a wave of evictions for nonpayment. In New York City alone, an estimated ninety thousand became homeless in early 1874. The new movement of social Darwinism provided an easy rationale against helping the destitute, where a convenient argument held that the tenants' present circumstances were evidence of laziness and character deficiency.[15]

The Homeowner Society

Over the course of hundreds of years, these historical events and cultural currents solidified the connection between property ownership—as exemplified by the yeoman farmer—and full citizenship. As small-scale farming diminished and the country became increasingly urbanized with more people making their living through wage labor, the detached single-family home was the new homestead. However, a coordinated effort to sell this specific American dream to the public didn't reach its full stride until the early twentieth century. After World War I, then Commerce Department Secretary Herbert Hoover was a major proponent of homeownership and supported the construction of single-family homes. He described it as fundamental to American independence and initiative; an essential component of connecting with one's national identity. These American ideals about homeownership and independence dovetailed nicely with Hoover's belief that the construction industry was a core component of the economy. Accordingly, his postwar housing policy focused on promoting homeownership over building affordable rental housing.

Under Hoover's direction the federal government endorsed and supported the work of organizations that promoted better living through the suburban ideal, such as the Architect's Small House Service Bureau and the public relations campaign, "Own Your Own Home," originally launched by the National Association of Real Estate Brokers (NAREB) after World War I and eventually taken over by the U.S. Department of Labor. The "modernization movement" addressed a leveling out in demand for new homes with the formation of the Home Modernizing Bureau, which was organized by members of the building industry, lumber companies, and building and loan associations. The organization's work was informed by a federal survey that found three in five residences were in need of upgrades. In 1934, this initiative was shifted to the new Better Housing Program, which provided federally backed funding for home improvements.

The Housing Committee of the NAREB was strongly against publicly funded housing of any kind and found a kindred spirit in Hoover, who believed private control of property and real estate was best. Hoover also worried that the housing shortage—combined with low homeownership rates—would result in a class system of landlords and tenants that would eventually lead to a revolution. Hoover moved the Division of Building and Housing from the purview of the Labor Department to the Commerce Department. This agency conducted research, engaged in advocacy efforts, and distributed educational literature to support the creation of owner-occupied housing provided by the private market. These campaigns spurred a boom in the construction of single-family homes, accounting for 60% of the family housing constructed in the 1920s, and 90% in the 1930s.[16]

Marketing was instrumental to the growing popularity of the detached single-family home, which was quickly becoming a commodity good that conferred status in the emerging consumer society. Unlike the agrarian yeoman homestead, this living arrangement didn't support independence from wage labor. Accordingly, developers aimed to redefine independence in their marketing by using language of masculinity and dominance over the home. In this incarnation, the owner-occupied house was both a proxy for the homestead ideal and a consumer choice in the emerging era of mass consumption. It was a means for the wageworker, who may not have any control over his labor, to feel like a master of his own domestic sphere.[17] In urban studies scholar Lawrence Vale's analysis, "The compensatory myth of homeownership is rooted in its cultural mystique, its ability to provide pastoral roots, and moral superiority."[18]

Marketing materials promoting urban homeownership emphasized the ideals of middle-class autonomy, reified gender roles, and preservation of social status.[19] In an extension of the homesteading ideal, it was inextricably bound up with good citizenship and moral character. Early advertisements for upper-class single-family homes in Boston even described them as homesteads. Conversely, renting was disfavored, carrying a social stigma reinforced by tenement conditions that were frequently reported on in the media. A 1920s homeownership promotion from the NAREB went so far as to suggest that the owner-occupied single-family home would protect one from unwholesome renters, who were described as "floating."[20] Through this kind of targeted messaging, homeownership became what housing researcher and advocate Michael Stone described as "the mark of full citizenship, the symbol of status, almost a civil right to anyone who saved up a little for the down payment."[21]

Throughout the twentieth century and into the next, the relationship between the primacy of homeownership and the policies that support it have been mutually reinforcing.[22] In addition to their sponsorship of early promotional efforts, the federal government has invested heavily in supporting ownership. The mortgage income tax deduction amounts to hundreds of billions of lost revenue each year, while renters are afforded no comparable financial assistance or benefits. In the mid-1960s, homeowner tax deductions were around $7 billion annually and, by 1984, had reached $53 billion, a sum almost five times more than all direct federal funding for housing during that year.[23] Because the deduction can only be used by households that itemize their expenses, it has little impact for low-income households. Federal Housing Authority mortgage insurance through Fannie Mae and Freddie Mac is the other major homeownership subsidy. Economic policy analyst Morris Davis estimated the total cost of these policies to be around $2.5 trillion.[24] Significantly, these subsidies function as *entitlements* rather than appropriations, the latter of which is how public housing and federal rent vouchers are funded. Policies that unfairly benefit homeowners persist. In 2024, Oregon legislators proposed two similar pieces of legislation that would freeze property taxes for homeowners who are over sixty-five years old, regardless of income. Policy analysts estimate this would result in a loss of around $140 million in tax revenue by the end of the decade.[25] Meanwhile, the state-level preemption on local rent control remains in place despite persistent efforts to eliminate it.

Homeownership comes with undeniable benefits, but, the question is, to what extent are those the result of something intrinsically superior about the tenure versus the product of policy decisions—especially those that have made renting precarious? In this vein, Jim Kemeny argues the seemingly self-evident superiority of homeownership is based on a principal myth in Anglophone countries that plays up its "natural" quality and security, which is to a great extent the result of policy decisions about renting that have rendered it insecure. This stratifies tenure by class and eliminates renting as a sustainable and desirable long-term option, which has far-reaching consequences for the state of housing in America and other "homeowner societies" like Australia and the United Kingdom.[26] This is especially problematic as homeownership becomes increasingly inaccessible to even middle-class households. Because fluctuations in home prices have a direct positive correlation with rent levels, that leaves renters even less money at the end of the month to save toward buying a home.[27]

While it is widely accepted that homeownership is the primary mechanism for building intergenerational wealth in America, the economic reality of homeownership for lower-income people doesn't necessarily follow that narrative. In some cases buying a home can put an economically vulnerable household in a more precarious situation than if it continued to rent. Planning scholar Meagan Ehlenz argues that low-income households are "often exposed to substantially greater risk and are less likely to reap the rewards of homeownership relative to their higher income counterparts."[28] Low-income households are less likely to see meaningful appreciation, dedicate larger portions of their income to mortgage payments, and are more susceptible to predatory lending and foreclosure due to fluctuating interest terms and financial precarity. Nonetheless, many households feel considerable pressure to stretch their housing budget if it means they can own. Low-income households may be just a few paychecks away from foreclosure and this stress can have a negative impact on mental health. For example, housing researchers Susan Saegert, Desiree Fields, and Kimberly Libman studied the impacts on potential foreclosure on homeowners. They found that both the material and the intangible social prestige of homeownership become "painfully inverted," ultimately leaving people and communities worse off than they were before.[29] Yet, despite the financial vulnerabilities of traditional ownership—as illustrated by the subprime mortgage crisis and ensuing foreclosure epidemic—it remains a cornerstone of the American dream while renting continues to be stigmatized.

Another touted benefit at the center of government homeownership policies and incentives is the tenure's stabilizing effect on households and communities. However, longevity of tenure may be more closely connected to the high transaction costs of moving for homeowners than some innately stabilizing characteristic of ownership.[30] In this sense, what looks like stability may actually be *constraints* on relocation to a more desirable locale or suitable home.[31] These high exit costs may also lead owners and neighborhood organizations to take action to prevent a decline in property values, which may be antithetical to the needs of other community members. For example, homeowner NIMBYism and concerns about property values may motivate opposition to affordable housing due to negative beliefs about low-income renters, as housing researchers Ed Goetz and Mara Sidney found in their study on two neighborhood associations in the Twin Cities.[32]

Higher levels of civic engagement and participation in community groups is another purported benefit of homeownership. Under the direction of President Bill Clinton in 1995, the federal Department of Housing and Urban Development implemented the National Homeownership Strategy—a public-private partnership to increase homeownership rates over the course of six years. "The desire for homeownership is deeply rooted in the American psyche," the policy brief begins. "Owning a home embodies the promise of individual autonomy and of material and spiritual well-being that many people sought in coming to this country." After introducing the topic with this familiar framing, the authors add that homeownership is thought to promote qualities like thrift, stability, neighborliness, and other "individual and civic virtues." The document outlines four fundamental benefits of homeownership underpinning the policy's rationale, one of which is stabilizing neighborhoods and strengthening communities. In this category, the authors point to connections in housing research literature between homeownership and length of residence, "neighboring" behavior, crime prevention, and sociopolitical activism.[33]

However, my research found correlations between rent-controlled housing and all of these attributes, with the exception of crime prevention, suggesting the *stabilizing* features of homeownership are likely more important than the "spiritual well-being" or any other mysterious benefit homeowners enjoy. Likewise, other research on the topic has advanced a multitude of sometimes conflicting theories to explain the connection between homeownership and community engagement. Some prominent variables identified are the presence of children in the household, education level, income, gender, and length of tenure. The complexity of various contexts and lack of consensus on motivation led housing geographer Richard Ronald to conclude, "Data on homeowner activism remains generally inconsistent and the rationalizations and sociopolitical responses of homeowners are varied."[34]

While there is a noticeable dearth of research on motivation for renter participation, research has illuminated some of the reasons renters do *not* participate. Housing researchers Arlene Carson, Neena Chappell, and Karen Dujela found the length of residency to be a more significant predictor of feelings of community membership than tenure status, but that feelings of influence and self-efficacy in making changes are strongly correlated with homeownership and not renting. Their research also exposed a discrepancy in the way homeowners viewed the level of renter attachment and the ways that renters experienced it, suggesting renters may not be participating in neighborhood groups due to the perception of inferior stakeholder status compared to homeowners.*[35] In the same vein, Michael Hooper and Jenny Cadstedt's research on participatory planning revealed how perceptions of transience and "inconsequentiality" held by both renters themselves and homeowners resulted in an unwillingness or inability to participate. This was a mutually reinforcing process, where homeowners' perceptions of renters led to renters' interests being ignored, which made them disinclined to participate and further marginalized their status in the process.[36] This is echoed in Kent Portney and Jeffrey Berry's study on mobilizing minority communities, where feeling a sense of belonging and community was a crucial variable leading to or away from participation.[37]

---

* Several of my interview participants described similar experiences attending their neighborhood association meetings.

Together, We Can Control the Rent

In America and abroad, for generations, tenants have advocated for rent control as a solution to rising rents and unfair eviction practices. As with the settlement of the American West, real estate investment speculation plagued the country's urban centers from the early days of the republic. Converging with other factors like low wages, these practices drove up housing costs, perpetuating poverty and ensuring a sizable number of residents would remain tenants. While tenant organizing took place in cities across the United States, New York City was the most significant flashpoint for tenant activism in America through the twentieth century and the only city where tenants won rent control until the 1970s. An affordable housing shortage emerged in New York City at the beginning of the twentieth century, resulting from a combination of the demolition of existing tenements and a slow rate of new building in the wake of the Tenement House Act of 1901, which aimed to reform poor housing conditions. The common practice of landlords subleasing their buildings to "listers"—who preyed on immigrants and created tenement conditions while raising rents even further to make a profit—was yet another mechanism through which wages were extracted in the form of rents.

These conditions, combined with increasing demand from a steady wave of immigrants arriving in the city, led landlords to propose May 1 (the traditional day for rents to increase, also known as "moving day") rent increases of 20%–30% in 1904. Inspired by strike tactics from the labor movement, a group of mostly Jewish residents in the Lower East Side organized a mass rent strike involving two thousand tenants in eight hundred buildings. They were largely successful in suspending evictions and rolling rents back to prestrike levels, and this action was a powerful lesson in the efficacy of solidarity and collective protest. Several years later, in the wake of the Panic of 1907, landlords proposed raising rents again. This sparked the even larger rent strike of 1907, which began on the Lower East Side and spread to Harlem and Brooklyn. This time the Socialist Party was heavily involved, which politicized tenants' rights struggles in the city from that point on.[38]

A housing shortage and rent increases during World War I precipitated another wave of rent strikes, organized by the Socialist Party, that swept across the city from 1917 to 1920. With the situation reaching a boiling point, the state legislature convened to pass the Emergency Rent Laws—a historic moment for tenants in America. With the exception of a federal statute governing the District of Columbia, passed several months earlier, it was the first rent control law in the nation, and it was hard-won through tenant organizing, creating a template for future campaigns. The law established rent control, with increases to be approved by municipal court judges based on the financial evidence presented by the landlord. It also restricted landlords' ability to deny lease renewals to tenants, an early form of "just-cause" eviction policy.

The outcome was a drastic reduction in the number of rent strikes, and tenant organizing and Socialist-led groups dissipated. Meanwhile, more moderate tenant assistance groups saw an increase in activity as their services were needed to navigate the bureaucracy of the rent appeals process. Renewing the legislation was the most pressing ongoing effort for activist groups in the years that followed. In advance of a 1923 hearing before the state's Commission on Housing and Regional Planning, tenant leaders conducted surveys of tenants in their neighborhood on vacancy levels, rents, and landlord-tenant issues. They presented this data before the commission, arguing that a failure to extend the law would exacerbate the deepening crisis, characterized by low vacancies in affordable apartments and "doubling up" (multiple households sharing one dwelling). They were granted an extension through early 1926, but, by 1925, the landlord and real estate lobby mounted vigorous opposition to extending the emergency law. Some frustrated landlords—like their contemporary colleagues—were resorting to tactics like decreasing maintenance and evicting tenants through false pretenses. Though the controls were extended several more times, they were lifted in the fall of 1929.[39]

The years of the Great Depression saw yet another housing crisis unfold for the city's tenant households. The weakened housing industry led to a subsequent failure of the market to provide safe and affordable housing to the third of the city's population that was unemployed or underemployed. This gave birth to another vibrant tenant movement, with activists demanding a reinstatement of the Emergency Rent Laws. Around this time, Black tenants joined the Jewish community as movement leaders, beginning with the Harlem Tenants League's 1929 protest campaign against expirations of the rent control law. The Black community would remain a major force in the city's tenant movement throughout the twentieth century to the present.[40]

The federal government's first foray into rent control policy took place during World War II, in the context of a nationwide decline in housing construction combined with mass migration of defense workers to urban centers. The federal government acted to prevent landlord price gouging, in response to surging demand, by passing the Emergency Price Control Act of 1942. This legislation established the Office of Price Administration, which had the power to open local offices that could elect to freeze rents in addition to regulating the price of other essential goods. Rent controls were not automatic, and, in some locations—including New York City—tenants had to advocate for their local OPA to establish rent control. Approximately

80% of the nation's rental housing stock was under a rent freeze until the late 1940s. The Emergency Price Control Act expired in 1947, and the Federal Housing and Rent Act of 1947 took its place. Under these regulations, new construction after February 1, 1947, was exempted from rent controls, while buildings constructed before that remained protected.[41] Some areas continued rent control into the 1950s, with New York City extending its rent control protections into the present day.

The 1970s and early 1980s were a high-water mark for the tenant movement in progressive cities across the country, and tenant activists expanded rent control out of New York City. During this time, cities in New Jersey, Massachusetts, Maryland, Virginia, Florida, California, and the District of Columbia implemented various versions of the policy, in response to unsustainable rent increases and affordable housing shortages. This wave of tenant activism ebbed, and the hard-won policies prompted an equally strong offensive by the real estate lobby. Over the course of the next few decades, renter protections were gradually eroded in many jurisdictions, with Miami, Boston, and Cambridge repealing their ordinances entirely.[42] During the neoliberal turn of the 1980s and 1990s, Massachusetts municipalities lost the ability to implement rent control in a 1994 statewide referendum. The residents in cities with rent control ordinances didn't vote in the majority for the referendum, meaning the real estate lobby found an effective way to circumvent local control by tapping into deeply held beliefs about private property rights that appealed to rural and suburban voters, in addition to a minority of urban voters. Santa Monica and most other jurisdictions in Los Angeles County retained their rent control and rent stabilization policies, but landlord trade organizations continue to challenge the regulations forty-five years later.

In the new millennium, tenant organizations attempted to hold ground against a consistent and well-funded landlord lobby. Washington, DC, voters defeated a 2000 attempt to repeal rent control, and New York City also successfully fended off an attempt to establish full vacancy decontrol in 1997, but new regulations in 2000 established a criteria for establishing base rent that was more favorable to landlords. New Jersey, another center of tenant activism, also saw a barrage of prolandlord legislation in the past several decades, which has resulted in vacancy decontrol for 80% of the state's 115 rent-controlled jurisdictions.[43]

The tenants' movement appears to be in a third wave that began in the years following the 2016 election. In 2019, Oregon became the first state to implement rent stabilization and ban no-cause evictions at the state level, with Senate Bill 608. Though the rent increase is generous for landlords at 7% plus the increase in CPI (with a maximum of 10%), and there are some substantial loopholes in the bill, the significance of this bill passing through a state legislature is undeniable. California followed suit shortly thereafter, enacting its own statewide legislation that caps rent increases at 5% plus CPI and, like Oregon, prohibits no-cause evictions with some key exceptions. Washington joined its West Coast neighbors in 2025, when the state legislature passed a similar bill. Renters in New York state achieved a major victory in 2019 with the passage of the Housing Stability and Tenants' Protections Act. The legislation addressed the impending expiration of the state rent control law and closed a number of problematic loopholes. State lawmakers also implemented legislation that enables rent stabilization to expand to other cities and counties.[44]

The Evolution of Our Modern Housing Landscape

During the same era that tenants on the Lower East Side were conducting the city's first rent strikes, progressive social reformers sought to improve tenement conditions through a program of publicly owned affordable housing. In addition to the rent issue, low-income households in urban centers like New York and Chicago were subject to extreme crowding and living conditions were dire. This impacted life for many recent immigrants, whose labor powered the factories that made the commodity culture of the Gilded Age possible. Social workers, planners, industrialists, and others visited progressive housing developments in Europe to study their structure. They were interested in building model developments to raise working-class standards of living from the slums and tenements that had become the dominant form of housing. Their concerns centered around cramped and unsanitary conditions and perceptions of resulting physical and moral degradation. In addition to general concerns about public health, reformers believed that proper homes were necessary for assimilation into the American way of life. Efforts were mainly focused on improving the housing stock rather than the landlord-tenant relationship. To that end, Lawrence Veiller released *Housing Reform: A Hand-Book for Practical Use in American Cities* in 1910.[45]

Until World War I, housing had been the purview of local governments, but this changed with the need to house defense workers. The federal government formed the Department of Labor's U.S. Housing Corporation (USHC) and the U.S. Shipping Board's Emergency Fleet Corporation in 1917. The resulting housing developments were a synergy of the government-mandated need for wartime worker housing and the community development philosophy of housing reformers, city planners, and architects. National leaders of the era identified a need to create social stability in wartime, which dovetailed with practitioners' vision of shaping the working class into something resembling middle-class respectability through the built environment. The provision of housing was framed by the latter not only as a matter of supporting social harmony but also as a critical link to supporting the labor force and preventing turnover. Thus, the driving force behind America's first national housing policy was meeting wartime production needs.[46]

Then (as now) affordable housing advocates in the prewar era attributed the dearth of housing for the working class to a reliance on the private market for its provision. Reformer Edith Elmer Wood opined that "Private initiative has failed lamentably,"[47] and called for policy that would offer federal funding incentives for greater private investment in this sector, along with more direct government involvement in the process. With the federal government's wartime intervention, the U.S. Shipping Board's Emergency Fleet Corporation disbursed federal funds to shipbuilding companies to build worker housing, while the USHC was charged with direct construction. Though progressive housing reformers hoped this intervention would be the beginning of a social housing program and these developments could be converted into worker cooperatives, concerns about socialism—combined with other factors—led the government to auction off all of the housing they created. The USHC sold its holdings for $27 million, compared to the $52 million it had spent.

Early New Deal housing programs like the National Housing Act (1934) aimed to stimulate housing construction rather than engage in its direct provision. The Federal Housing Administration was created and empowered by the act to offer federally insured mortgages through private financial institutions to both individual homeowners and developers. The Better Housing Program provided government-backed funding for home modernization, which was a vestige of the Hoover era, situated in the suburban ideal. Funding was available through a set of guidelines under which housing in the urban core was generally not eligible, which furthered suburbanization.[48] Meanwhile, the Public Works Administration was tasked with the construction and renovation of low-cost housing and slum clearance projects, resulting in twenty-five thousand residences being built in four years, many of which were of high quality. While these homes were ostensibly targeted toward low-income renters, there was growing apprehension among the real estate industry that the government was competing with private market housing, due, in part, to the fact that public housing was not "means tested" (restricted to residents with low incomes).

During this time, housing activist Catherine Bauer noted the emergence of a national "dual" or "two-tiered" housing policy; the federal government generously subsidized commercial enterprise around the development of housing for middle- and upper-class consumers, while funding for public housing was anemic. In response, Bauer and the Labor Housing Conference (LHC) offered a vision for government housing policy in 1934, which they coined "modern housing." This plan proposed that the public finance large-scale nonprofit housing developments in collaboration with groups of workers and potential residents. This housing was intended to serve both low- *and* moderate-income households, rather than the two-tier approach that addressed households differently by income. The idea was to make quality housing available to everyone rather than just to those who can afford it, thus avoiding the stigmatizing effects of housing that was specifically for the poor and looked like it. While this alternative economic model of modern housing didn't take off, the emphasis on thoughtful design and fostering community was a key aspect of housing policy under the New Deal.

In 1935, Bauer and her LHC allies collaborated with Senator Henry Ellenbogen on a new housing policy bill in response to a more conservative piece of legislation that had been introduced by Senator Robert Wagner. The Ellenbogen Bill called for replacing the Public Works Administration's Housing Division with a permanent U.S. Housing Authority that would manage a federally supported affordable housing program with funding from an initial appropriation supplemented by bond sales. Critically, this included the means for nonprofit, limited equity, and cooperative housing to be created using federal funded grants and loans. The intention was for people of all income levels to have the means of creating their own decommodified housing,* independent from the real estate industry. Receptive of Bauer and Ellenbogen's critiques of his proposed bill, Wagner invited them to help draft new legislation for the 1936 congressional session, but it failed to pass. In 1937, he introduced a third version of the bill.[49]

Meanwhile the real estate lobby—a group of trade organizations—was mounting stiff resistance to a program of federally owned rental housing with the rationale that homeownership was closely tied to Jeffersonian visions of American independence. To this point, the president of the NAREB argued that "widespread ownership of land . . . is the bulwark of a democratic form of government."[50] NAREB feared that living in this housing may prove so attractive that homeownership would lose its luster. In addition to NAREB, the U.S. Chamber of Commerce, the U.S. Building and Loan League, and the National Retail Lumber Dealers Association also lobbied against government-funded and publicly owned housing. The lumber lobby objected on the grounds that public housing would use concrete and steel because it was more affordable.

When Congress passed the U.S. Housing Act in 1937, it had been significantly compromised. Provisions for nonprofits and cooperatives were eliminated, and all authority for siting and tenant selection was left to local

---

* Decommodified housing is removed from the housing market by way of the legal framework governing its use. This includes public housing and limited- or shared-equity housing, where the resident owns their home but receives limited profit from its sale.

jurisdictions. This last piece meant both that low-income public housing would tend to be situated in less desirable neighborhoods and that prospective tenants had no federal protection against discrimination. It also focused housing development on the lowest income segments of the population only, rather than the mixed-income social housing program promoted by the LHC. The "equivalent elimination clause" was a key piece of the bill, mandating urban renewal and slum clearance in equal measure with new construction. This helped reduce the competition between private developers and the public sector for desirable land on the urban periphery. Senator Harry Byrd of Virginia also introduced an amendment to cap construction costs at $5,000 per unit, dashing Bauer's vision of high-quality public housing with appealing architecture and design. These austerity measures, along with the ambitious thriftiness of the U.S. Housing Authority (with the altruistic motivation to create more housing and win the public's trust), resulted in the massive apartment towers like the Cabrini-Green in Chicago that have become the face of public housing in America.

Housing historian Gail Radford ultimately attributes the failure of a European-style social housing program like the one Bauer envisioned to a combination of the powerful forces shaping consumer choice and the power of the real estate lobby. Union members responded enthusiastically to the LHC's housing program when Bauer traveled around the country presenting it, suggesting there was a real possibility for alternatives to both the design of the detached single-family home and the traditional ownership model. But the majority of Americans had never heard of these housing models, and the real estate industry's influence in Congress assured that they wouldn't. Though the Housing Act of 1937 remains an exceptionally liberal piece of housing policy by American standards, it firmly established the nation's public housing program as a limited one, available only to households who couldn't afford housing on the private market. In this sense, it was designed to supplement the private market rather than provide a true alternative, as is the case in many European countries. According to urban planning scholars Peter Marcuse and W. Dennis Keating, this compromise avoided direct competition between public and private housing providers.[51] Radford's analysis of this turning point and the role of the real estate industry's power in shaping policy holds true for the provision of housing in America today:

> In the United States, with its long tradition of land speculation as a central economic activity, the configuration of political forces was very different [from Europe]. Here, property investors possessed much greater political power than did those in European nations, especially at the local level where more political decisions were made.[52]

During the Great Depression and its aftermath, the economic policy in the United States and several European nations shifted from a classical economic model to one developed by the British economist John Maynard Keynes. This restructuring was known as the "class compromise" and aimed to create social stability by balancing the competing interests of capital and labor as an alternative to the extreme inequality produced by the capitalist excesses of the Gilded Age. Keynes and his supporters were concerned that continuing down the path of an economically bifurcated society would eventually lead to a complete upending of the status quo, possibly resulting in a turn toward communism or totalitarianism. Under the Keynesian economic system, the private sector still played a key role, but market activities were tempered by strong regulatory mechanisms. Policy focused on creating full employment, economic growth, abundant housing, improvements in public health, and increased educational opportunities. Labor unions had power and influence within the state apparatus. The core principle of Keynesian economics was the belief that the government can and should intervene when necessary to protect the well-being of the people.

This "welfare state" approach was effective in creating prosperity and relative social stability for several decades, but, by the end of the 1960s it had begun to falter. Unemployment and inflation surged internationally, and an era of "stagflation" set in for most of the 1970s.[53] While some Keynesian nations addressed these challenges by leaning further into regulation and the provision of social welfare, including social housing,[54] the United States took a different path. The early neoliberal economic doctrine was developed by economists Milton Friedman, Friedrich Hayek, Harold Luhnow, and others, in the late 1940s. These economists envisioned an end to the Keynesian welfare state and the New Deal model and a return to laissez-faire, as the realization of true liberalism. In this vein, President Ronald Reagan's "trickle-down economics" inverted the Keynesian principle that the key to economic prosperity comes from below, not above.[55] The main tenets of the new economic order—neoliberalism—were (and remain) strong individual property rights, rule of law, and institutions that maintain the free market and free trade. Privatization, public-private partnerships, deregulation, and competition were key components. Early tactics included government-sponsored union busting and an overall weakening of organized labor, tax breaks for the rich, and corporations outsourcing labor to cheaper markets outside of the United States.[56] It was a return to the primacy of property in American policy and economics and the end of the class compromise.

The President's Commission on Housing, appointed by President Reagan and composed of members primarily drawn from the real estate industry, articulated the administration's vision for the provision of housing in America in their 1982 report. According to Marcuse and Keating's synthesis, the document's core principles encourage free and deregulated housing markets, rely on the private sector with minimal government intervention, decentralize authority from the federal government to local jurisdictions, promote homeownership as a major goal, and stimulate the accumulation of private wealth to foster economic growth. It also established the tenant-based federal housing voucher program, enabling recipients to use their rent subsidy in private market housing.[57] While housing choice is of undeniable benefit to households, this pivot to focus on directly helping people (demand side) rather than investing in new public housing (supply side) meant the deficit of affordable housing stock would deepen over time and reliance on the PRS would increase.[58] While the values underpinning these principles were a departure from the liberalism of the Keynesian era, the role of the private sector and emphasis on supporting homeownership was a continuation from the previous era.

The limited appetite among policymakers around federal spending for public housing and their preference for public-private partnerships led the federal government to create a new investment mechanism to facilitate the development and preservation of privately developed affordable housing. Congress passed the Tax Reform Act of 1986, creating the federal LIHTC program to incentivize private equity in the development of affordable housing. Under the program, nonprofit and private sector developers sell tax credits to investors to raise equity for residential projects that have income restrictions. The tax credits do two things for investors: offset federal tax liability and enable saving on taxes through operating losses and building depreciation.[59] According to the U.S. Department of Housing and Urban Development's website, the LIHTC program is "the most important resource for creating affordable housing in the United States today," with $9 billion going toward the program annually. Funds can also be used to buy or rehabilitate existing structures. Over 3.5 million homes have been created since 1987 under this program.[60]

However, the program has faced criticism around several key areas. One is its inability to achieve spatial equity in the siting of low-income housing absent specific federal guidelines. For example, housing researcher Casey Dawkins's study on LIHTC siting revealed clusters of LIHTC housing in seven of ten metropolitan areas in the sample. These tended to be located in dense areas with higher poverty rates and percentages of minority populations.[61] Additionally, the minimum affordability period for these developments is thirty years (some jurisdictions have longer requirements), with half a million apartments set to lose their affordable status between 2020 and 2029 alone.[62] Unless local housing authorities or nonprofits intervene to purchase these buildings (at great cost), residents will face major rent increases while communities lose hundreds of affordable homes, setting back progress in state and local housing programs.

The income qualification system also differs from the federal Section 8 voucher program, or other voucher–based housing, where the resident pays 30% of their income no matter what the rent is. With LIHTC, tenants qualify for apartments designated for the area median income bracket at or above their income, which has a set rent. This means many LIHTC tenants pay more than 30% of their income for rent. How much more depends on how far their income is from the nearest bracket. Last, the program is best suited to serve households in the mid- to low-income range, with very low-income households often relying on federal rent assistance to afford the rent.[63] Meanwhile, the federal public program received another blow from legislators: in 1998, the Faircloth Amendment to the 1937 Housing Act established a firm limit on the number of affordable homes federal authorities could build and own.

In the neoliberal era, real estate is enmeshed in the web of global capital more so than, perhaps, any other physical commodity. From micro- to macroscales, the impact of global capital flows and loose government regulations are evident in everything from individual residential evictions and foreclosures to federal housing policy.[64] Observation of these processes led Marxist geographers and economists to develop the theory of "capital circuits." According to David Harvey, capitalists tend to invest first in the production of goods and services (the first circuit), which leads to an accumulation of capital. This excess can then be siphoned off by financial and state institutions through the creation of fictional capital within the credit system and then channeled into the built environment in the form of investments (the second circuit). This circuit switch may happen either in the course of a financial crisis or in a smoother and more deliberate fashion.[65]

In light of this, Harvey argues that capitalism is "addicted to geographical expansion as much as it is addicted to technological change and endless expansion through economic growth."[66] This led him to theorize a "spatial fix" for dilemmas of capital flow. He conceives of a "fix" in two ways: in the literal sense, as an object secured in space, and in the metaphorical sense, as a temporary solution to an ever-evolving problem that must also evolve to remain effective. The fix can take the form of changing location to take advantage of favorable conditions, like a labor surplus and/or resources, or it can mean rearranging the local environment through projects like suburban expansion or the construction of an airport to bring tourists to an area. In this way, the built environment functions both as the facilitator of further capital accumulation *and* as the investment vessel of capital surplus. Because the political economy is inextricably tied to geography, the result is uneven development: a phenomenon where already prosperous regions grow more affluent while other locales become increasingly marginalized.

Uneven development, produced by the "spatial trajectory of investment and disinvestment, economic growth and decline," creates urban spaces of impoverishment and deprivation located adjacent to thriving commercial and business centers.[67] As investors shape space over time, lucrative upscaling opportunities emerge from rent gaps created by disinvestment.[68] Uneven development was a key factor in the foreclosure crisis of the early twenty-first century, when the neoliberal policy decisions of the 1980s and 1990s enabled home mortgages in disinvested neighborhoods to become Wall Street trading commodities. Through this mechanism, risky mortgage lending connected spatialized inequities with global capital flows.[69] Many of these homes would later be purchased by corporations like Invitation Homes, with backing from private equity firms like Blackstone. These large institutions own about 5% of the single-family rental homes nationwide, with one projection estimating that this share may increase to 40% by 2030,[70] leading several federal lawmakers to call for regulatory legislation. Not surprisingly, Invitation Homes made a sizable contribution to a PAC to defeat a 2018 California ballot initiative (Proposition 10) that would have given localities the power to extend rent control protections to single-family homes.

Multifamily rental housing also emerged as a major investment frontier in the mid-2000s. This unfolded concurrently with the subprime mortgage boom and, though not directly related, was an outcome of the same search for new capital circuits enabled by deregulation or lack of regulation and oversight. In addition, weakened rental protections have shaped the nature of financialization (defined as private equity investor–owned property) in urban space, by creating opportunities to transform affordable multifamily housing into a new global asset class financed by private equity funds.[71] These Wall Street investors look for multifamily housing with "value add" potential (e.g., tenants paying low rents in a housing market where higher rents could be charged) to extract returns far beyond what a more traditional long-term landlord would expect, generally on a short-term basis analogous to the single-family home flipping model. The complicated institutional arrangements of landlords, creditors, investors, and managers often obfuscate decision-makers and entities that hold responsibility, making it difficult for tenants or jurisdictions to remedy issues.[72] As housing researchers Desiree Fields and Sabrina Uffer explain, "Areas of high demand afford a strategy of upgrading, modernizing or otherwise developing properties, yielding profits from increased rental income and/or the sale of upgraded properties to tenants or new investors."[73]

For example, the erosion of rent control in New York state by conservative lawmakers in the 1990s created an environment of speculative investment. In the early 2000s, investment firms and banks bought about one hundred thousand of these dwellings, which represented roughly 10% of New York City's city's rent-stabilized housing stock. Financial yields for shareholders were based on 20%–30% projected turnover in tenancy in contrast to the actual rate of 5%–10%. Fields and Uffer found that ensuring investment returns under these circumstances often requires the removal of long-term renters paying below market rents through a suite of harassment tactics that include building-wide eviction notices, frivolous lawsuits against tenants in the housing court, aggressive buyout offers, threats to contact immigration officials, and refusal to make repairs inside the home. In California, investors—from small landlords to corporate entities—have taken advantage of state law to evict longtime tenants of rent-controlled housing in order to close the "rent gap" and charge market rents to new tenants or Airbnb guests. The City of Los Angeles alone lost almost thirty thousand rent-controlled homes to evictions under the Ellis Act between 2001 and 2023.[74]

Decades of decisions to prioritize homeownership while stigmatizing renting and underinvesting in public housing have created conditions where renting on the private market means living in a state of material and perceptual precarity. In most U.S. locales, regulation of the rental market is minimal and the power imbalance between landlords and tenants is significant. As such, precarity exists in tandem with other stressors associated with the lack of control over housing quality, management, and cost. Research on risk and security in the U.K. rental housing market showed widespread involuntary mobility among renter households. The researchers concluded that the "experience of such precariousness has a notable impact on the experience of private renting and the extent to which individuals feel 'at home' in the tenure."[75] Similarly, a study of long-term renters in Australia found that most low-income renters experienced "perpetual insecurity" in the form of constant anxiety about having to move at any given time and being unable to find another home that meets their needs. One in four long-term renters interviewed experienced constant anxiety about housing insecurity.[76]

As housing research shows, housing precarity—regardless of the tenure type—has a range of negative consequences. A study of Milwaukee renters found low-income renters who experience forced mobility often must accept substandard housing, which then results in further moves.[77] In particular, evictions can present a substantial barrier to accessing housing, leaving households with few options.[78] A comprehensive literature review on housing insecurity identifies a higher likelihood of food insecurity, poor physical and mental health, low birth weight, antisocial behavior among youths, and developmental risk in children as common costs to families and individuals.[79] In this same vein, researchers in the health field identified a connection between difficulty paying for housing and self-reported poor health, hypertension, and arthritis as well as the deferral of health care visits and buying medication.[80] Similarly, mothers who experienced "housing disarray" (dark, crowded, and noisy) and instability were more likely to suffer from depression, while those experiencing only instability were more likely to have generalized anxiety disorder.[81] Another study compared the relationship between diminishing housing affordability and mental health for both homeowners and renters. The researchers found tenure to be a significantly mediating variable, concluding that "private renters appeared to be more vulnerable than home purchasers to mental health effects of unaffordable housing."[82]

Displacement often results in a loss of social networks of reliance and support that are especially crucial for lower-income households and communities, in addition to cultural resources and attachments. Displaced residents lose things like reciprocal expectations (favors), trustworthiness, and social norms and sanctions. Culturally, forced mobility can mean a loss of shared languages and traditions, systems of belief, and values "used by members of a group to ascribe meanings to events and experiences, to define roles and their distribution among members of given social groups, and to set norms for social interactions."[83] This is reflected in a study on mobility among low-income households, which identified relationships as the driving factor in locational decision-making. Support networks are an essential resource for low-income families to meet their basic needs, which leads to the prioritization of neighborhood relationships over other locational characteristics.[84] Research on the HOPE VI redevelopment of a public housing community in Portland confirms the importance of social capital for low-income households. Despite outside perceptions of deprivation and dilapidation, the majority of residents didn't want to leave their homes and described conditions of a "socially-well functioning community" that "allowed residents to lay down roots, form place attachments and create bonds of mutual support with neighbors."[85]

The ever-increasing cost of rent (in contrast to a mortgage with a fixed interest) is another negative feature of renting that impacts tenants with a range of income levels. Households who spend over 30% of their income on rent—and are, therefore, considered "cost-burdened"—reached an all-time high in 2023.* This affected just over 22% of all renter households, with more than 12% experiencing a severe cost burden, meaning they spend more than 50% of their income on housing.[86] Faced with these constraints, households

---

* This is the most recent year for which this data, from the U.S. Census Bureau and the American Community Survey, is available.

respond by spending less on food and health care, working more hours, moving, or adding additional residents to the home. Rent burden is associated with income, household composition (larger households and households with children), and location (metropolitan areas), above all other factors. Though rent burden is, not surprisingly, most prevalent among low-income households, it's on the rise for middle-income households as well. As housing researchers Gregg Colburn and Ryan Allen note, there are a significant "lack of policy responses that address hardship among renter households in contrast to the privileged status enjoyed by homeowners in the policy domain."[87]

Conclusion

From the earliest colonial settlement to the present day, private property rights have been a cornerstone of American culture and identity. But, at some point, the original concept of a Lockean ownership claim based on *use*—followed by the Jeffersonian yeoman homestead and then the detached single-family home—expanded to include the rights of anyone with the capital to purchase property, regardless of what they intend to do with it. As a result, in most of America, there is no restriction on tearing an apartment building down and leaving the lot vacant for decades, on raising a tenant household's rent by 100%–200%, or on building an apartment building and leaving it half-empty rather than lowering rents to what people will pay.

This explains why rent control, public housing, and nontraditional ownership models are still so controversial, even to nonlandlords: they threaten fundamental American values and beliefs related to property rights and the free market. From this perspective, government regulation of real estate investment feels deeply unjust. Oppositional rhetoric from the real estate industry evokes what David Harvey described as the "creative tension" between neoliberalism in theory and neoliberalism in practice. As he points out, the state's role is ostensibly to refrain from interfering with free market enterprise. In actuality, it has evolved in different local and national contexts to suit corporate and entrepreneurial priorities, which *is* a form of market interference.[88] For example, landlords are able to take advantage of elements in the tax code, like depreciation and operating cost write-offs, which enable some owners to leave apartments empty if they can't secure the desired rent. Meanwhile, tenants can't deduct their rent payments the way homeowners benefit from the mortgage interest deduction. The steadfast belief that landlordism is simply good old-fashioned American entrepreneurialism, and should be minimally regulated at best, persists today, including in the nation's most progressive enclaves.

The People's Republic of Santa Monica

The rent control initiative has developed a new spirit of
unity and strength in this silent majority. . . . A permanent
change in the political structure of the city is presently
taking place, and rent control is the catalyst, the vehicle for
such change. The tenants are preparing to take their
rightful majority place in guiding the city into the future.

—SYD ROSE, TENANT ACTIVIST[1]

In 2011, the FBI's number one most wanted criminal, Whitey Bulger, was identified and taken into custody by bureau agents at the Princess Eugenia Apartments. The unassuming three-story dingbat-style building is located just blocks from Santa Monica's vibrant commercial core and the popular Third Street Promenade. Bulger had lived there with his wife for fourteen years under a fake name, in a rent-controlled apartment. In a *60 Minutes* report on Bulger's arrest, journalist Steve Kroft described Santa Monica's distinctive social mix:

> This low-key, seaside suburb of LA is shared by tourists and transients, hedonists and hippies, celebrities and lots of senior citizens, attracted to the climate and an abundance of rent-controlled apartments just a few blocks from the ocean.[2]

In Kroft's view, the city's large senior population and affordable rent (at the time Bulger began renting) made it the perfect place for an elderly fugitive to hide.

Santa Monica's rent control legacy has indelibly shaped the city's social fabric and identity. The small city made national headlines in the late 1970s when a coalition of activists pulled off a radical political and ideological coup, upending the previous regime's "growth machine" ideology and replacing it with a progressive vision of a vibrant community, underpinned by a partial decommodification of privately owned rental housing.[3] This

Figure 2.1 Front page of the *Santa Monica Evening Outlook*, April 11, 1979.

history remains deeply embedded in the city's political culture, even in the face of dramatic socioeconomic shifts, the recent political realignment, and the gradual erosion of housing affordability.

From the inception of this local revolution to the present day, city policymakers and tenant advocates have been locked in a prolonged battle with real estate and landlord interests over rent control and other tenant protection policies. This struggle is, ultimately, about controlling land and the profits that can be extracted from it. Though it is sometimes focused locally on Santa Monica, it also plays out on larger scales, from the county to the region to the state. Sometimes the fight takes place on the national level. In early 2024, the Supreme Court of the United States declined to hear a case brought by New York state landlords challenging the constitutionality of rent control on the federal level. It wasn't the first challenge of its kind and likely won't be the last.

The legacy of tenant activists, and the sea change they catalyzed, continues to shape policy in Santa Monica, informing renters' relationships with the places where they live, and the extent to which they feel at home. At the same time, this sustained effort by the real estate investment industry to tear down tenant protections creates an environment of tenuousness and uncertainty that inevitably impacts the real lives of tenants in Santa Monica, whether through policy or by informing the behavior of individual landlords.

The Bay City

Unlike older urban areas across the nation that typically formed around industry and trade routes, in Southern California, the land itself—with the exceptional climate and natural beauty—was always the region's best product. Fueled by boosters who extolled the region's positive attributes, real estate speculation and railroad entrepreneurship (often in coordination) were intrinsic to settlement and rapid expansion after the Spanish rancho period. Seminal California historian Carey McWilliams described the land speculation boom in Southern California as beginning in the 1870s and continuing unabated. "Buying a slice of one of the ranchos," he wrote, "the promoters would build a hotel, lay out a few streets, sidewalks, and curbs, and start the construction of a local railway." As one San Diego real estate firm explained, "This boom is based on the simple fact that hereabouts the good Lord has created conditions of climate and health and beauty as can be found nowhere else." Between 1884 and 1888 over one hundred towns were platted in Los Angeles County, two-thirds of which no longer exist.[4]

The place we now know as Santa Monica occupies a part of Tovaangar, the ancestral homeland of the Tongva people. The Tongva called this place Kecheek. Much of the modern city's footprint was part of the Spanish land grant ranches Rancho Boca de Santa Monica and Rancho San Vicente y Santa Monica. The land was purchased by Colonel Robert S. Baker who soon brought on Nevada Senator John P. Jones as his investment partner. The two aspired to create a town that would be a major commercial center in the Southwest. They platted the town in 1875 and put the first lots up for auction that same week, with buyers coming from as far away as San Francisco to invest in what was touted as the next great seaport on the West Coast.[5] The auctioneer Tom Fitch—who McWilliams describes as one of the "poets" of the Southern California land boom—auctioned off the first lots. He described Santa Monica as the "Zenith of the Sunset Sea."

City residents voted to incorporate Santa Monica as a city in 1886, with 168 men casting their votes. Though Jones and Baker initially aspired to develop the city into a prosperous port town, they lost their bid for the county's harbor and Santa Monica was primarily a resort destination from its inception through the first half of the twentieth century. By the 1800s, the city had a reputation as a party destination for residents of neighboring Los Angeles. Saloons and bathhouses proliferated. City leaders attempted to crack down on this activity with little success.[6] In 1909, the Pacific Electric

2510 – Port Los Angeles, from the Palisades, Santa Monica, California.

Figure 2.2 Postcard depicting what is now known as the California Incline, which connects Ocean Avenue and the Pacific Coast Highway. The Incline was completed in 1905 and the postcard is from a few years later. *(Author's collection.)*

Streetcar company opened the Santa Monica Air Line, which offered public transportation from Los Angeles (then still centered in what is now Downtown Los Angeles) to the seaside resort town. It operated on the same tracks as the steam-powered train that began passenger service to Santa Monica around 1875. At the time, much of the area between the two cities was undeveloped. The municipal Santa Monica Pier opened September 9, 1909, and was an instant success, attracting large crowds from throughout the area. Amusements entrepreneur Charles Looff constructed an adjoining pier in 1916, which included the Looff Hippodrome, now a National Historic Landmark and home to Santa Monica's famous carousel.

The piers' popularity diminished during the 1930s as amusement attractions were decommissioned, and the pier went through an extended period of decline.[7] Author Horace McCoy used the pier for the setting of his Depression-era novel *They Shoot Horses, Don't They?*,[8] a story about Hollywood hopefuls competing in a hellish dance marathon that was a popular form of entertainment at the time. For noir author Raymond Chandler, Santa Monica was the Bay City. This seaside burb at the end of Wilshire Boulevard, where the water was dotted with gambling boats and the police had a light touch, was, in Chandler's world, somehow even more corrupt

Figure 2.3 Santa Monica Pier and Beach circa 1924. *(Fred Bastien Collection, Santa Monica History Museum.)*

than neighboring Los Angeles. Later, the pier's faded resort town atmosphere would be the setting for the films *Inside Daisy Clover* (1965), *Night Tide* (1961), and *The Sting* (1973), among others.

Santa Monica became an important defense industry production center during World War II, when Douglas Aircraft employed about forty-four thousand workers. This influx of residents transformed the city, requiring thousands of new homes to accommodate the increase in population.[9] By 1968, the Douglas plant had closed, and the 1960s and 1970s saw a flourishing of skate and surf culture in what was at the time a relatively affordable part of greater Los Angeles. Though neighboring Venice was more widely known for its counterculture scene, Santa Monica, and the Ocean Park neighborhood in particular, also attracted artists and political and community activists, setting the stage for the renters' revolt of the late 1970s.

In the early 1970s, Santa Monica City Council proposed demolishing the piers, and residents organized the Save Our Pier Forever campaign, successfully staving off demolition. Today the pier is a popular tourist destination and part of what brings people to the city. The year before the pandemic over

Figure 2.4 Santa Monica postcard from the mid-twentieth century. *(Santa Monica History Museum.)*

eight million people visited Santa Monica, half of whom were coming from outside the United States.[10] This same spirit of grassroots community organizing would later drive the campaign for rent control. Somewhere along the way, and through unknown origins, the city acquired its motto: *Populus felix in urbe felici.** The phrase is captured in the terrazzo city seal in the lobby of the 1938 city hall, displayed under a coastal scene featuring a coy mermaid, two small ships, and the sun beaming radiantly over the Santa Monica mountains.

One of LA County's eighty-eight municipalities, Santa Monica is 8.3 square miles and is surrounded by the City of Los Angeles on three sides and the Pacific Ocean on the fourth. A comparatively small city, it's home to about 93,000 of the county's 10 million residents.[†] Today the city has a relatively high percentage of renters, at 71% of the population. This is a slight decline from 80% in the late 1970s, when voters passed the city's rent control law. Comparatively, the county's percentage of renters is 54.2%, while the city of Los Angeles is 43.2%. Santa Monica also has higher education levels,

---

* The title of this book is taken from a participant interview and is one of several translations. Another common one is "happy people in a happy city."

† All data is contemporaneous to 2021, when the interviews were conducted, unless otherwise noted.

Figure 2.5 Santa Monica tourism billboard circa 1960. *(Santa Monica History Museum.)*

median income, rents, density, and racial and ethnic homogeneity, with 64.6% of residents identifying as white only, compared to 26% of county residents. Significantly, only 15.4% of Santa Monica's residents identify as Latino as compared to 48.6% countywide.[11] It has the most expensive average rent for a market rate one-bedroom apartment in the Los Angeles Metro Area.[12]

Santa Monica has an at-large city council system, which means its seven council members are selected by the entire electorate, rather than by district, as in neighboring Los Angeles.* Every two years, the city council selects one of its members to serve as the mayor and another to serve as the mayor pro tempore. Council member terms are four years, and council members often hold full-time jobs in addition to their position. The city manager's office

---

* The city council's at-large structure was the subject of a 2016 lawsuit from the Pico Neighborhood Association and neighborhood resident Maria Loya, alleging that the system dilutes Latino voting power. After an initial judgment in favor of the plaintiff, followed by a reversal in favor of the City and subsequent appeals, the lawsuit is still making its way through the courts. At the time these interviews were conducted, Loya's husband, Oscar de la Torre, was serving as a city council member.

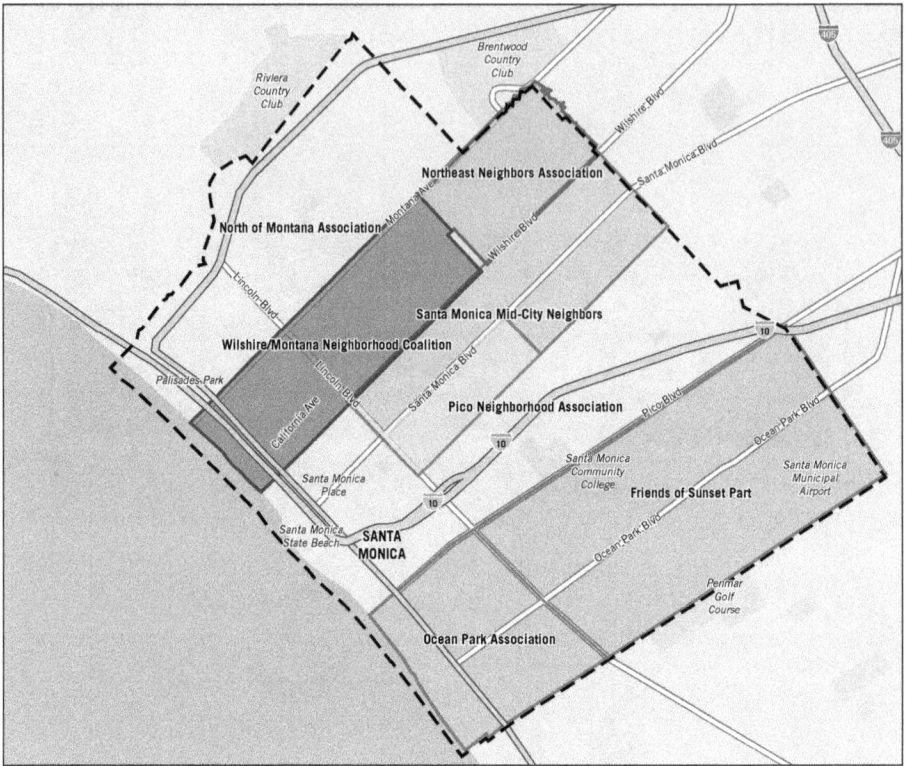

Figure 2.6 Santa Monica neighborhoods by neighborhood association boundaries. *(City of Santa Monica.)*

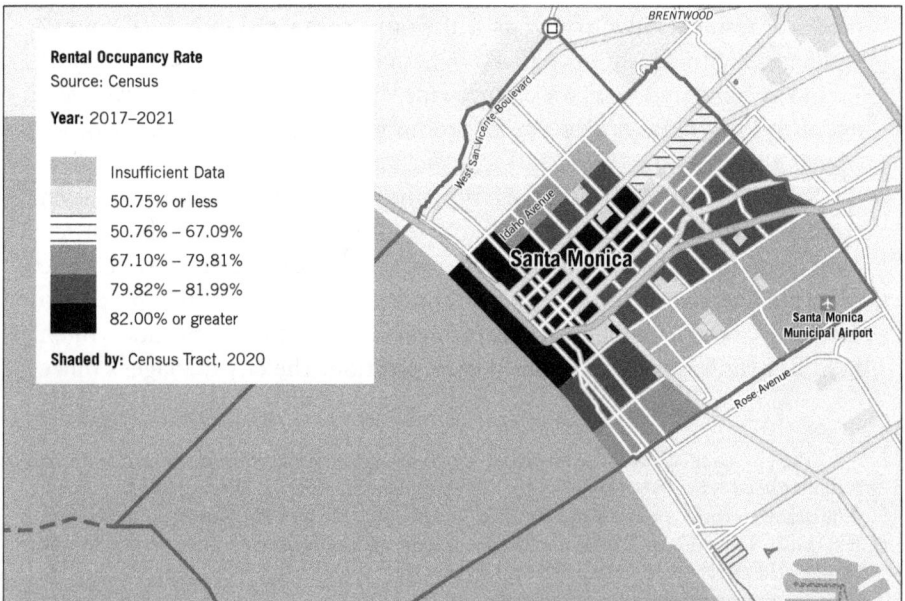

Figure 2.7 Distribution of renter households in Santa Monica between 2017 and 2021. *(PolicyMap based on data from the U.S. census. Source: available at www.policymap.com.)*

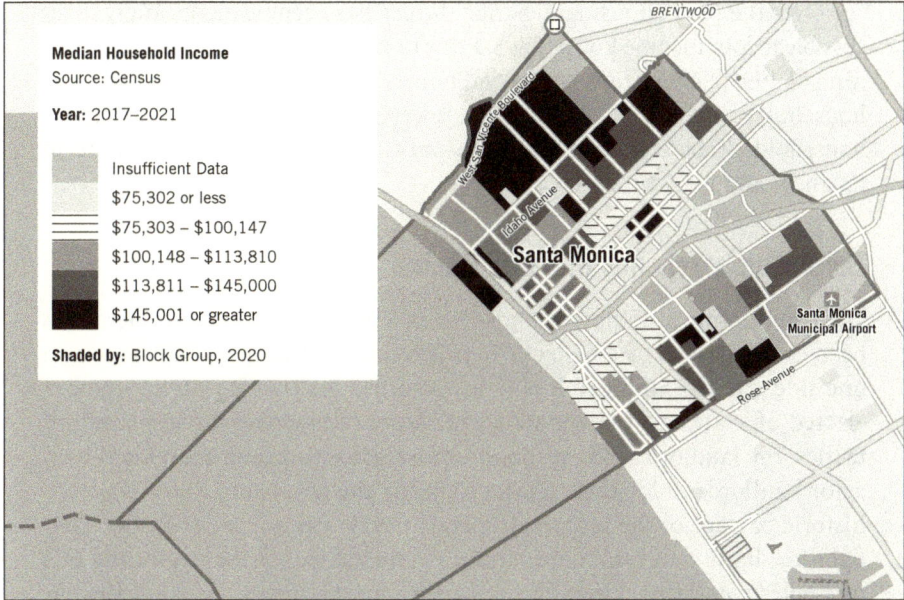

Figure 2.8 Median household income in Santa Monica between 2017 and 2021. *(PolicyMap based on data from the U.S. census. Source: available at www.policymap.com.)*

leads the various city departments and staff in implementing the city council's vision.

The majority of the city's renters live in one of its 27,429 rent-stabilized dwellings. Of those households, 24.7% have lived in their homes since before 1999. More than half of all rent-controlled apartments have been rerented since 2011, with almost 40% turning over tenancies between 2016 and 2020. A staggering 81% of tenants who moved into a rent-controlled apartment in 2015 have already moved out.[13] According to the RCB's 2020 annual report:

> With starting rents at rates that would not be considered "affordable" for many tenants, and without deep roots in the community, recent tenants appear more mobile. Tenants who have been renting in Santa Monica for a longer time, likely feel more connected to the community and realize the financial benefits of remaining in place.[14]

As my interview findings show, this high level of turnover has a negative impact on the social fabric of individual apartment buildings. It also produces housing insecurity and anxiety for longtime tenants who are aware of the significant gap between their rent and market rent, presenting strong incentives for their landlords to find a way to end their tenancies. Policy loopholes that enable and exacerbate this are discussed later.

Over the years, housing in Santa Monica has become increasingly inaccessible to low-income households. Prior to vacancy decontrol* at the beginning of 1999, 84% of rent-controlled homes were affordable to low-income households, whereas in 2020 only 4.2% were considered affordable to those households. Table 2.1 illustrates the disparity between the average long-term tenancy† and market rate tenancy.

The People's Republic of Santa Monica

The tenant protection policy landscape in Santa Monica (as elsewhere) has been characterized by a dialectic between the city and tenant advocates on one side and the landlord lobby on the other. As the city and protenant elected officials enact new policies in response to ever-evolving landlord tactics, the landlord lobby responds with legal action, and individual bad-actor landlords tailor their tactics to evade the law. Santa Monica voters' historic passage of the rent control law in 1979 was not the end of renters' fight for dignity and full community membership, but the beginning of a new one: Over the next four decades a protracted struggle unfolded for control over the city's housing stock, and, by extension, between the competing objectives of a vibrant and healthy community and the right to extract profits. The tension between the Marxian dichotomy of use value and exchange value continues to play out in the political landscape of the small city, and, by extension, in every renter's home.

Revolt!

Though California didn't have a strong tenant movement until the 1970s, there were two prior instances of rent control in the state. The first was a short-lived 1921 rent control law in Los Angeles, which was adopted by the city council in response to tenant advocacy. The Apartment Association of Greater Los Angeles (AAGLA) and their attorney were instrumental in ending the law, which state courts ruled as unconstitutional that same year.[15] The federal Emergency Price Control Act of 1942 was more difficult to defeat. Though the controls were initially generally accepted in the patriotic spirit of the time, landlord opposition started building in 1945 after the war ended. According to historian and policy scholar Alisa Belinkoff Katz, the

---

* Vacancy decontrol is mandated by state law and means that when one tenant moves out a landlord can charge market rate rent to the new tenant. Prior to the law's passage, rent increases were regulated between tenants and throughout the tenancy. This preserved housing affordability over the long term.

† Long-term tenancies are homes that have been occupied by the same household prior to January 1, 1999, and have thus never been subject to vacancy decontrol.

TABLE 2.1. "RENT GAP" BETWEEN RENTS PAID BY LONG-TERM TENANTS AND MARKET RATES

Area	0-Bedroom units			1-Bedroom units			2-Bedroom units			3-Bedroom units		
	Long term	Market rate	Diff.	Long term	Market rate	Diff.	Long term	Market rate	Diff.	Long term	Market rate	Diff.
A	$702	$1,677	$975	$929	$2,364	$1,435	$1,155	$3,034	$1,879	$1,350	$3,651	$2,301
B	$603	$1,425	$822	$826	$1,922	$1,096	$982	$2,572	$1,590	$1,350	$2,874	$1,524
C	$811	$2,413	$1,602	$842	$2,784	$1,942	$982	$2,958	$1,976	N/A	N/A	N/A
D	$549	$1,500	$951	$770	$1,922	$1,152	$862	$2,275	$1,413	$1,062	$3,113	$2,051
E	$704	$1,635	$931	$839	$1,979	$1,140	$1,092	$2,627	$1,535	$1,373	$3,449	$2,076
F	$827	$1,707	$880	$1,014	$2,432	$1,418	$1,330	$3,134	$1,804	$1,537	$4,197	$2,660
G	$757	$1,758	$1,001	$888	$2,215	$1,327	$1,202	$2,938	$1,736	$1,563	$3,918	$2,355
Citywide	**$745**	**$1,707**	**$962**	**$888**	**$2,166**	**$1,278**	**$1,106**	**$2,795**	**$1,689**	**$1,421**	**$3,595**	**$2,174**

Note: Aside from 1221 Ocean Ave., there are only five three-bedroom units in Area C, so the median is not reported here.

Source: Santa Monica Rent Control Board. (2020). *2020 Annual Report Santa Monica Rent Control Board. City of Santa Monica.*

group argued the rent ceilings were so low they weren't able to cover costs, and the law hurt small landlords, with many threatening to pull their properties off the market in protest. Landlord rhetoric opposing rent control during the period centered on a narrative of "communistic" and "un-American" ideological underpinnings, which would be echoed in landlord opposition to the rent control movements of the 1970s and through to the present day.[16] In July 1950, over two thousand members packed Los Angeles City Hall to support a resolution requesting the end of local rent control. When the federal government amended the law later that year allowing for voluntary continuation of rent controls, Los Angeles ended its local policy, as did all other California jurisdictions.*

In tenant movement historian Allan David Heskin's analysis, "Aspiring tenant organizers considered the California tenant to be too individualistic and too mobile to be organized." In California, "housing conditions were considered to be too good, the weather too mild, urban settlement too spread out, and densities of renters too low for collective mass action."[17] Several events turned the tide, setting the stage for California's successful tenant movement of the 1970s. A population increase early in the decade strained the existing housing stock and outpaced the construction of new rental housing, but rent increases remained moderate for several years. In the mid-1970s, the construction of new multifamily housing declined significantly, and rents began to increase substantially, with yearly average increases over the annual CPI increase (already high with inflation of the time) for several years in a row. California's real estate industry mobilized around the growing threat of tenant organizing statewide, and their lobbyists introduced a legislative bill to preempt local rent control legislation at the state level. Though the bill passed in the senate, the California Department of Housing and Community Development convinced Governor Jerry Brown to veto it. The attempt to supersede local control and needed tenant protections galvanized tenant advocates statewide and resulted in the formation of the California Housing Action and Information Network, whose strategy was to build tenant power through local organizing.

In Santa Monica, median rents rose 125% between 1970 and 1980.[18] One factor was a spike in real estate speculation that led to a tenfold increase in the number of rental properties sold between 1972 and 1977. By 1977, rent

---

* The AAGLA continues to engage in advocacy and lobbying efforts, with the AAGLA Legal Fund, the AAGLA PAC, and the AAGLA Issues PAC. They have an advocacy and lobbyist team in Los Angeles that works in the three counties they serve as well as three full-time lobbyists in Sacramento and they help fund lobbyists in Washington, DC. In addition to submitting comments and testimony on policy proposals and meeting with elected leaders, the group has been the plaintiff in numerous lawsuits against various municipalities, including Santa Monica.

control was already being debated in the public sphere, with a burgeoning tenant movement led by labor arbitrator Syd Rose. In an article printed the day after a rally at Santa Monica High School that was attended by about three hundred people, the *Evening Outlook* described the issue as having "the potential for erupting into the hottest political battle Santa Monica has ever faced."[19] In addition to unsustainable rent increases, condominium conversions were also a major issue for Santa Monica renters, with over five hundred rental homes converted from apartments to condominiums in 1978 and 1979.*

The orientation of Santa Monica's political establishment was traditional and conservative, with Council Member Seymour Cohen remarking, "Some people wisely invested in property and I don't condemn them for their actions. Some of you are too lazy to go out and do the same thing."[20] Mayor Donna Swink, who was vice president of a local bank that financed real estate acquisitions, opined that the problem in the city was not high rents but rather too many renters and not enough homeowners. According to the Reverend Jim Conn—who led the progressive Church in Ocean Park during the time and was deeply involved in the movement—one council member informed him that poor people were just going to have to learn to accept that they would not be able to live in the city anymore. Conn made it his mission to advocate for policy and programming that would enable low-income households to remain in Santa Monica.[21]

In 1978, a group of seniors who had already been involved with Rose's efforts, together with younger activists who had been involved in community organizing like the Save Our Pier Forever campaign and other initiatives opposing redevelopment around the city, channeled the momentum of the movement and formed the Santa Monica Fair Housing Alliance. Working together, they succeeded in qualifying a rent control charter amendment for the November 1978 ballot. Landlord interests outspent tenant organizers by twenty to one, and local voters failed to pass the policy, with 54% of voters voting against it. Santa Barbara voters also failed to pass their local rent control measure. Los Angeles City Council passed a rent control ordinance that same year, making it the first major West Coast city to adopt the policy.

Meanwhile in the same election cycle, homeowners statewide rallied against unprecedented spikes in property taxes, resulting in voters passing Proposition 13. This legislation limits property taxes to 1% of the assessed value of property—both owner-occupied and leased—with maximum increases of 2% per year unless the property is sold or improved through new construction.[22] Because the property value is only assessed at sale or new construction, the benefit to owners increases over time to become a

---

* My parents were evicted from their rental home for a condominium conversion.

Figure 2.9a Flyer from the Santa Monica rent control campaign, 1977. *(Santa Monica Committee for Fair Rents.)*

- Ignoring the hundreds of angry tenants who twice appeared before them;
- Ignoring the many rent increases in Santa Monica since the passage of Proposition 13;
- Ignoring the example of cities like Los Angeles, Beverly Hills, and El Monte;

THE SANTA MONICA CITY COUNCIL VOTED TO TAKE *NO ACTION* TO PROTECT RENTERS HERE!

RENTERS LAUNCH NEW

RENT CONTROL DRIVE

Refusing to be ignored, a coalition of community groups has announced a joint effort to place a rent control initiative on the April 1979 ballot.

IF WE ARE TO WIN, WE MUST HAVE YOUR HELP!

COME TO THE RALLY!
Retail Clerks Auditorium
1410 2nd St.
(near Santa Monica Blvd.)

OCTOBER 23, 7:30 P.M.

Sponsored by:
Santa Monica Fair Housing Alliance
Campaign for Economic Democracy
Santa Monica Tenant Union Council

FOR INFORMATION CALL: 829-2484

Figure 2.9b Flyer from the Santa Monica rent control campaign, 1978. *(Santa Monica Committee for Fair Rents.)*

significant tax break. Under Proposition 13, owners are insulated from fluctuations in the market, while, without rent control, tenants are not. According to the National Bureau of Economic Research, Proposition 13 creates "obvious distortions in the marketplace" and decreases mobility among homeowners—an outcome also intrinsic to the landlord lobby's critique of rent control.[23] Landlords engaged in an intensive campaign to garner tenant support for Proposition 13, promising more stable rent increases if the measure passed.

These promises temporarily defused the demand for rent control, but when landlords continued to raise rents after the bill passed, tenant organizing and agitation escalated in Santa Monica and beyond. SMRR formed as a coalition of Santa Monica Fair Housing Alliance, Tom Hayden's (along with Jane Fonda) national organization, the Campaign for Economic Democracy, the Santa Monica Democratic Club, and the Committee for Fair Rents. Drawing on Campaign for Economic Democracy's substantial organizational resources and knowledge, along with a small army of committed volunteers, SMRR ran a second, more sophisticated, campaign to pass a rent control ballot measure in April 1979. In the weeks and months leading up to the election, panicked landlords engaged in what local media described as a "demolition derby"—demolishing around five hundred rental homes, mostly in the Wilshire corridor neighborhood. Not surprisingly, the biggest increase in support came from tenants in that area who had voted against the previous measure.

Despite intensive countercampaigning by the opposition, Proposition A passed with 54.3% in favor—nearly the same percentage of voters that had previously voted against it. SMRR candidates Ruth Yannatta Goldway and William Jennings were also elected to the city council. The measure amended the city charter, freezing rents for 120 days and then rolling them back to April 1, 1978, levels. Reporting in the *Evening Outlook* described how "the rent control victory was seen by some election-night observers as a 'revolution' which will mark the beginning of significant changes in the social and economic make-up of the community." Santa Monica became one of the few cities in California where rent control was adopted by voters. Los Angeles's ordinance was implemented by its city council, and similar ballot measures in San Francisco and Santa Cruz had recently failed. At the victory celebration Jane Fonda thanked campaign volunteers, who had "given their lives, some of them for years," to the cause.[24]

The landlord lobby's foiled victory party at the Miramar Hotel's Starlight Ballroom had a decidedly different tone. John Jurenka, a landlord advocate and former prowrestler who had been the leading proponent of the drive to demolish the Santa Monica pier and had just lost his own bid for the city council, vowed that Santa Monica landlords were "not going to take this sitting down. We're going to challenge this and we're already prepared to file

A-6—Wed., April 11, 1979   EVENING OUTLOOK

Evening Outlook Photo by James Ruebsom

CENTER STAGE — New Santa Monica City Councilwoman Ruth Yannatta (right) is joined on the stage at the victory celebration of pro- rent control forces by actress Jane Fonda (left), rent control campagin treasurer Cheryl Rhoden and political activist Tom Hayden, Miss Fonda's husband. Miss Fonda and Hayden, whose Campaign for Economic Democracy backed rent control, live in Ocean Park.

Son of former   SM rent controls approved

Figure 2.10 Coverage of the rent control campaign victory featuring Jane Fonda, Cheryl Rhoden, Tom Hayden, and Ruth Yannatta in the *Santa Monica Evening Outlook.*

a lawsuit."[25] Sure enough, the AAGLA filed suit within twenty-four hours of the ordinance's passage to prevent it from moving forward, on behalf of four landlord plaintiffs. The suit argued the law denied owners the right to a fair return on their investments, as guaranteed by the state and federal constitutions. Several initial rulings in the superior court found different parts of the law to be unconstitutional, but then, in 1986, a state court of appeals overturned those rulings. Shortly thereafter, the U.S. Supreme Court rejected the AAGLA's request to hear the case on the grounds that it did not contain a "properly presented federal question." The lawsuit ended up costing the AAGLA nearly $800,000.[26]

Tenant organizers didn't have a moment to rest. The next struggle would be to fill the five elected seats on the Rent Control Board, which was to be formed as part of the charter amendment. The city was required to hold a special election for the five board commissioners within ninety days of the measure's adoption. The commissioners serve four-year terms and meet at least one time per month. The board is empowered to change the regulations that dictate the implementation and enforcement of rent control. They also hold hearings about rent decreases or increases and occasionally file suit against landlords. Two months after Proposition A passed, all five SMRR candidates were elected to the newly formed RCB. The following November, voters elected SMRR candidate Cheryl Rhoden to the city council, continuing the progressive coup with three of the seven council members now in the tenants' corner. The landlord-sponsored Proposition Q—which would have weakened the rent control law by exempting single-family homes, permitting higher rent increases, and allowing rent increases to market rates between tenancies—was defeated by voters in that same election.[27]

SMRR gradually increased its political power with a series of electoral victories, achieving a majority on the city council in 1981 with the election of Jim Conn, Ken Edwards, Denny Zane, and Dolores Press. By the end of 1979, Los Angeles County and El Monte joined Santa Monica, Los Angeles, and Beverly Hills as jurisdictions with rent control. The new West Hollywood City Council would follow suit in 1985 after area residents voted to incorporate as a city for the purpose of preserving rent control, in response to the LA County Board of Supervisors vote to phase out the county ordinance in 1984.[28]

In the midst of these historic victories, the landlord lobby's opposition was relentless. Local landlords formed a trade group called ACTION,* in the wake of the tenant movement's dramatic 1979 victory. Their website describes the original 1979 policy as "radical," and over the past four decades, ACTION has initiated numerous lawsuits against the city. Around this time, the landlord lobby started referring to the city as the "People's Republic of Santa Monica." Though surely not all landlords were opposed to rent control, there was a current in anti–rent control discourse that portrayed it as radical to the point of being communist. The involvement of Tom Hayden and his wife "Hanoi Jane" Fonda contributed to this framing, but ultimately, it was the challenge to the primacy of private property and the right to profit that was most objectionable. The influx of Eastern Europeans who emigrated to escape communism and became mom-and-pop landlords was also a contributing factor.

In their comprehensive account of Santa Monica's tenant movement, Stella Čapek and John Gilderbloom describe the expansion of SMRR's agenda from rent control to other progressive priorities as "a vision of community . . . that was much broader than the single focus on rent control."[29] According to former SMRR cochair Nancy Greenstein, the organization's vision for Santa Monica represented a fundamental ideological departure

---

* They updated their name to ACTION Apartment Association in 1991.

from the former regime. Prior to the city's progressive awakening, Santa Monica was largely run by the Chamber of Commerce and established families concerned with maintaining the status quo of business interests' hegemony and "growth machine" ethos. In contrast, SMRR focused on environmental issues, increasing social services, women's rights, workers' rights, preserving diversity, and economic vitality, among other priorities. After rent control passed, "There was a sense of ownership, even though you didn't own it," said Greenstein. "There was a sense of, this is my community, this is where I live. We had a voice."* [30] As Conn explained, "We had a whole vision for what we wanted the city to be like. We had a whole vision of the elements that needed to be in place for this to be a livable place for everybody." [31]

Robert M. Myers authored the Rent Control Charter Amendment a mere three years after graduating from Loyola Law School, while working as a staff attorney with the Legal Aid Foundation of Los Angeles. According to the amendment's statement of purpose, it aims to address the following:

> A growing shortage of housing units resulting in a low vacancy rate and rapidly rising rents exploiting this shortage constitute a serious housing problem affecting the lives of a substantial portion of those Santa Monica residents who reside in residential housing. In addition, speculation in the purchase and sale of existing residential housing units results in further rent increases. These conditions endanger the public health and welfare of Santa Monica tenants, especially the poor, minorities, students, young families, and senior citizens.

Myers went on to serve as Santa Monica's City Attorney from 1981 to 1992. Longtime tenant lawyer Elena Popp credits Myers with creating a culture within the city attorney's office of proactively enforcing consumer protections and laws that protect vulnerable people, which contrasts sharply with the City of Los Angeles's approach. [32]

Heskin attributes SMRR's victory to their successful ideological framing of what was at stake:

> Tenants repeatedly asserted their attachment to the community. They denied that tenants were second-class citizens and asserted the

---

* Due to the economic and residential stability created by rent control, Greenstein was able to save enough money to eventually purchase a condo in Santa Monica. This stability also enabled her to make choices about her career and volunteer commitments that led to her cofounding the Public Policy Institute at Santa Monica Community College as an elected member of the college's board of trustees.

rights and status of full citizens. They referred to their apartments as homes, and indicated that they felt these homes were threatened. They emphasized their desire to stay in Santa Monica, where some had lived all their lives.[33]

This rhetoric was the foundation of Santa Monica tenants' successful moral claims to their neighborhoods, communities, and city. It challenged home-owner ideology by asserting that the people who actually live and work in a community—who *create* community—are its rightful owners, regardless of whose name is on the property deed. Elders were a critical component of both the movement and its messaging. Flyers often featured seniors who faced or had already experienced displacement. They evoked not only the cruelty of uprooting someone on a fixed postretirement income but also the irreplaceable loss of one's *home* environment. As Čapek and Gilderbloom write, this "change in the identity of tenants is one of the most tangible re-sults of the social movement in Santa Monica."[34] In their analysis, the dif-ferentiation between "home" and housing as a commodity was at the crux of the paradigm shift that repositioned tenants as full members of society in Santa Monica and beyond.

Over forty years after its formation, SMRR remains a powerful—though contested—player in local politics. Despite the rapid expansion of LATU, SMRR remains the primary voice for tenant interests in Santa Monica. SMRR is a voluntary membership organization with no paid staff. Accord-ing to their official platform, "All residents are entitled to stability, safety, privacy, dignity and peace in their homes. A primary goal of SMRR is to support, defend and enhance rent control and tenant protections locally, regionally and statewide." In addition to this core mission, their platform also includes a number of other progressive initiatives. The majority of elect-ed officials in Santa Monica since SMRR's inception have been endorsed by the organization, including all RCB commissioners. Eleven of the past twelve mayors are SMRR members, and candidates endorsed by SMRR have held a majority on the city council most years since their initial electoral victory in 1981. Each year SMRR holds its Annual Membership Convention, where candidates seeking endorsement make speeches and members vote on who will receive the SMRR endorsement. These include not only candi-dates for the city council but also those for the school board, the commu-nity college board, and state representatives.

After the Revolution: Santa Monica Housing Policy, 1981–2021

Santa Monica's rent control law is an amendment to the city charter and can only be modified by city voters. The major provisions of the law are that it:

1. Controls the amount that may continue to be charged for a rental residence and provides remedies for the collection of excess rent
2. Determines the amenities and services that are included as part of the rent and provides remedies for removal or reduction of those amenities or services
3. Provides for only "just cause" evictions*
4. Limits removal of controlled residences from the rental market

The law applies to most multifamily residential buildings built before April 10, 1979, and, in some circumstances, buildings constructed after. It also applies to certain single-family homes and condominiums. Duplexes and triplexes are under rent control by default but are eligible for removal if the owner moves into one of the residences. Annual rent increases are limited to 75% of the increase in the CPI for the region, and the RCB may also set a dollar-amount limit, which is calculated using a set formula. The Rent Control Agency (RCA) supports policy implementation, outreach, and enforcement. The RCA maintains a website and public database of all rent-controlled residences, their maximum allowable rents (MAR), and the associated documents for each residence. It also conducts landlord and tenant information seminars, sends out a twice-yearly newsletter for landlords and tenants, proactively pursues delinquent landlord registration fees, and sends information to new landlords, among other services. The RCA-run rent control office (RCO) answers questions and assists with other businesses for both landlords and tenants.

In 1984, city voters enacted the Tenant Ownership Rights Charter Amendment (TORCA),† which allowed rent-controlled apartments to be converted to condominiums in certain circumstances. Conversation was only allowed if all tenants consented. Each resident would have the opportunity to purchase their home for a below market price, and any resident who chose not to buy was able to remain in their home under rent control. A tax associated with TORCA conversions funded the program and provided assistance to low- and moderate-income households who wished to

---

* It permits exemptions for the (a) occupation of the landlord or an immediate family member, (b) removal of the property from the rental market, (c) nonpayment of rent, and (d) violation of a "material and substantial" obligation of the tenancy that has not been previously waived through the landlord's past behavior or statements. Owners are also allowed to offer a tenant money to move out, which is commonly known as "cash for keys," provided they furnish the tenant with certain information about their rights.

† One of the tenants interviewed for this book lives in a TORCA complex. Her situation dealing with both a property manager/landlord and a homeowner's association is unique in the study.

purchase their homes. The amendment had a "sunset" provision to expire in 1996 unless voters opted to extend it, which did not come to pass.

The California Association of Realtors scored a major victory against rent control in 1985 when the state legislature passed the Ellis Act, and Santa Monica was at the center of it. It was catalyzed by a lawsuit filed against the City of Santa Monica by eighteen-year-old Jerome Nash* [35]—a UCLA student who inherited a six-residence apartment building and was denied permission by the city to demolish it. Nash won in superior court, but the state supreme court reversed the decision, and the U.S. Supreme Court refused to hear the case. The California Association of Realtors lobbied Jim Ellis (R-San Diego), a state senator, to sponsor a bill that would guarantee landlords the right to evict their tenants and "exit the rental business," which would preempt any local prohibitions on demolition such as those encountered by Nash.[36]

The law prohibits local governments from requiring landlords to continue renting their residential properties if they choose to "go out of business." Yet, oddly, the landlord needn't leave the real estate investment business altogether, as the law applies to the individual property not the proprietor. Moreover, there is no requirement that the owner have purchased the property prior to the rent control law's passage, which means that despite their knowledge of the regulations at the time of purchase, landlords are still permitted to evict tenants at their convenience. Under the law, owners have a number of options for their Ellis'd building, including condominium conversion, demolition, a change in usage (e.g., residential to commercial), or simply letting the building sit empty.

The landlord lobby had carved out a very effective loophole: to the present day, the Ellis Act is one of two statewide policies that have been most detrimental to the efficacy of local rent control. An article in the *Los Angeles Times* right before the law went into effect described how conservative legislators had successfully circumvented local control:

> Not having done well in the courts, not having an outstanding batting average in local elections (earlier this month, voters defeated a measure that would have allowed vacancy rent hikes and cash benefits to remaining tenants), the landlords have found success with a different approach—the state Legislature.[37]

---

* According to a 1992 story in the *Los Angeles Times*, the Nash family engaged in a prolonged internal legal battle over their real estate portfolio, which was valued at about $8 million in the late 1980s. Jerome's mother, Hannah Nash, purchased all of the properties with her earnings as a travel agent.

With its passage, rights for Santa Monica renters took a step backward: there was now a relatively easy way to evict tenants. In response to the Ellis Act's passage, the city enacted the Condo Conversion Ordinance in 1988. This ordinance stipulates owners who use the Ellis Act may not *convert* the property into condominiums, though they may demolish the property and redevelop it as condominiums or for other uses.[38] In the years since the Ellis Act went into effect a considerable number of rent-controlled homes have been withdrawn, with a net loss of 2,075 residences in 483 buildings as of 2020. Condominium redevelopment accounts for 24.3% of withdrawals, followed by conversion to single-family homes (12.8%) and leaving the property unoccupied (15.5%).[39]

The city council directed the city attorney's office to examine legal strategies in response to the Ellis Act,[40] which resulted in the City filing four lawsuits to challenge the law.[41] Its 1986 lawsuit against landlord Henry Yarmark, who was in the process of evicting thirty-five households under the act, argued that the law intruded on its local authority as outlined in the California constitution. Specifically, the City claimed that the act does not authorize landlords to evict tenants in violation of local law. The City lost in superior court and the state appellate court, with the California supreme court declining to hear its appeal. Then, in 1989, the California supreme court refused to hear the City's appeal of a lower court ruling that stated that landlords do not have to obtain a removal permit from the RCB to remove property from the rental market.[42] Two other lawsuits were filed against groups of apartment owners who purchased buildings and then moved in en masse, converting the buildings into "de facto condos." Carl Lambert of ACTION argued that the City "being radical and holier than thou, is trying to block the landlord's right to use his property as he sees fit." Conversely, the City Attorney Robert Myers described the Ellis Act as "an abuse of tenants' rights" and a "state statute bought and paid for by the real estate industry."[43] The City lost the other two suits as well.

That same year SMRR proposed a measure to close one of the rent control law's loopholes, which allows a two- or three-apartment building to be decontrolled if the owner or a family member moves in.* The rationale was that the loophole created "speculative opportunities," in the words of the SMRR activist and Council Member Denny Zane. Landlords were apoplectic, staging a demonstration with around 150 attendees from both Santa Monica and West Hollywood marching in a circle around Santa Monica City Hall. Event organizers played heavily on symbolic imagery, using American flags, red, white, and blue balloons, and a brass quintet to portray the property owners as representing classic American values. In contrast,

---

* This problematic provision remains intact.

several signs featuring a hammer and sickle declared Santa Monica "Soviet." Another sign read, "Rent control and drugs: Both destroy neighborhoods."[44]

In 1989, the City prevailed in federal court against a ninety-three-year-old landlady who sought to overturn rent control on the grounds that it was unconstitutional. Her attorneys argued that the law prevented her from evicting a tenant, in violation of the Takings Clause of the Fifth Amendment. However, U.S. District Judge Ronald S. W. Lew wrote in his ruling that there was no evidence that the rent control law deprived owners of the use and control of their properties.[45] On the occasion of rent control's tenth anniversary, several months later, the city hosted a celebration in a courtyard at city hall. Outside, landlords protested with signs and chanted, "Rent control for the rich! Help the needy, not the greedy!" While a World War II armored car circled city hall with its turret gun aimed at the building that many protesters referred to as "the Kremlin."[46]

In early 1990, the RCB's annual report showed rapidly escalating rates of Ellis Act apartment withdrawals and evictions. Most of the apartments' residents were paying rents far below the average rent-controlled apartment, suggesting owners were simply using the law to capitalize on unrealized profit rather than to truly exit the rental market. Even more troubling, many of the properties had been purchased in the previous two years, meaning individuals and corporations were purchasing rent-controlled multifamily housing with the *intention* of evicting the tenants. These trends emerged in contrast to the supposed spirit of the law, which was to protect landlords who had owned their property before rent control passed.

In response, the RCB called a special meeting to hear testimony from tenants who had been evicted under the law. Instead, the meeting was dominated by landlords, who were united in their claim that the only way to slow down the Ellis Act evictions would be to allow "vacancy decontrol," or unlimited rent increases between tenancies. Around the same time, the city council approved a second reading for an ordinance that would increase the minimum relocation amount for tenants facing an Ellis eviction. One landlord who testified had purchased a five-residence building just after the passage of the Ellis Act and opposed the increase on the grounds that the RCB had "forced" her out of the rental business by not allowing her to pass $40,000 in repairs through to her tenants.[47]

Four years after the passage of the Ellis Act, and as November elections approached, an article appearing in the *Los Angeles Times* in the summer of 1990 described rising tensions between landlords and tenant advocates in Santa Monica: "Santa Monica's rent control law is at a perilous crossroads. A group of its staunchest supporters is trying to save it by giving landlords a little of what they want—more leeway to raise rents."[48] The proposal to offer a compromise bill authored by tenant advocates was accompanied by considerable debate within SMRR and among SMRR-backed members of the city council and the RCB. As Mayor Denny Zane explained, this strategy aimed to diffuse the momentum of a landlord-backed initiative to weaken rent control by crafting their own compromise proposal. The City Attorney, Robert Myers, opined that both of the proposals in development were unlikely to have any real impact on stemming Ellis Act evictions.[49]

In that year's election cycle, the landlord lobby and SMRR both authored measures in response to the growing trend of landlords removing residences with low rents from the rental market under the Ellis Act. According to City housing officials, over the previous four years about one thousand of Santa Monica's thirty thousand rental homes had been either taken out of the rental market or were scheduled to be removed.[50] The landlord-sponsored ballot measure Proposition U would have established vacancy decontrol between tenancies. The tenant-backed Proposition W would allow landlords a one-time rent increase between tenancies to a set level. While Proposition W would result in an increase in rents for some residences, they would remain well below market rates. All four RCB commissioner seats were again filled by SMRR-backed candidates.[51] Proposition U lost by a significant margin, and Proposition W lost more narrowly by a margin of 266 votes.[52]

In response to the growing landlord pressure around vacancy decontrol, combined with the threat of Ellis Act evictions as a means to a similar end, the RCB implemented the Threshold Rent Program, which went into effect January 1, 1992. The program was specifically intended to help landlords who were already charging below market rents when rent control was initially implemented. It provided landlords with the opportunity to apply for a limited rent increase in the event of a change in tenancy. The city was divided into seven zones, with different rents set for each zone and number of bedrooms. Landlords had to submit an application to the RCB and prove the vacancy was voluntary and not the result of harassment. Though the new rents were still far below market rates, attitudes toward the policy among tenant advocates were divided.[53] In the program's first eighteen months, it received 1,862 petitions for rent increase, with an average monthly adjustment of $103. Additionally, 183 residences were returned to the rental market after a year or more of vacancy.[54]

Meanwhile, Santa Monica's rent control policy withstood another challenge by the local landlord lobby when a federal court of appeals in San Francisco ruled in favor of the City. Deputy City Attorney Barry Rosenbaum speculated the group was hoping to take advantage of the conservative shift in the courts, with two Reagan appointees out of the three judges hearing the case. In the 3–0 ruling, the Ninth U.S. Circuit Court of Appeals explained that the landlord group's argument about the failings of rent control—that it was "economically damaging, did not help the poor, and was unjustified by any demonstrated evidence of housing shortages or rising rents"—was misplaced.[55]

The landscape of rent control in California was transformed dramatically in 1995 with the passage of Assembly Bill 1164 in the state legislature. More commonly known as Costa-Hawkins, the legislation was the culmination of over a decade of landlord lobbying and finally achieved the lobby's dream of eliminating vacancy control in California. This meant cities like Santa Monica and West Hollywood were legally obligated to permit owners to increase rents without limit when a tenant moved out. State Senator Jim Costa (D-Fresno) commented that the new rules would "create a positive business climate for the construction of rental housing throughout (the) state." Herb Balter of ACTION stated, "We're ecstatic, after 16 years of being held hostage, we are finally free." Rent increases for new tenants were to be phased in over a period of three years at 15%, after which landlords would be free to charge new tenants market rent.[56] In addition to establishing statewide vacancy decontrol for jurisdictions with rent control ordinances, Costa-Hawkins limited the type and age of residential structures that could be subject to rent control. The law excluded single-family homes and condominiums, and all new construction. Though Santa Monica's rent control law already limited the policy (in most cases) to housing built before April 1979, this meant that other municipalities throughout the state were restricted from applying rent control to housing built after 1995.*

Meanwhile, tenant advocates were bracing themselves for the deleterious effects of vacancy decontrol. Santa Monica Mayor Denny Zane predicted the city would become more upscale, while West Hollywood Council Member Paul Koretz worried that "affordable housing is out the window now and there's not a thing we can do about it." The ability to instantly increase profits when an apartment was vacated created strong incentives for landlords to remove long-term tenants by any means necessary. There were lawful tactics like buyout offers, but with the landlord's powers under the Ellis Act, these offers contained an unspoken threat that, if the landlord wanted a tenant to leave, they could make it happen eventually with or without their consent. At the same time, the Ellis Act route had its drawbacks, as the landlord was limited in what they could do with the residence afterward.

---

* Assembly Bill 1482, also known as the California Tenant Protection Act, was passed by lawmakers in 2019, extending moderate rent control protections to renters statewide. This legislation caps rent increases to the lower of 5% plus CPI or 10%, limits evictions without cause, and establishes relocation fees for allowable no-fault evictions. It applies to rental housing constructed that is at least fifteen years old (on a rolling basis), and to single-family homes that have three or more bedrooms that are rented separately.

Simply making the tenant feel unwelcome or uncomfortable in their home was easier and cheaper.

In anticipation of these harassment tactics, West Hollywood and Santa Monica enacted tenant anti-harassment ordinances.* [57] Unlike other tenant protections, which are enforced through the RCB/RCA, the anti-harassment ordinance is enforced by the Public Rights Division (PRD),† which is situated within the city attorney's office. The housing wing of the PRD has an investigator, a community liaison, a consumer specialist, and five attorneys dedicated to the agency's housing work. Their scope includes taking questions and complaints from tenants about policies like the Tenant Harassment law and Fair Housing law and performing investigations in situations where a landlord or property manager may be in violation of those laws. They also enforce the law through court actions on behalf of the City in selective cases where the violations are particularly egregious.

Vacancy decontrol played out exactly as tenants and advocates anticipated, incentivizing some landlords to harass their tenants with the intention of persuading them to leave their homes. This began during the interim period when the 15% increase was permitted, prior to 1999 when landlords were allowed to fully increase the rent to market levels between tenancies. A 1997 *Los Angeles Times* article on changing landlord behavior reported tactics such as attempting eviction for an oil stain under a car, suddenly enforcing no-pet rules on pet owners, attempting to evict one roommate with the hope that the other will not be able to afford the rent, refusing to accept rent checks, delaying repairs, and making numerous requests to inspect the same apartment. According to Denise McGranahan of Legal Aid, "There have always been bad landlords, but now we're seeing more frequent cases of harassment. Landlords are bolder because they think they can get away with it." One landlord, after the RCB ordered her to reinstate tenant parking spaces she had recently removed from use, complained that "being

---

* Santa Monica's Tenant Harassment law prohibits the following behaviors if they are done with "the intent to harass":
- Taking away services provided in the lease (such as parking or laundry)
- Entering the apartment without proper notice
- Using lies or intimidation intended to make a tenant move out
- Issuing a "three-day notice" or other eviction notice that's based on false charges, where the landlord does not intend to take the case to court
- Using fighting words or threatening bodily harm
- Refusing to do make repairs that are required by law
- Intentionally disturbing a tenant's peace and quiet
- Interfering with a tenant's right to privacy
- Refusing to acknowledge receipt of a lawful rent payment

† This division changed its name to the Consumer Protection Unit shortly after this research was conducted.

a building owner is not a piece of cake. These people should be grateful they have someone to provide them housing."[58]

The City filed its first lawsuit under the harassment law in 1997. It alleged that landlord George Bassiry began harassing his tenants shortly after purchasing a nineteen-residence building. Bassiry's behaviors included verbal harassment; taking away parking spaces, storage areas, and personal belongings; illegally increasing rent; and threatening not to perform any repairs for two years. Bassiry countered that the tenants had been harassing *him*, ever since he asked them to clear out a hallway.[59] In 2013, Bassiry and building manager Gilbert Rodriguez later received an injunction and judgment for harassment behavior against a resident with thirty-two years of tenancy at the same building.[60]

The financial windfall of potential rental earnings under vacancy decontrol was illustrated by the 1999 sale of the 532-apartment Santa Monica Shores. The building had been constructed in the mid-1960s and changed hands in 1971 for $14 million. In preparation for the 1999 sale, the owners strategically left many apartments vacant as residents moved out and paid some tenants $20,000 or more to move out. As broker Ron Pelleg explained, the $20,000 could be recouped in less than a year with market rents, which were projected at around $2,500 versus the current range of $600 to $1,100. Ultimately, the $95 million sale was the most expensive apartment sale in the city's history at the time, and calculations around vacancy decontrol, vacancies, and sale value were prescient for future real estate trends and landlord tactics.[61]

Earlier that year, the City won a major case in the California supreme court, when the majority decision affirmed the constitutionality of its rent control law. The plaintiff's lawyers, the Pacific Legal Foundation, argued that rent control should be disallowed because it had failed to achieve its purported goal of preserving low-income rental housing. They cited census data that apparently showed a loss of low-income renter households in the city, as compared to an increase in many Southern California cities without the policy. In his majority opinion, Judge Stanley Mosk wrote, "The notion that a court may invalidate legislation that it finds, after a trial, to have failed to live up to expectations, is indeed novel." Out of fear that such an argument could open the floodgates to lawsuits about a range of other policies, sixty-five other California cities sided with Santa Monica in court. Tenant advocates hailed this decision as a major victory.[62]

Around the same time, the city council directed the city attorney's office to prepare a city charter amendment that would address the growing issue of evictions based on "immaterial and insubstantial violations of rental agreements and against evictions based upon covenants or obligations which the landlord has previously waived or is precluded by conduct from enforcing." This proposal targeted new landlord tactics to evict tenants paying below market rent. One common story was the sudden enforcement of pet prohibitions when the landlord was unquestionably aware of the pet's existence previously and had taken no action. Another was a scenario where the tenant had made substantial improvements or modifications to the home under the assumption of having an understanding with the landlord based on past conduct, only to receive a notice to "cure" the lease violation by removing the modifications, which may be "costly or difficult."[63] Voters passed Proposition 1 in April 1999, which prevented a landlord from evicting a tenant for a violation of a rule if the landlord had never enforced it before.[64]

In 2002, Measure FF proposed extending eviction protections in rent-controlled residences to spouses, children, or domestic partners of tenants who die or become incapacitated, in addition to other miscellaneous tenant-related adjustments to the city charter. It passed with 62.74% of the votes.[65] A group of landlord plaintiffs brought a legal challenge to the measure, arguing that the eviction restrictions were an "irrational response" to the housing crisis. In 2007, the case was decided in the City's favor when the three-judge panel of the Ninth U.S. Circuit Court of Appeals wrote that it "declined to second-guess Santa Monica's chosen means of implementing its indisputably legitimate goals."[66]

The Ellis Act continued to decimate Santa Monica's rent-controlled housing stock and wreak havoc on its residents, requiring constant vigilance from the city. In 2009, the City's Ellis Act Task Force found fifty-nine properties containing 245 apartments that were withdrawn under the law but had not been demolished or converted as required, and 42 of them were occupied without an occupancy permit.[67] That same year, the number of rent-controlled apartments increased, due to the outcome of an appellate court's decision in a lawsuit filed by the AAGLA. The case established that the RCB had authority over apartments that had been offered for rent less than five years after withdrawing them using the Ellis Act. This included new construction that replaced rent-controlled properties, and 168 newly built apartments became rent-controlled following the decision.[68]

In 2010, the RCB introduced a ballot measure to broaden the scope of tenant protections in Santa Monica in response to a finding in the RCA's annual report that 74% of evictions between 2005 and 2009 were for breach of contract or nuisance.[69] Measure RR was approved by voters with 65.36% of the vote and establishes that landlords must give tenants a "reasonable time" to correct rental agreement violations (excluding nonpayment of rent). It also stipulates that landlords may not evict elderly, disabled, or terminally ill tenants to move into the residence unless they themselves also meet one of the those criteria.[70]

The RCB approved a new formula to determine rent increases in 2012. The formula resulted in smaller increases than in the previous year (1.54% vs. 3.2%), which an ACTION spokesperson speculated was in response to the lawsuit the group won that allowed owners to pass taxes through to residents. The landlord group described the new mathematical formula, which bases the annual increase on a higher average rent than in the past, as "black magic."[71] Several months later, the city council voted to put a measure on the November ballot that would change the increase calculation method from the "pie method" to 75% of CPI, with a maximum increase of 6%.[72] It passed with 60.52% of the vote.[73]

In 2012, Jerome Nash of Ellis Act fame was once again embroiled in a lawsuit—this time as a defendant. A private attorney filed suit on behalf of tenants living in a building that he owned, which was infested with mold and termites and had leaking gas lines and broken plumbing. Nash was accused of berating tenants and calling them names, in addition to threatening one of their jobs. The plaintiffs were asking for repairs and to be compensated for stress and other damages.[74] The following year, the owner and manager of a sixty-apartment complex agreed to stop harassment behaviors or risk reopening an investigation by the city attorney's office. The settlement required the owner and manager to rescind restrictive new rules (e.g., keeping items on porches and balconies) and unreasonable lost key fees ($250) and to create better communication with tenants around construction and tenant complaints. The city attorney conducted three mediation sessions. As part of the agreement, the city attorney's office monitored the companies for a year to make sure they complied.[75]

In 2014, the city attorney collaborated with Legal Aid and a private attorney to settle a particularly egregious harassment case at a historic building downtown, which was home to a number of formerly unhoused disabled tenants with federal Section 8 rent vouchers. The owners of the forty-nine-residence building agreed to adopt a written antidiscrimination policy, complete a training in fair housing law, restore parking spaces for disabled tenants, clarify their guest policy, improve repair response times, get rid of bedbugs, and more. The City added $2,500 in penalties for any future violations of the harassment law. The owner and manager entered into the agreement without having to admit liability, fault, or guilt, with the understanding that the city attorney and Legal Aid would monitor certain provisions of the agreement for ten years.[76]

Harassment complaints increased by about 30% in 2014 compared to the previous fiscal year. In a brief to the RCB, Deputy City Attorney Gary Rhoades summarized the city's involvement in resolving harassment complaints. In the previous fiscal year, the city pursued sixteen cases out of thirty-eight total complaints, all of which were solved through phone calls, meetings, conferences at city hall, discussions with the landlords and their attorneys, and written settlement agreements. Rhoades felt the City's efforts were sufficient, but Legal Aid attorney Denise McGranahan countered that many tenants feel there's a lot of unaddressed harassment going on, particularly with "frivolous eviction" cases. Several tenants also testified about their harassment experiences.[77]

Several months later the city council discussed the issue. Chief Deputy City Attorney Adam Radinsky attributed the increase in complaints to the changing housing market and rising rents as well as new owners who don't know the law. He pointed to an emerging trend of sudden enforcement of lease provisions to persuade tenants to "self-evict." Another trend was landlords falsely claiming not to have received rent payments. An SMRR hotline rep and a Legal Aid attorney said they no longer refer tenants to the city attorney's office because they take too long to address complaints. Council members gave the attorneys several suggestions, including looking into how long-term construction can become a harassment tactic.[78]

Three months later, the city council took up the harassment issue again, hearing testimony from dozens of tenants who had experienced harassment. City Attorney March Moutrie attributed the harassment to the Ellis Act and explained that while the city attorney can enforce harassment laws, they cannot represent tenants in eviction court. Thus, she argued that more private attorneys were needed to address harassment. Nicole Phillis, RCB candidate, criticized the city attorney's response. She countered that "would-be tenant harassment plaintiffs are not bringing these cases because the legal standard for intent (malice) is too high" and that the city attorney has done a poor job of enforcing the ordinance. In response, city attorneys suggested hiring a half-time employee to help with claims, and Councilmember Gleam Davis suggested training lawyers to pro bono defend tenants in court. Legal Aid suggested increasing penalties for harassing seniors and people with disabilities.[79]

Having heard these arguments, the city council voted to tighten harassment laws two months later. The unanimous vote increased penalties, prohibited landlords from entering apartments for specific reasons, and modified the standard for what is considered harassment. Significantly, they changed the word "malice" to "bad faith," which was intended to give the City more leverage when litigating against bad landlords. The penalties increased from a fixed $1,000 to starting at $1,000 and extending up to $10,000. They also approved a requirement that landlords file buyout agreements with the city.[80]

In 2015, the city council decided to focus on initiatives that would maintain an inclusive and diverse community.[81] In line with this mission, the city council voted unanimously to disallow discrimination against Section 8 voucher holders, which was not yet protected under state law.[82] The city council also targeted Airbnb and other short-term rental platforms with its Home-Sharing Ordinance. The rule prohibits renting an entire residence for less than thirty days and requires individuals who choose to take part in allowable home sharing to obtain a business license and pay a 14% hotel tax. Significantly, the ordinance draws a conceptual distinction between "home sharing" and "vacation rentals." As Mayor Kevin McKeown explained, "When a landlord or other property owner takes a unit off the housing market and uses it for vacation rental, there is no permanent resident on the site. We've lost that part of the fabric of our community." He also cited resident concerns about noise and disruptions.[83]

Meanwhile, the median monthly rent for a rent-controlled studio apartment* increased 16% between 2016 and 2017 and 7% for a one bedroom. Addressing the rent increase data, RCB Commissioner Todd Flora commented, "This annual report scares the shit out of me, because the affordability crisis gets worse and worse and worse." The board voted unanimously to support AB 1506, which was introduced by Santa Monica Assemblyman Richard Bloom and two other members from the Bay Area, and would have overturned Costa-Hawkins.[84] It was unsuccessful, but it wouldn't be the last attempt. The same year, the city approved the Preserving Our Diversity pilot program, which provides financial assistance to very low-income long-term tenants (defined as households that moved in before January 1, 2000), who are aged sixty-five and older and live in rent-controlled apartments. The funds are generated from local sales taxes raised through Measure GSH in 2016 and the program is still in place.

In 2017, code enforcement officers started training to identify tenant harassment scenarios. The city had received 74 written and sworn complaints about harassment since July 2016, and 117 in the previous fiscal year. This new initiative was "in direct response to experiences that we've had recently where it seems on the face there is harassment taking place, but it is difficult for the City Attorney's Office to find enough evidence to initiate litigation." The City's code enforcement manager also requested that the council raise the code violation fine from $75 to $1,000 a day.[85]

Naomi Sultan was sworn in to the RCB in 2018 with the intention of reevaluating the City's approach to preventing tenant harassment and enforcing the anti-tenant harassment ordinance. Harassment had been on the rise as property values continued to skyrocket. According to Sultan, "They

---

* This includes apartments with the full range of tenure lengths, from apartments that were occupied at the time rental control was implemented in 1979 to apartments that were recently rented at market rates.

really have a financial incentive to turn over tenants, especially tenants who have been there longer, which means elderly folks who often have disabilities are particularly vulnerable." Other issues cited were landlords beginning construction without offering tenants another place to live and refusing to fix maintenance issues. Sultan proposed addressing the deficit in harassment enforcement by adding more staff to the Code Enforcement Division or creating a separate group to focus on enforcing the law.[86]

That same year, the RCB established that landlords cannot exceed the maximum allowable rent for a residence by engaging in Ratio Utility Billing Systems, which divides a building's master meter bill evenly by the number of units. ACTION had filed suit against the board on the grounds that utilities are not rent and are, therefore, not subject to rent limits. The case was settled in Los Angeles Superior Court, which agreed with the board that ACTION was essentially making a policy argument rather than a legal one.[87] Later that year, the city council passed an ordinance protecting students and educators against no-fault evictions during the school year.[88]

In 2018, a coalition of social justice advocacy groups spearheaded by the AIDS Healthcare Foundation gathered the requisite voter signatures to place Proposition 10 on the November ballot. The measure would have overturned Costa-Hawkins, giving municipalities the power to end vacancy decontrol and extend rent control to newer housing and to single-family homes. The Santa Monica City Council voted unanimously to endorse it. As the Councilmember Kevin McKeown explained:

> Even with the strongest rent control law in the state, Santa Monica has seen housing affordability undermined by twenty years of sudden jumps to market-rate rents under Costa-Hawkins. Our vote to support Proposition 10 is a vote for working families, students, fixed-income seniors, and everyone else whom Costa-Hawkins has been pricing out of Santa Monica.[89]

Real estate investment PAC mailers targeted homeowner fears about diminishing property values, with one projection warning voters that property values could drop by an average of $60,000.[90] The landlord and real estate lobby raised a stunning $76 million—almost three times the $26 million raised in supporter contributions—and the measure was defeated with 59.43% of voters against it.[91] According to the *Los Angeles Times*, it was one of the most expensive campaigns in California history. Much of the funding came from national investors with California portfolios,[92] illustrating David Harvey's concept of land as the "second circuit of capital" for investment. In the days leading up to the election, the *Los Angeles Times* reported on the opposition campaign's astonishing fundraising efforts:

Many of the landlords are publicly traded real estate investment companies with portfolios that span across the country. In earnings calls and investor conferences over the last year, company executives have spent significant time reassuring Wall Street they're doing everything they can to defeat Proposition 10. Their goal, the executives and market analysts say, is not just winning in California, but also preventing a wave of rent control measures that might follow nationwide.[93]

Some of the largest donations included $2,761,840 from the Western National Group, $642,050 from Invitation Homes (at the time owned by Blackstone), and $562,725 from United Dominion Realty Trust. The investment firms that own the massive rent-controlled Parkmerced complex in the Bay Area donated $322,100 to the campaign.

In 2019, the Santa Monica City Council increased the amount landlords are required to compensate tenants for "no-fault" evictions, such as Ellis Act evictions or owner move-ins. The compensation for a typical studio went from $9,950 to $15,020, while a one bedroom went from about $15,300 to $20,705.[94] The city council also voted to give affordable housing wait-list priority to qualifying households displaced by owner move-ins.[95] The RCB urged the city council, in response to bad faith "renovictions," to create a new law limiting cosmetic upgrades to situations in which the apartment is already vacant or the tenant agrees. They also asked the city council to pass a law barring landlords from subdividing rent-controlled apartments, which had been a common practice for Airbnb and other vacation rental ventures.[96]

Meanwhile, the rents in Santa Monica continued to increase. The RCB's annual report revealed that a household making the median income in the greater Los Angeles area could not afford even a studio apartment in Santa Monica without being rent burdened. "People know the value of staying in place," explained the RCA's Executive Director Tracy Condon, "They can't leave these affordable units and find something comparable, particularly in Santa Monica. There are fewer people in rent-controlled housing than there were twenty years ago, but they're staying as long as they possibly can."[97]

Later in the year, Council Members Sue Himmelrich and Kevin McKeown asked the city council to develop a Right to Counsel ordinance, which would provide low- and moderate-income renters with legal representation in the event of an eviction. They cited similar laws in San Francisco and New York City as well as one in development in Los Angeles.[98] The city attorney's office launched its pilot Right to Counsel program in 2021. Counsel is available to tenant households with incomes at or below 80% of LA County's area median income. Legal Aid is the contracted service provider, and the program is implemented through Stay Housed LA County.[99]

The city attorney's office continued to pursue egregious cases of landlord harassment. In 2019, they filed a criminal complaint against landlord Miesha Charnae Grant, charging them with five counts of tenant harassment. The behavior included disobeying a previous court order, interfering with the tenants' right to quiet use and enjoyment of their homes by entering without permission, vandalizing properties, and battering a tenant.[100] Later that year, the city attorney's office brought a suit against two landlords who had harassed a tenant by repeatedly parking in their space, going through their storage area and disposing of items, and filing an untenable eviction case against them that was quickly dismissed. A judge in Los Angeles Superior Court ruled in favor of the plaintiff and fined the landlords $35,000.[101]

In early 2020, a new ordinance took effect that targeted "medium-term" leases. In response to the growing issue of businesses leasing apartments for corporate housing, council members adopted an ordinance requiring leases to be for a minimum of one year, the tenant to be a person (rather than a corporation), and the home to be unfurnished. Corporate housing was already unlawful per a previous ordinance, and the new one aimed to close some loopholes.[102]

Two years after the real estate investment lobby defeated Proposition 10, the Rental Affordability Act (Proposition 21) met with the same fate, with only 40.15% of voters supporting the measure statewide, compared to 57% of Santa Monica voters.[103] The proposal would have replaced (though not explicitly repealed) Costa-Hawkins, enabling local governments to establish rent control on homes that are fifteen years old or older, including single-family homes and condominiums if the landlord owns more than two properties. It would have also introduced a more moderate form of vacancy control similar to what exists in New York City, with set increases permissible within a certain time frame. Though the will of Santa Monica voters was clear, local control was superseded yet again at the state level. Supporters of the ballot measure raised almost $41 million in contributions; just less than half of the opposition's $83.5 million, but almost double what was raised for the Proposition 10 campaign. The Issues PAC of AAGLA contributed $112,790.[104]

In the same election, the RCB Commissioners Anastasia Foster and Caroline Torosis were elected for a second term, easily defeating the non-SMRR endorsed candidate Robert Kronovet, who received only 14% of the vote. On the importance of rent control in Santa Monica, Foster said:

> If we didn't have a hot market we wouldn't need as stringent of protections. But money is unapologetic, capital seeks to increase itself, and what we are saying is that there are human lives and families at the other end of that capital. Owning a multifamily building is not

like owning a strip mall, you don't just have tenants who pay rent, these are human lives.[105]

Foster identified three forces lowering the availability of rent-controlled homes in Santa Monica: landlords pushing tenants out to raise prices, landlords pushing tenants out so they can sell the building with empty apartments, and landlords converting their properties to short-term vacation rentals. Foster and Torosis characterized the majority of landlords as good actors but said there are some bad actors who require the RCB's intervention.

During the early days of the COVID-19 pandemic, Santa Monica tenants were protected by California's eviction moratorium, which was in place from March 2020 through September 30, 2021, and applied to cases where households were unable to pay rent due to a COVID-19-related income loss. They were required to submit a declaration of financial impact each month and pay 25% of rent due for the months of September 2020 through September 30, 2021, by September 30, 2021. There was also a state rental assistance program for both landlords and tenants. The City implemented several additional policies to protect renters. No-fault terminations for Ellis Act withdrawals were mostly prohibited, in addition to for-cause terminations for unauthorized occupants or pets or for nuisance. Additionally, the penalty for harassment increased from $10,000 to $15,000.[106]

While nonpayment of rent due to COVID-19-related income loss and other difficulties arising from the pandemic added a new layer of protection for Santa Monica renters, much remained the same. In early 2021, the city attorney filed suit against two local landlords for deceiving their tenants with a false renovation plan (which they claimed had been approved) and then filing for eviction against the tenants when they refused to leave for fear they would be giving up their tenancy. Attorneys from both the RCB and the City wrote to the landlords informing them that their letter contained multiple false and misleading statements and that the tenants were not required to leave. At least two of the apartments were listed on Airbnb, and the property was also advertised for sale with the information, "only five units are currently occupied and Seller is in the process of completing the buy-outs." All five households were paying significantly less than the other apartments in the building,[107] illustrating that closing the rent gap continued to be a business model for some Santa Monica landlords.

Later in the year, the City and the RCB filed suit against NMS Properties Inc., alleging that they purchased rent-controlled properties and then began deliberately disruptive repairs, which led two tenants to move out of their homes. The owner subsequently evoked the Ellis Act to evict the remaining three tenants after they refused cash for keys offers and listed the apartments for rent shortly thereafter in violation of state law. Additionally, several of the apartments were fully furnished and advertised as vacation rentals in violation of city law. Rent Control Commissioner Caroline Torosis commented, "These corporate actors intentionally evicted tenants and then marketed furnished short-term rental in blatant violation of our Rent Control law." Several of the company's owners are involved in a separate city lawsuit that alleges tenant harassment, maintaining a public nuisance, and violating local zoning laws.[108]

Conclusion

Rental market conditions—along with loopholes codified within the Ellis Act, Costa-Hawkins, and even allowable reasons for no-cause eviction in city law—support and encourage speculative investment activity in one of Los Angeles County's most expensive and desirable areas. These combined forces have had a devastating impact on the city's renter households and housing affordability.

Over the past forty years, SMRR, the city attorney's office, and elected officials on the city council and the RCB have demonstrated a sustained commitment to supporting tenants, even in the face of fierce landlord opposition. Santa Monica has some of the strongest tenant protections in the country, with an impressive breadth of resources available. But no matter how much time and effort goes into strengthening tenant protections by addressing legal loopholes and outmaneuvering evolving landlord tactics, some property owners remain committed to extracting the maximum possible profit from the city's rent-controlled housing by any means necessary. Meanwhile, the AAGLA and ACTION's relentless legal battles against the city continue to send an unambiguous message that rent control will always be under attack from the landlord lobby.

This prolonged struggle has real implications on the extent to which Santa Monica renters can feel at home in their residences, and by extension, their ability to envision a future in the city. For some renters who follow this "politics of place,"[109] knowledge of the city's sustained commitment to support renter households has the effect of making them feel valued as community members and stable in their homes. On a practical level, many tenants I interviewed also had positive experiences accessing the resources available to them when they needed to learn about or enforce their rights. On the other hand, constantly reading and hearing about other renters whose homes are threatened by Ellis Act evictions, habitability issues, harassment, Airbnb conversions, owner move-ins, and other circumstances can seriously undermine those feelings, leading to perpetual insecurity for some.

The knowledge of market conditions, landlord tactics, and legal loop-holes means even the sale of a building is likely to trigger anxiety about housing instability. Most long-term tenants are aware that receiving a buy-out (or cash for keys) offer signals that the owner's next move will likely be to serve them with an Ellis Act eviction or, perhaps, simply harass them until they leave. This can be used to the landlord's advantage, as it may result in the tenant accepting the offer and leaving their home simply to avoid the stress of a battle they feel unlikely to win. This saves the landlord the trouble and expense of proceeding with the Ellis Act process and also means they can immediately rent the apartment at the market rate. To this end, even deep knowledge of tenant protections and resources may not mitigate the perception of housing instability when a building is sold or a tenant other-wise perceives that the owner would like them to leave, especially for long-term tenants paying below market rents.

3

An Industry at War

Landlord Discourse and Market Language

The culture, rhetoric, and business practices of the real estate investment industry—which is situated in the sacrosanct ideology of private
property—impact the residential experience of many tenant households. AAGLA's monthly magazine, *Apartment Age*, serves as a rich resource
for gleaning insight into this world. The themes discussed here are drawn
from an in-depth review of the magazine's monthly issues from August
2019 and July 2021. This time period was selected because it was contemporaneous with when the participant interviews were conducted, but the content is consistent in issues from the years before and after this period. Issues
from 2022 to the present are available online.* My analysis reveals the deeply held perceptions of unfairness from an industry that views itself as em-
battled. These perceptions arise from a commodity view of land and housing, wherein both the right to profit should take precedence over a right to
housing or a home and government regulation of private property is *un-
American.*

While there is no way to know what percentage of landlords and property managers in the region hold these views,[†] both the longevity of this

---

* PDFs of past issues are available at https://aagla.org/apartment-age-magazine/. The website previously included many more years of issues.
  [†] A study on this is desperately needed. Understanding more about landlord business
models and decisions, including variations across portfolio size, would shed light on the ve-
racity of conventional wisdom and assumptions about this industry.

organization and the consistency of its rhetorical tone and political stances suggest these are mainstream perspectives in the local real estate industry. That means this ideology has a direct impact on shaping policy, including the prolonged struggle in Santa Monica and beyond.* AAGLA Executive Director Daniel Yukelson is a prominent industry spokesperson on issues concerning rental property owners and is frequently interviewed for relevant articles in the *Los Angeles Times* and other local publications. His style is sometimes flamboyant, as when he characterized a proposed anti-harassment ordinance in the City of Los Angeles as "like open hunting season on landlords by unscrupulous lawyers."[1] Yukelson has also authored some of the magazine's most bombastic pieces.

AAGLA was founded in 1917 and is a membership trade organization that serves landlords and property managers throughout Southern California. The organization has over ten thousand members who own or manage about three hundred thousand rental homes in Ventura, Los Angeles, and San Bernardino counties. AAGLA offers their members numerous monthly education seminars both on practical aspects of property ownership and management and on broader topics like What Are Tenant Advocate Groups Teaching Tenants? which promises to "help you formulate and deploy a winning strategy to fight back against tenant attacks and win in court." Membership includes free attendance at these events, access to an extensive library of legal forms, operational advice, a subscription to *Apartment Age*, and discounts on various services from a number of vendors. They also serve in a lobbyist capacity at all levels of government and raise money for landlord advocacy issues through their PACs.

Much of the magazine's content is practical advice and information presented in a neutral or mostly neutral tone. It includes articles on property management, legislative and lobbying updates, overviews of lawsuits against eviction moratoriums and other tenant protections, legal questions from readers, best practices for maintenance, industry trends, tenant screening tips, updates on local ordinances, earthquake preparedness, best practices for interacting with tenants, humor pieces, and a section for Korean owners. There are a multitude of advertisements for various goods and services, such as cabinetry and other fixtures, seismic retrofitting, financial planning, mold abatement, electrical infrastructure, tenant screening, and HVAC infrastructure. Each issue includes multiple ads for eviction services, in addition to political advertisements and solicitations for the organization's PACs, which tend not surprisingly to be more prominently featured when there are important ballot initiatives in the coming months.

---

* The Santa Monica landlord group, ACTION, uses identical language in their content.

There are also numerous articles that articulate a holistic worldview on the state of the residential rental industry and being a landlord. Each issue opens with messages from the president and from the executive director. Yukelson has served as the executive director for the duration of the review period, and Earle Vaughan was the president until January 2021, when the role was assumed by Cheryl Turner. As the organization's leaders, their columns speak directly to the membership, and they often use strong and galvanizing rhetoric that concludes with an appeal for member donations. In addition to these monthly columns, there are also guest editorials and articles presented as reportage but that contain extensive editorial language beyond what is generally accepted within basic journalistic standards. These authors are sometimes economists or attorneys and are usually associated with conservative institutions and publications like the Howard Jarvis Taxpayers Association, *Patriot Post*, the Charles Koch Institute, the Heritage Foundation, the Cato Institute, the Foundation for Economic Education, and the Ayn Rand Institute.

Many of these articles focus on the unfairness, unlawfulness, or misguided nature of the various protenant policies and practices and their threat to the industry's sustainability. Concerns about socialism and communism also make frequent appearances. The tone and content over the time period remained fairly consistent, with topical variations relating to COVID-19 policy, challenges, and best practices. Industry views expressed in *Apartment Age*—on both pre- and COVID-19-era policies and practices— articulate a narrative of unfairness and undue burden framed as un-American in its denial of property rights. The five themes that follow were drawn from this discourse.

An Industry at War

The editorial articles in *Apartment Age* often contain language that paints a picture of an industry engaged in a battle against forces (tenant organizers, elected officials, etc.) who wish to destroy or subjugate it. For example, in the "Legal Corner" section of the August 2019 issue, attorney Stephen Duringer describes "right to counsel" policies as an "assault on housing providers" and the industry itself as being "under attack from all sides."[2] Similarly, in his monthly column, Yukelson calls rent control a "continuing war on rental property owners"[3] and attributes to it both the end of the golden age of California and his decision to sell the investment property his family purchased in the 1940s. In his November 2020 column, President Vaughan frames the previous three years as a noble fight against the injustices of rent control, using the words "defense," "skirmish," "battle," "attacks," and "war." He describes COVID-19-era eviction moratoriums as the industry being "attacked by a new housing policy," never acknowledging that the policy was an emergency response with a public health rationale.[4] Board President Turner pursues a similar rhetorical strategy in her May 2021 column, evoking a picture of an industry under constant assault by unsympathetic forces. She closes the column with a solicitation both for donations to AAGLA and for her campaign for state assembly.

The omnipresent threat of tenant activism, an overzealous government, and the actions of other misinformed actors create an environment in which property owners must perpetually fight for their rights. As Vaughan writes in his August 2020 column, "There are so many attacks against our livelihoods, retirements, and security which each of us have worked so hard for."[5] A common narrative thread is that tenant groups are gaining power and present a formidable threat to the future of the industry. In another column, Vaughan warns that, thanks to tenant rights organizations' successful electioneering in New York State, "these draconian rent control measures continue to spread like a cancer on the multifamily housing industry."[6] Similarly, Yukelson warns that tenants are highly organized and elected officials love to "pander" to them.[7] Nearly a year into the pandemic, Yukelson writes that professional renter-activists are "at it again," assisted by unspecified socialist organizations and taking advantage of the crisis by using "doomsday scenario" tactics.[8]

Narratives of Unfairness and Oppression: The Landlord's Burden

The magazine's editorial contributors perceive virtually any policy that regulates the rental market or provides support to tenants as unfair. One article argues that "just-cause" eviction policy, rent boards, tenant unions, and relocation benefits are even worse than rent control and describes relocation benefits as an "involuntary redistribution of wealth from housing providers to renters."[9] Other injustices, as outlined in Yukelson's August 2019 column, include being "forced" to accept Section 8 vouchers being "forced" to disclose rents on rental registries and a proposed vacancy tax.[10] Yukelson's March 2020 column paints landlords as victims, demonized by public opinion and persecuted by policy. He complains that elected officials "pander" to "vocal tenant groups that for the most part merely want something for less or in some cases for free." Meanwhile, landlords don't have the same luxury of asking mortgage lenders and insurance brokers for cost breaks. The situation is "never fair. We are just trying to do the best job we can by keeping our renters, who are our customers, in their homes, safe and sound. We are, in fact, the ones providing roofs over the heads of those living in the communities we ourselves live in and own rental properties."[11] He closes the column with a pitch for donations to AAGLA's political advocacy

PAC. The language of persecution appears again in Yukelson's May 2020 column, where he describes rent control as a "public policy focused on villainizing and overregulating property owners to achieve affordable housing."[12]

The magazine's contributors perceive the pandemic as having ushered in a new era of unfair policies and landlord martyrdom. In his first column of the pandemic era, titled "A Moratorium on Evictions? No F-ing Way!" Vaughan exclaims, "Sometimes, I just wish that California would really sink into the ocean!" He describes eviction moratoriums as a "punishment" and complains, "We property owners' investments and livelihoods are always expendable in the eyes of our political leaders."[13] A strikingly tone-deaf article in the May 2020 issue rails against COVID-19-era eviction moratoriums, on the grounds that renters "have no stake in this game, have no reason to budget, no reason to cut back on other discretionary spending, and now no reason to pay rent," while landlords assume the brunt of the pandemic's financial burdens.[14] The previous board President, Harold Greenberg, argues that eviction moratoriums are politically motivated and "inequality at its worst"—simply another way to punish the much-maligned landlord.[15]

Yaron Brook of the Ayn Rand Institute uses similar language of martyrdom to describe the plight of landlords: the "property owners who make it possible for us to rent rather than buy a home."[16] Under COVID-19 eviction moratoriums, landlords are the "sacrificial lambs who will bear the brunt of the economic devastation of the pandemic." Brook suggests a moratorium on government regulation instead. In a guest editorial, titled "San Francisco Cannot Foist the Pandemic's Economic Burden onto Landlords," the author argues that the city of San Francisco "targets innocent property owners for special—unfair—treatment," and asks, "Why are landlords singled out to bear the burdens of the pandemic?"[17] In "Essential Workers: Landlords Are Heroes Too!" Irma Vargas valorizes landlords' contributions to the collective well-being during the pandemic. Explaining that there have been increased maintenance requests, neighbor issues, and other responsibilities, she likens their role to that of nurses and doctors. Returning to the rhetoric of unfairness, she argues that landlords are only wealthy "in the minds of our ignorant politicians and renters."[18]

While many of the articles during the pandemic era focus on eviction moratoriums and other pandemic policies, some authors continue to address pre-COVID-19 policies. Attorney Harold Greenberg decries the unfairness of Los Angeles's Systematic Code Enforcement Program, initiated by the "tenant activist retired professor" Gary Blasi and supported by "tenant-biased Council members" Jackie Goldberg and Mike Feuer. He portrays owners as existing at the whim of code enforcement inspectors and city attorney's offices, who have been charged with a protenant and antilandlord agenda, and wonders, "Why is it fair or just that the City can spend taxpayers' monies to pay these tenants' rights advocates and attorneys to harass own-ers?" He concludes that it "is not right, it is not just, and it is not fair."[19] Similarly, real estate attorney Joshua Stein argues that rent control is unfair because a building owner cannot simply move their asset to a more favorable business environment to elude regulations.[20]

Yukelson's appeals to members for financial support often engages in this rhetoric of oppression and the quest for freedom and fairness. His Sep-tember 2020 column outlines the tribulations landlords face due to COVID-19-era tenant protections like eviction moratoriums, writing, "Our crusade against the tyranny of injustice and unfair rent regulation is justified."[21] An ad for AAGLA membership the following month features Yukelson's reas-surance that "we are always here for you, standing by your side, monitoring and aggressively fighting back against the tyranny of ill-conceived state and local regulations."[22] Anti-harassment ordinances—which have been enacted in Santa Monica, West Hollywood, and recently Los Angeles—are an "or-deal that has been inflicted on rental property owners."[23] The following month, Yukelson complains that California landlords are the only industry that has "been required to bear the brunt of the State's shut down of the economy without receiving any state monetary relief."[24] In a particularly flamboyant rhetorical flourish, Yukelson connected the traditional Passover song *Dayenu*—which is essentially about gratitude at having survived op-pression with God's support—with the unfairness and burden of regulations on the rental housing industry.

The Undesirable Tenant

While the magazine *does* include articles that stress the importance of re-sponding to tenant complaints in a timely manner and cultivating a conge-nial relationship, there are other instances where renters who advocate for themselves are described as problematic and to be avoided. In "The Prop-erty Manager's Guide to Renter Selection," the author guides readers to iden-tify "difficult renters," who "complain about nonexistent problems, and in some cases wrongfully sue" landlords.[25] This fear of predatory legal action was echoed in the November 2019 "Ask Kari" column. Kari outlines several "dirty tricks" and "sleaze ball tactics" typically practiced by tenant attor-neys. These include claiming every habitability issue possible, that a notice wasn't served properly, or that the building or residence wasn't in compli-ance with code enforcement or the rental registration requirement. In con-clusion, "There is no limit to how tenant rights attorneys will twist the law and exploit the process to the benefit of their non-paying client." This builds on a popular landlord trope about predatory tenant attorneys (*all* tenant attorneys) who initiate frivolous lawsuits for their own enrichment.[26]

Other authors adopt a paternalistic view toward tenants. An article titled, "Learn How to Deal with Dirty Tenants" by the Fast Evict Law Group includes a list of evidence that indicates a property is in distress due to a problem tenant. In addition to hoarding and some other behaviors that can be reasonably attributed to the resident, they also list things like pests and mold, which can just as easily be connected to other causes. They advise owners and managers to "make it your responsibility to visit the property frequently after tenants move in or whenever you feel that there are issues and point out the locations that require regular cleaning."* [27] An article by the similarly named Fast Eviction Service, titled "Obvious Signs That Should Cause You to Avoid Accepting a Tenant," lists eight red flags to be aware of during the screening process. While a few of these seem fairly standard (e.g., hesitating to fill out an application or appearing intoxicated), others contain value judgments and assumptions far beyond typical screening criteria. Multiple employers in two years may signal that "the tenant does not have a serious attitude towards work," being in a rush to find a home to rent may indicate they are "looking for a place to hide," arriving to view the residence with many people may mean they are "planning something," and someone who offers a large sum of money in advance is potentially suspicious. [28]

Housing as Commodity, Property as Freedom

Tenant protections' encroachment on sacrosanct private property rights is a consistent rhetorical thread in *Apartment Age*. One author aptly describes the founding fathers' vision of property and liberty as "inextricably entwined." [29] In a guest editorial, Jon Coupal of the Howard Jarvis Taxpayers Association frames the landlord struggle against rent control in the context of the larger struggle against government interference that is the cornerstone of American ideals about individualism and freedom:

> Rights, properly understood, are restrictions on government actions, not an entitlement to free stuff. We have a "right" to speak, to assemble and to practice our religious beliefs. We have a right to be free from unreasonable searches and seizures and, yes, a right to bear arms. This is the reason we have a Bill of Rights, not a Bill of Freebies. [30]

In "California's War on Private Property Rights," Susan Shelley of the Howard Jarvis Taxpayers Association writes about the threat posed by Oakland housing justice direct action collective, Moms 4 Housing, as well as by regulatory policies like rent control and minimum wage. She argues that the

---

* This approach may be unlawful in jurisdictions with anti-harassment policies.

rhetoric of "housing as a human right" is merely a right to someone else's property and that there "can't be a right to anything that has to be provided by other people."[31] In "Prediction for 2030: A Government Take Over of Rental Housing," Roger Valdez references David Madden and Peter Marcuse's *In Defense of Housing*—an instant classic in housing justice circles—and speculated that the "housing is a human right" ethos will lead both to a nationalization of housing and to America becoming a socialist country. He writes, "This is where we're heading as a country, a government housing system driven by resentment, entitlement, and political power instead of abundance, opportunity, risk, and reward. Would a system like this make life better for people who need housing?"[32] In the sequel to this article, Valdez predicts that "anger about housing prices, socialist activism, and an incurious media and academia will lead to so much incremental regulation that, in effect, the government will be running all rental housing in the country by 2030."[33] The February 2021 edition of the "Ask Kari" column echoes this fear, with Negri claiming that calls to "cancel the rent" are analogous to living in a communist country.[34]

The magazine's contributors continue to evoke the red menace in reference to Santa Monica. Over the two years of issues reviewed, the city is referred to twice as the People's Republic of Santa Monica. The first appearance is in the April 2020 issue, in the headline of a news item about the city establishing a moratorium on evictions.* In one short update on the RCB's annual rent increase in the June 2020 issue, the author opines that "most of the members of the Rent Control Board must not believe in private property ownership" because they were also considering a rent freeze.[35] The accompanying graphic uses a red background and yellow stars, evoking imagery from the People's Republic of China.†

While some articles acknowledge that housing is a necessity of life, the magazine's contributors still view it as a commodity within a free market framework. In his third and final installment of the "Prediction for 2030" series, "Can We Stop the Government Take Over of Rental Housing?" Valdez exalts the free market as the basis of civilization. He refutes the notion that housing produced by the private market is "exploitive and that the people who earn a living from housing are avaricious," and, adopting a classical economic framework of supply and demand, blames the high cost of

---

* The Trump administration later implemented a federal eviction moratorium, showing, beyond the shadow of a doubt, that eviction moratoriums are not a radical policy.

† Lest there be any doubt these sentiments are evergreen for AAGLA, a February 2024 blog post described Santa Monica City Council's recent expansion of tenant protections as a "Socialist takeover of our local government." While I don't disagree that the city and electorate's orientation toward protecting tenants does have a spirit of socialism, it's a mystery why AAGLA is reeling from it forty-five years later, as though it just happened.

housing on government regulations that constrain development.[36] In the COVID-19-era, analogies between tenants not paying rent under eviction moratoriums and tenants receiving free food from a grocery store made a number of appearances in *Apartment Age*. Former state senator Roderick D. Wright employs this comparison, arguing that eviction moratoriums are akin to a grocery store being forced to give food away.[37]

In "A Comparison between Artichoke Hearts and Residential Rental Real Estate," Stein draws out an extended metaphor in which the specialty food and rental housing are analogous commodity goods that should be subject to the same market logic. He conflates modern rent control with price fixing—similar to the price controls of World War II—arguing that, if the grocery store cannot cover the cost of purchasing the artichoke hearts but is forced to sell them anyway, it will go out of business. He concludes that not paying rent is the same thing as shoplifting.[38] Turner agrees, employing the grocery store shoplifting analogy in her April 2021 column. She also evokes the rhetoric of fairness, writing, "As housing providers who have sacrificed to make investments in rental property, we are the ones who are *fiscally responsible 'adults'* [italics mine]."[39] This statement about the renters and responsibility echoes some of the views held by pro–real estate, anti–rent control incumbents in the Santa Monica City Council in the late 1970s.

Similarly, economist Walter Block likens nonpayment of rent to stealing a service, like a haircut or massage, and wonders, "What is it that is so special about domiciles that failure to pay for them should be singled out for kid glove treatment . . . ?" He begins to answer his strikingly obtuse question by speculating that "maybe we are hard-wired by evolution to see 'home and hearth' differently from all other items."[40] He then discards this insight by evoking Adam Smith's "invisible hand" of the market, which, if allowed to take its natural course, will reallocate rental housing by sorting those who cannot afford their current residences into smaller and cheaper dwellings. This is portrayed as a win-win because households will ostensibly consolidate, resulting in more available rental housing. Seen through the lens of market logic:

> Evictions economize on space; they are a necessary condition for downsizing. Preventing them means more homelessness, not less. . . . Evictions seem callous, but they are not. Rather, they are the way the market maximizes human welfare when we face economic difficulty.[41]

The concept of a value-neutral free market that allocates resources and people in the Pareto optimal way goes hand in hand with the adage that "all economists agree" rent control is a bad policy. Attorneys Burrus and Spiegelman expand on this discourse with the assertion that, under rent control, people do not "economize" their housing choices, which results in two people each having their own home rather than "cramming" into one. This lack of economizing behavior reduces supply. They conclude that rent control is a price ceiling and thus achieves the predicted result, which is that "consumers over use the product and producers under produce it."[42] This abstraction of economic language and frameworks can also be found in much of the quantitative research about rent control, which uses concepts like the "housing misallocation" argument to obscure the complex lived experience of human beings.

Rent Control: A Perennial Thorn in One's Side

Despite over forty years of local rent control and rent stabilization in California, the efficacy and legality of the policy continues to be a topic of vigorous debate. Instead of regulations on the rental housing market, *Apartment Age* authors advocate for a free market and loosened restrictions on zoning and building permits, ostensibly to increase housing supply to the point that there would be no issues with affordability. In his monthly column, Yukelson blames rent control for severe housing shortages, skyrocketing rents, gentrification, and even homelessness. He further offers that it disincentivizes homeownership, ignoring the economic reality that homeownership opportunities are nonexistent for most renters in the Los Angeles area, especially in a market like Santa Monica. Yukelson also evokes the "housing misallocation" critique of rent control, arguing that tenants will be "reluctant to give-up their rent-controlled units, forgoing opportunities to buy property of their own, forgoing job opportunities, commuting long distances to work, or staying in place long after their children have gone and the 3-bedroom unit no longer suits their needs."* [43]

A common trope is that many rent-controlled homes are inhabited by the wealthy, which is ostensibly the opposite of the policy's stated intent.† In his October 2019 column, Vaughan protested both that even the mayor of San Francisco is rumored to reside in a rent-controlled apartment and that 12% of households residing in New York City's rent-controlled housing earn

---

* This observation is supported to some extent by the findings from my interviews. However, they illustrate that this reluctance is usually based on the strength of the relationship between the resident and their home environment (apartment, building, neighborhood, social network, and city) combined with a lack of options, rather than purely financial motives.

† Rent control policy traditionally does not state or intend that rent-controlled homes should be exclusively occupied by residents within a specific income range.

over $200,000 a year. In "Rent Control: A Cautionary Tale of the City of Santa Monica," the author wonders why cities cannot "means test" prospective tenants of rent-controlled housing so that owners do not subsidize wealthy tenants.[44] Libertarian-conservative writer Hannah Cox echoed this sentiment, writing, "It is often the wealthy who *hoard* [italics mine] the rent-controlled properties. A select few benefit from rent control—while the rest of the city pays the price."[45] Like other authors who have advanced this narrative in *Apartment Age*, she did not cite a source to support it.

In his November 2019 column, Vaughan evoked the "virtually all economists agree" rent control doesn't work argument, because "rather than forcing us to rent out units at below market rates, we often look for 'outs' like converting our rental units into condominiums or business properties that are not subject to rent control laws."[46] This admission of the landlord's role in undermining rent control's goals is unusual in the magazine's discourse. In a similar vein, the article "More Rent Control in California Will Make Housing Problems Worse" argues that the policy exacerbates existing shortages by further reducing supply. It references a much-cited study[47] that found that rent control in San Francisco reduces available housing due to the landlords' tendency to remove their properties from the market using the Ellis Act and other tactics. The article was reprinted in *Forbes* several months later.[48]

Apartment Age contains a number of pieces that outline potential legal challenges to the policy. In his September 2019 column, Vaughan optimistically hopes that once Ruth Bader Ginsburg is no longer on the U.S. Supreme Court, the conservative majority composition of the bench will lead to a decision that rent control is indeed unconstitutional. He is heartened by how the "majority of current justices have shown a willingness to overrule past decisions that impair property rights and keep us off the beaten path to socialism and the ultimate destruction of property rights."[49] Attorney Frank Weiser is similarly hopeful that California's various rent control ordinances may be challenged under the Fifth Amendment's takings clause.[50]

Market Language and the Rent Gap

Language used in sales materials for multifamily housing in Santa Monica reveals common industry practices around increasing rents. For example, Rent Control Commissioner Anastasia Foster pointed to the practice of emphasizing how many apartments will be "delivered vacant" in multifamily real estate listings. Listings often use language like "long-term upside potential" of a given percentage and include charts that compare current rents with potential market rents. The implication is clear: remove the current tenants, close the rent gap, and increase your profit margin.[51] This observation is supported by research about the financialization of housing, which examines how real estate investors adopt strategies to maximize returns.[52]

I surveyed all of the Santa Monica multifamily sale listings on LoopNet .com for the week of August 2, 2021.* The average price per apartment for this time period was $587,157, compared with $464,966 from January through May 2019. All except one of the properties were "Class C," which are typically over twenty years old and in need of renovation and other improvements. This 26.27% increase in value over a period of about two years contrasts with the rental housing industry's narrative of persecution. In this snapshot, nearly half the listings included language like *value-add* and *rental upside potential*, which suggests the new buyer can increase their profit, whether through redevelopment, owner occupancy to trigger a rent control exemption in duplexes and triplexes, or other means of removing the tenant to charge market rents to a new tenant. The listings touted proximity to various amenities and worksites, the transience of the target demographic (high earners), and the inaccessibility of the housing market—all of which underscore the role local context plays in determining property values and rents.[53] A sample of language from the LoopNet.com listings:

> At the epicenter of Silicon Beach, Santa Monica is home to world-class technology, media, and entertainment companies such as Google, Facebook, Hulu, Electronic Arts, among many others, providing a steady source of high-income professional renters.

> This exceptional hi-growth, hi-employment market provides a steady source of high-income professional renters.

> A savvy investor will be able to capitalize on the renter's neighborhood that is Sunset Park for decades to come. With a median home price of $2.2M, residents enjoy the affordability and flexibility of renting as opposed to buying a home.

As the data in Table 3.1 illustrates, there is substantial speculative potential for increased profits in some of these properties through various policy loopholes. The value is inflated accordingly, which creates a status quo of buyers removing long-term tenants by using cash for keys, the Ellis Act, or harassment tactics. This potential to yield higher returns by maximizing

---

* I excluded two- and three-residence properties that may be exempt from rent control due to owner occupancy, unless the listing noted otherwise.

TABLE 3.1. MULTIFAMILY BUILDINGS FOR SALE ON LOOPNET.COM FOR THE WEEK OF AUGUST 2, 2021

Asking price	"Upside potential" language	# of apartments	# of vacant apartments
$15,800,000	"Significant rental upside potential!"	20	9
$7,250,000	*	11	*
$3,500,000	"Value-added component—approximately 36% in rental upside."	8	*
$4,598,000	"Meaningful rental upside."	6	100% occupied, with a waiting list
$1,650,000	"Tremendous value add potential—51% projected upside."	4	*
$2,950,000	*	6	5
$1,799,777	*	5	*
$1,400,000	"Great owner user opportunity—rent control exempt if owner occupied."	3	*
$3,250,000	*	7	*
$3,650,000	"45% rental upside potential."	6	*
$2,675,000	*	6	*
$3,700,000	*	6	1
$2,150,000	*	4	1
$6,000,000	"Presents a significant value-add opportunity to investors, as current rents are approx. 75% below market value."	12	*
$3,400,000	"Presents a significant value-add opportunity to investors, as current rents are approx. 56% below market value."	4	*
$2,296,000	*	5	*
$4,985,000	"Redevelopment potential" and "upside potential of 29% in total rental income."	12	5
$5,195,000	*	7	*
$3,800,000	*	10	*
$6,400,000	"This 16 value-add deal has nearly 20% upside in rents, once units are rented for the market."	16	*
$3,489,500	*	4	1
$3,150,000	*	4	*
$9,250,000	*	7	*
$3,350,000	"This is an excellent corner lot for new multifamily condominium or apartment development opportunity."	7	*

* This information wasn't offered for the listing.

rents is what policymakers and activists continue to respond to with the implementation of various policies on tenant relocation, Ellis Act guidelines, and tenant harassment. As Fields and Uffer write, "Areas of high demand afford a strategy of upgrading, modernizing or otherwise developing properties, yielding profits from increased rental income and/or the sale of upgraded properties to tenants or new investors."[54]

Conclusion

While the rhetoric of AAGLA's leaders undoubtedly doesn't resonate with all Santa Monica landlords, it is hard to imagine how AAGLA members who choose to read *Apartment Age* year after year would not be influenced by its ideology to some extent. The framing of housing as a commodity, in particular, is probably self-evident to most landlords (and nonlandlords). To that point, ACTION's website characterizes Santa Monica's rent control policy as "radical," and their pitch for membership implores local landlords to "enlist in the army—fight Santa Monica's war on owners." This perspective is diametrically opposed to SMRR's progressive vision of tenants' moral right to their communities and homes (rather than "units"). This is exactly why the "housing as a human right" discourse of the past several years is so threatening to *Apartment Age*'s contributors. If one believes that housing is a commodity comparable to an artichoke heart—and *not* a home as a homeowner might experience it—it's easy to understand how regulations that limit returns on that commodity could be perceived as deeply unfair and burdensome. To add fuel to this fire, the discourse of private property rights is evoked as a direct connection between the landlord's unjust plight and the foundational principles of America.

This market logic also applies to framing like the "housing misallocation" argument, which proposes that people who rent their homes should live in residences that are matched to their family size and work location, in a Pareto optimal way, and continue to change dwellings as these circumstances evolve—much as one would purchase a new pair of jeans if they gained ten pounds. However, this logic does not seem to apply to owner-occupied homes, which are valued for their purported effect of stabilizing households and communities. Meanwhile, landlords are rebranded as "housing providers," who heroically offer an essential service to people who may not wish to own, rather than investors.

This commodity view of housing, combined with the perception of injustice at the hands of the People's Republic of Santa Monica, may result in some landlords feeling a certain reluctance to do more than the bare minimum of maintenance and upkeep, if that. It may also encourage some landlords to attempt to circumvent the tenant protections entirely, through either legal or extralegal means. Additionally, the combination of policy loopholes and lucrative rent gaps makes this an attractive course of action. These conditions have grave repercussions for the residents of Santa Monica's rent-controlled housing.

Figure 4.1 Ocean Avenue looking east on Washington Avenue. *(Author's collection.)*

4

The Person-Place Relationship

"It's More Than Just an Apartment"

> A meditation upon human dwelling reveals our primal
> embodied existence, our being-in-the-world. The notion of
> dwelling is the most taken-for-granted aspect of human
> existence. For this very reason, inhabitation, our familiar
> though enigmatic circumstance, is the most obscure
> problem upon which we may reflect.
>
> —RICHARD LANG (QUOTED IN *DWELLING, PLACE AND
> ENVIRONMENT*)

When viewed through the lens of economic theory and the market logic of real estate investment, the Pareto optimal allocation of residential units should be the primary objective of policy around rental housing. This implicitly assumes that mobility among renter households is desirable and necessary and the aim of housing policy should be to match residents with certain material features of the dwelling and location (e.g., number of bedrooms, proximity to work), along with a rent proportionate with their income. In contrast to homeownership, with its connotations of rootedness, renting is therefore viewed as an inherently transient form of tenure, and renters are expected to change residences periodically as life conditions (income, family size, job location, etc.) or landlord plans change. In actuality, most renters would like to have at least the *option* to experience the stability and longevity of tenure that homeowners typically enjoy, regardless of circumstances that inevitably evolve over the course of one's life. Moreover, when it comes to home, the whole is greater than the sum of its parts. Material features that meet residents' needs *are* important, but this limited view misses the significance of the wider context in which the dwelling and the dweller exist.

A more just society would be one in which renters and owners could both enjoy not only material stability but a sustained relationship with their home environment and community for as long as they choose. Contrary to the argument that rent control is specifically intended to benefit low-income households (and is thus ineffective as a method of Pareto optimal resource allocation), moderate-income households also derive real benefits from stable and predictable rent increases and restrictions on lawful causes for evictions. The examination of rent control and other tenant protections through the lens of the residential experience—rather than economics—reveals a different set of priorities, benefits, and challenges. An essential component of the residential experience is the person-place relationship. The extent to which someone feels attached to and integrated with their home environment, on multiple scales, correlates to both their well-being and their likelihood of staying long term. Moreover, it also informs the amount of time and care they invest both in maintaining and improving their home and in participating in the social fabric of their community. Both of these aspects have positive impacts beyond the benefits to the individual or household.

The early theory on the person-place relationship was developed by the human geographers of the 1970s, most notably Yi-Fu Tuan, Anne Buttimer, Edward Relph, and David Seamon, whose seminal writing explored the difference between the concepts of *space* (geographic location) and *place* (the added layer of meaning). They were inspired by the philosophy of Heidegger, whose conception of dwelling (or simply "being in the world") "involves the process by which a place in which we exist becomes a personal world and home."[1] Theory on the person-place relationship soon expanded to the field of environmental psychology, where it remains primarily situated today. As environmental psychologist Susan Saegert wrote, dwelling "points to a spiritual and symbolic connection between the self and the physical world. . . . It emphasizes the necessity for continuing active making of a place for ourselves in time and space."[2] In other words, dwelling is the process of *fully inhabiting* a place and is characterized by a symbiotic relationship between dweller and place. She notes that, though dwelling is often conceptualized as occurring in the home itself, it can also be experienced at the neighborhood and city scales (among others). Broadly speaking, to dwell is to be grounded in one's environment in such a way that one can reach their full human potential. As Lang wrote, dwelling is intrinsic to the human experience. To dwell is to be "at home."

If dwelling (or at-homeness) describes a holistic inhabiting of place, constructs like place attachment, sense of community, and sense of place are both the building blocks and the outcomes of that state of being. These describe attitudes, emotions, and behaviors, with respect to places and the people in them. Place attachment consists of emotions, thoughts and beliefs, and practices—such as caretaking, volunteering, and taking action to remain in a place in the face of a threat.[3] Sense of place and sense of community are closely related, specifically focusing on the environmental (e.g., nature, architecture, infrastructure, climate) and social dimensions of the person-place relationship. This chapter looks at the relationships these thirty Santa Monica renters have with their homes, buildings, neighborhoods, city, and neighbors.* Examining these relationships and the value they bring to both the individual household and the wider community offers a more nuanced and human-centered understanding of the benefits of rent control and other tenant protections.

Relationships with the Residence

At its most elemental, place attachment can be defined as an affective bond between people and places.[4] Participants expressed their attachment and sense of rootedness to their residences in different ways, ranging from pragmatic to emotional considerations. Katya is in her early thirties and has lived in her apartment for five years. She would only consider leaving her apartment if she were to move in with her partner, in which case the couple would need a bigger residence. When asked what she would miss most if she had to move, at first she thought of practical things like having an outdoor area and being able to drill holes in the wall to hang things. Reflecting further, she evoked her relationship with a favorite tree outside of her apartment: "The tree is very big and the leaves are really gorgeous when they blow in the wind," she explained. "Sometimes I just like to stand at my door and stare at them and breathe and kind of like center myself."

While almost all participants plan to stay in their homes for the foreseeable future, some spoke emphatically about never wanting to leave. Older individuals with long-term tenancies and participants on fixed incomes were especially determined to remain. Vanessa is in her early sixties and moved into her home over forty years ago so her son could attend Santa Monica's highly regarded public schools. She recalled how when they initially moved in, she immediately decided she was never going to move: "They'd have to drag me out with my fingernail scratches on the wall right there. They'd literally have to drag me out kicking and screaming. Until I have something that is substantively better there's no way I'm leaving this: [it's] exactly where I want to be." Diane is eighty, retired, and planning to stay in her apartment where she's lived for thirty-five years: "I'm going to stay here until I die and they carry me out." Joyce is in her sixties, has lived in her apartment for almost fifteen years, and has one of the lowest incomes among study participants. She can also see "dying here" in her apartment, "because where would I go where it would be better?"

---

* In alignment with social science conventions about respecting research participants' privacy, all tenant names are pseudonyms.

Christina and her husband have only lived in their Pico Neighborhood bungalow courtyard apartment complex for eight years, but in this time they've become close with their primarily working-class Latino neighbors and enjoy the community feeling. Her children attend or have attended Santa Monica public schools, but the family had been using a friend's address to qualify, as they were previously living outside the city limits. Despite some issues with the landlord around maintenance, her family is comfortable in their home. " I love our courtyard," she said. "I love our neighbors. . . . I just love it. I love our home." Christina could see herself and her husband "riding into the sunset" there.

Selena is sixty and has lived in her apartment for three decades. In that time, she's become close to not only her neighbors but also her on-site landlords, and she will never give up her apartment willingly. She has heard about people who give up their rent-controlled apartments to move in with a romantic partner, and that's a mistake she's not willing to make. In the event that she does lose her apartment, she would "literally mourn" it, and it would be a "huge emotional loss." She knows people who have been displaced from their rent-controlled apartments after decades and have been moved to tears: "I know that's exactly how I would feel because that's my attachment to it. . . . It's more than just an apartment."

Nearly half the participants expressed gratitude for their housing situation at some point in the interview. Stability and affordable housing in an expensive location they otherwise may not be able to afford was a dominant theme. Heather is in her seventies and has lived in her home for over four decades, during which she's been highly involved with her community. Despite some historical conflicts with the property manager, "I do absolutely every day say, you know, 'thank you God for my apartment,'" she said, "because I have a stable place that I can live in. It's a haven." She went on to compare her situation with other renters who are struggling financially after the first year of the pandemic and in "horrible situations. They're worried about how they're going to pay."

Nate is in his midthirties and has lived in his apartment for almost ten years. When he moved in with a friend who already lived there, he was just getting started with his career in the entertainment industry. As his relationship with his current partner became more serious, she moved in and eventually his friend moved out. The couple was married and later had a son. According to Nate, he feels "fortunate" that they "lucked out basically into getting this apartment," which has been a significant source of stability as his family's first home. Gina, who is in her midthirties and has lived in her apartment most of her adult life, feels "special" and "lucky" that she lives in a place where other people come for vacation, and her rent-controlled apartment facilitates that access.

Despite the occasional stresses of her living situation, Sharon feels "really grateful to live here" in the apartment that was previously her grandmother's home for over twenty years, and where she has resided for the past twenty-six years. Sharon grew up in Santa Monica and moved into her apartment after a divorce when she was in her midforties. Her grandmother had formed a friendship with the on-site landlord and after her grandmother passed away—around the same time Sharon was moving back to Santa Monica—the building manager offered her the apartment. She wouldn't be able to stay in Santa Monica without it: "Whatever the stressors are, I feel extremely fortunate to be here."

Katya feels very "privileged" to have a relatively affordable rent, along with a job that pays enough for her to be able to live alone. Having immigrated from Eastern Europe as a child, she has a unique perspective: "A safe, stable place to call home is a major part of like, achieving the American dream quote unquote, right?" she pointed out. "Having a home is important to be able to really work on yourself and become . . . the person you believe you should be." One of the youngest tenants in the study, Katya participates in a dizzying array of voluntary organizations citywide.

Other participants expressed gratitude and appreciation for specific features of their housing or neighborhoods. Nicholas is in his early forties and has lived in his apartment for thirteen years. Most of that time was with a roommate, but when his last roommate moved to the Midwest to save money during the pandemic, Nicholas decided to live alone for a while as a health precaution. He feels "fortunate" to be living in an apartment where he has ample space to be comfortable. In addition to Selena's general attachment to her apartment building and home, she feels "lucky" to have a parking space and storage. Diane appreciates the ocean breeze and living within walking distance of the ocean, which she feels "very lucky" to have enjoyed for the over three decades she's been in her home.

Feeling at Home or Not at Home

Twenty-six participants reported feeling at home in their residences, while three have mixed feelings and one doesn't feel at home at all. The most common factors that make an apartment feel like home are the ability to personalize the space and the social fabric of the building. Long-term neighbors, friendliness, mutual support, and a sense of community are aspects of the building's social environment that contribute to feelings of being at home. Personalization elements include creating a cozy or comfortable space, filling the home with items that have personal meaning, and the ability to paint or make other modifications. According to the sociologist Perla Korosec-Serfaty, these kinds of interventions are different types of "spatial appropriation," which is one of the main components of dwelling.[5]

Daphne has lived in her apartment for almost twenty-five years. Over that time, she has made a number of aesthetic modifications to her space. She explained:

> When it's four white walls it's really so generic and sterile and it's harder to make an environment feel like home. Whereas if you can paint the walls or put carpet down or whatever colors that you like, you can make it feel more like it's more like your own home. Then you stay longer.

For Katya, feelings of safety and stability, combined with the ability to personalize the space, are what makes her apartment feel like home: "It feels safe. I feel like I can just exist. I don't feel like I'm imminently at risk of losing it. I feel like I have the capacity and resources and permission to make it my own space." Luis has lived in his apartment for thirteen years and echoed this sentiment about the importance of personalization: "The way I've decorated it and organized it and the furniture I've added . . . it's your stuff, and it's your personality that you've added to it."

The role of time was also a significant component of feeling at home for participants, which aligns with the importance of time in environmental psychologists Carol Werner, Irwin Altman, and Diana Oxley's conceptualization of dwelling.[6] A few participants mentioned raising children in the residence as an integral aspect of what makes it feel like home. In addition to her positive relationship with neighbors in the bungalow courtyard complex, Christina explained, "My kids growing up here now definitely makes it feel like home." For Nate, the apartment feels like home because it has been the setting of several important milestones over time: it was where he and his wife lived when they got engaged and married, and later, where their son was born. Evoking the role of both time and spatial appropriation through decoration and modification—which his landlord allows—he said, "We've been here for so long. . . . We have kind of done the best we can to kind of shape it to what we want it to be." Similarly, what makes the apartment feel like home for Vanessa is how she's "made it my own," over the past four decades, and that her son grew up there. Though Patrick doesn't have kids, he has lived in his home for almost forty years—since he was in his early twenties—through three landlords. As he pointed out, that's two-thirds of his life.

Mixed feelings about home were attributed to several factors that differed for each participant. Lisa has lived in her apartment for almost thirty years and feels at home most of the time but described some "outside elements that aren't so nice" in the alley behind her apartment and adjacent areas. She theorizes these are probably related to homelessness in the area, which was a major theme for many tenants interviewed. The behaviors include yelling in the alley, scoping out the complex's carport through a window, breaking into residents' possessions in the carport, and banging on a neighbor's door in the middle of the day.

Amy, who has lived in her home for the same amount of time, has a truly contentious relationship with her landlord/manager, and has struggled with maintenance issues, described her feelings toward her home as a "begrudging acceptance." She explained that she didn't envision this apartment as a long-term residence when she first moved in but can't afford to stay in Santa Monica otherwise. "It's not the apartment I would want to be in," she said, "It's not how I pictured my life." Karli, a young renter who has lived with her partner in their apartment for three years, attributes her mixed feelings to the limitations on the feasibility of personalizing what is most likely a short-term space that they do not own.

Estelle, who is in her sixties, was the only participant to report not feeling at home in her residence of almost four decades. In addition to the detrimental impact of the conflicts Estelle experiences with the building's management and the hostile environment they have created, she feels deep frustration around being unable to afford a bigger apartment at this stage in her life. The question "do you feel at home?" evoked tears, as Estelle recounted how she was never quite able to afford purchasing a home despite multiple degrees and professional accomplishments. "It's not the home that I would like, and I actually hate it here," she said. She described her situation as "stuck" and added, "I hate it and I have nowhere to go."

Overall, the pandemic didn't have a significant impact on the extent to which participants feel at home or not at home in their residences. Even individuals who had difficult relationships with their landlord or manager didn't report experiences in this area that they attributed to the pandemic. Notably, only two participants deferred rent under the provisions of the COVID-19 eviction moratorium, so this may have been different had that been more prevalent. Both of those individuals were able to make arrangements with their landlords without incident. Two other people who had diminished income due to COVID-19 elected to continue paying rent because they were able to.

Several participants developed a deeper relationship with their home during the first year of the pandemic. Georgia is retired, in her late seventies, and has lived in her home for about twenty-five years. She described how her small balcony was her "saving grace" during the pandemic. While the city and county were under mandatory stay-at-home orders she was able to sit on her balcony in the sunshine, listen to the wind chimes, and enjoy the view. During this time she had a realization that Santa Monica—and not the country she is originally from—is where she feels most at home: "I've ensconced myself here so much that I realized I don't want to leave this. I'm very happy in this house." Working from home during the early days of COVID-19 made Daphne reflect on how lucky she is to live in her neighborhood, with what she described as its natural beauty. Both Sharon and Amy became more familiar with their neighborhoods by taking frequent walks, which led to their deeper appreciation.

Attributes

In contrast to tenants who experience elements of residential alienation to the extent they don't feel at home, study participants were mostly satisfied with their homes. When asked to describe their residences, about half of participants expressed generally positive sentiments in their descriptions, pointing to aspects like the layout, amount of space, availability of outdoor areas to relax, character or "feel," social atmosphere of the building, presence of personal decor, location, walkability, and natural light. This contrasts with elements of housing that researchers have found to have negative effects on physical and mental health, such as inadequate space for the number of residents or lack of natural light. Two of the three participants who expressed negative attitudes in their descriptions pointed to physical elements of the apartment (e.g., "the stove sucks"), and the third explained that she would prefer to live alone but has to have a roommate for financial reasons. The remainder described their homes in a neutral way, identifying various physical and locational features.

Participants also were asked what they liked best about their apartment. The ways in which the apartment meets one's needs was a common thread, which includes elements like storage, parking, a good floor plan, and adequate space. Some people framed the strengths of their home in comparison to past residences. Bonnie, a tenant in her early forties who has lived in her apartment for five years, appreciates having enough room to store a large package of toilet paper after living in much smaller apartments on the East Coast. Katya enjoys having a more substantial kitchen than in her previous residence, which was a studio apartment.

Location is also important. Participants mentioned the area's temperate climate in the context of the home's proximity to the beach, having cross ventilation and access to an ocean breeze, and having a private outdoor area. Many participants also enjoy the amenities around their home, such as shops, restaurants, libraries, and parks. Several participants who are or have been parents of school-age children value having access to Santa Monica's highly regarded public schools. Joyce, who lives in the upscale Wilmont neighborhood, painted a vivid picture of what she likes about her home's location, ending with a description of the neighborhood's sense of place:

> The location is magnificent. It is nice on Montana [Avenue]. I'm across from Pavilions, I'm like next door to Wells Fargo, I can walk nine blocks to the beach. I'm surrounded by coffee shops, restaurants, and the breeze of the ocean. I can see a sunset every night. And it's basically kind of like a village. It's villagey, and I like that.

In addition to these ways in which their homes meet their needs, many participants also described various ways their apartment makes them feel. The words "quiet," "safe," "home," and "comfortable" were all used several times and were connected to location, security features, and decor. Katya described the process of decorating her patio with potted plants and a hammock found on the sidewalk, connecting the space with feelings of comfort and well-being: "It just makes me feel comfortable to have a nice outdoor space, even if I don't use it as much as I can or should. The roses blooming in it—it just makes me smile." Her patio took on a new level of utility in the early pandemic when she started cooking more and was able to start an herb garden. Vanessa appreciates that her hands-off landlord gives her free rein to personalize and improve her apartment. Others enjoy the social atmosphere of their building, whether they are just on friendly terms with neighbors or are actually friends. Several participants who live in older properties, built in the 1920s through 1960s, mentioned the home's interior architectural character as a positive feature. Georgia fondly remembers how her apartment looked like a "bordello" when she moved in, with red floral carpet and seagrass wallpaper.

Some participants value the connection to nature as experienced through views of trees and sunsets and appreciation of the local flora and fauna. Nate articulated feelings of peacefulness that he sometimes experiences looking out of the window above his bed:

> What is nice is that that's kind of my view when I lay in bed, if I'm reading or just waking up from a nap or something. And all I can see is the treetops and the blue sky. And that, you know, that's something that I do like about the apartment is that you know, Santa Monica still feels pretty urban, but . . . looking out that window makes me feel like we do kind of have our own space, even though we live in an apartment, and it's just kind of a peaceful thing, you know, not too much noise.

The themes of "meets my needs" and "how it makes me feel" illustrate different (and sometimes overlapping) ways that participants are supported by their home environments.

Participants were also asked about aspects of the apartment that could be improved. The question was phrased in an aspirational way rather than prompting them to list negative elements. Only half of interviewees were able to think of an answer to the question and the majority expressed a general level of satisfaction alongside their suggested interventions, which were mostly physical in nature. Desired minor improvements include updated bathrooms, new floors, removing "cottage cheese" from the ceiling, having an on-site manager, being able to live alone, more space, and more light. Four participants mentioned noise from the neighbors, but with the exception of one person who has called the police about the noise multiple times, this was characterized as a feature of apartment life that was to be expected.

Several participants conveyed a discontent that extended beyond these minor issues. The quality of maintenance was a recurring theme. Nate is frustrated with the extent of deferred or improperly performed maintenance with the building's infrastructure, which sometimes manifests as rusty water or flickering lights. He explained that the owner seems to instruct the maintenance team to do only the cheapest and easiest solutions, instead of properly addressing structural issues. Mariana has lived in her apartment building for forty-seven years, since she was three years old. While she has no intention of leaving, she's dismayed by the owner's lack of effort toward maintaining the aesthetics of the building's exterior. She recounted a beautiful grove of trees that used to be in front of the building and was cut down several years ago, leaving the building looking barren and subjecting tenants to increased temperatures in their apartments. Unrepaired facade damage and neglected landscaping add to the general effect.

Amy, who has a very contentious relationship history with her landlord, transitioned from discussing the material aspects to the underlying issue of the relationship itself. Her final point about the quality of the work echoes Nate's frustrations:

> [What would you change?] Yeah everything . . . carpets need to be replaced, needs to be repainted, all of those things. And it becomes how hard do I fight? . . . Because I'm busy. . . . There was a flood upstairs, it ruined my walls. . . . It took my landlord over a month of having his things in my apartment to do this work, that would have taken anyone else a day. And he still did not do a very good job.

The frustrations of Amy, Nate, and Mariana reflect a deeper issue, which is the landlord's business model and lack of responsiveness and professionalism.

Social Environment

Neighbors are an important component of the residential experience. In their conceptualization of dwelling, Werner, Altman, and Oxley identify "social rules and relationships" as one of the three processes through which people form attachments and realize a state of dwelling in the home.[7] Ross, Talmage, and Searle's study on the predictors of sense of community—a contributing element of dwelling—found a positive relationship between sense of community, exchanging favors with neighbors, and length of tenure.[8] Hiscock et al. also identified psychosocial benefits for people who exchanged favors with their neighbors.[9]

Two-thirds of participants mentioned neighbors who were friendly or considerate, and over half appreciate being able to exchange favors with their neighbors. More participants are friendly with their neighbors than actually friends with them, and this more casual relationship is valued for its low-maintenance but supportive nature. For example, Luis appreciates being able to engage in pleasantries with his neighbors and work together to solve issues with the landlord without the social obligations that a more substantial relationship might entail. "I like the ability to be social when I want to be social," he said, "and kind of keep to myself when I want to keep to myself." Not surprisingly, mentions of favors often coincided with descriptions of a friendly or considerate rapport. Favors include caring for pets and plants, bringing mail inside, helping change lightbulbs and other small maintenance tasks, rides to the grocery store, tending to landscaping, and sharing food. Several participants said that while they don't regularly exchange favors with neighbors, knowing one or more of them would be *willing* to do so if necessary gives them a sense of security. For Selena, this feeling is intertwined with feelings of stability and at-homeness. "I just feel stable in this apartment," she said, "I feel secure. I know my neighbors and they know me. So, if anything bad happens they'll help me."

At the same time, some participants have formed real friendships with neighbors. Over the years, Selena has become friends with the family that owns her building and lives on-site. She described the importance of that relationship and its connection to her feelings of attachment and dwelling: "Well I mean I almost feel emotional about it. . . . This is my home. The owners of the building—the daughters now run the building—I mean I feel close to them and to their dad." Heather befriended a couple who moved in when their now eighteen-year-old son was a toddler, and the two households hosted each other frequently in their homes. When Heather was in a dispute with the property manager about passing through the cost of replacing a decaying porch in the form of a rent increase, one of these neighbors helped her calculate a fairer amount, and she was able to get the amount reduced.

Sharon is close friends with her next-door neighbor, who was one of the only people she spent time with during the early pandemic. While Sharon's neighbor is working long hours in the film industry, her cat is free to walk over to Sharon's apartment. "That's a big part of being here for me," she said, "the relationship with my neighbor next door and our shared cat."

Not surprisingly, given that 24% of residents in Santa Monica's rent-controlled housing have resided in their apartments since before January 1999,* [10] longevity of tenure was a common attribute when discussing neighbors in the building. Several participants described how minimal residential turnover and the presence of long-term residents creates a positive effect of stability, trust, and community within the building. Additionally, residential stability in the building is part of what makes the apartment feel like home for some. This is an important element for Sharon, who has lived in her home for nearly three decades:

> Up until recently, the other tenants in the building had been pretty static in terms of turnover. And so I have great neighbors . . . [but] it's changing a little bit. . . . It was very much a feeling of a community in our building. Like everybody would always be there to help you out or you know just or like if there had been any kind of disaster there's no question that we would all be like "okay, what do we do, we got to turn off the gas." It would have definitely been a communal response.

For Joyce, longevity and shared norms about how to coexist in a dense environment are also part of what makes her residence feel like home: "A lot of the people once they move here . . . because it's such a great location, they won't leave. So part of it is the same people have been living here forever, and they don't want to move. So that's why—it's your neighbors." One of the things Nate most likes about his apartment is having "really good" neighbors in the apartments below and next to his. These neighbors are older couples, and he attributes their tenure to rent control. Christina feels similarly about the community feel of her apartment complex, which is a bungalow courtyard style with a shared common space in the center: "I love the community. I love being part of the community. No, I don't think I ever felt this [before]."

Some participants developed closer or new relationships with their neighbors during the early days of the pandemic. The residents of Bonnie's building started a text chain where neighbors could let the group know

---

* This data is contemporaneous to the time period when the interviews were conducted. As can be expected, the percentage of longtime tenants has since diminished slightly.

when they were going to the store and ask if anyone needed anything. Selena and her neighbors have become closer since the pandemic began. To illustrate this, she recalled an occasion where the building's residents came together to celebrate a child's birthday:

> Within the first two months of the pandemic, there was a little girl in our [building], she was two years old, and she had moved in about a month or two before. And it was going to be her birthday. And we didn't really know the parents, but the landlord sent around a little notice to all of us—it's a small building only ten units—do we want to meet in the courtyard at five o'clock to celebrate her birthday? And so, at five o'clock on that particular day we all went outside and that little girl walked out to the balloons and a little party. Perfect—it was really wonderful.

In addition to participants who described the presence of longtime residents as a positive aspect of the home environment, many others included it as a neutral descriptive detail. No one had a negative opinion of long-term tenancies. Conversely, the majority of participants who mentioned a high level of turnover—whether from short-term tenants or vacation rental guests—offered some kind of critique or concern about the phenomenon and its root causes, which were attributed to speculative landlord business models. This echoes the finding on the residential experience in multifamily housing of the geographers Sharda Rozena and Loretta Lees, and how "the transience of Airbnb guests has an affective impact on everyday sociocultural interactions, including the ability to create meaningful home-making practices."[11]

Caretaking the Home

While all participants engaged in some kind of decorative practice, a third made renovations or improvements to their homes at some point in their tenancies. These ranged from minor modifications—like painting one wall blue with a stripe of green—to extensive remodeling throughout the residence. Flooring replacement was the most common type of improvement, followed by replacing bathroom and kitchen fixtures and finishes, decorative painting, and constructing a deck, porch, or patio. Sometimes the work was done without asking the landlord for permission. When Gina's sink needed to be replaced she was unhappy with the proposed replacement and paid several hundred dollars for a sink that was more to her liking. She made this arrangement with the maintenance worker and still doesn't know if the landlord is aware this has taken place. She explained that it was worth investing the money because she doesn't have plans to leave.

Vanessa's professional background includes the skill set to make significant cosmetic modifications, and she has remodeled many features of her apartment by herself over the past four decades without seeking approval from the property manager. She attributes this freedom to the manager's relatively laissez-faire approach, combined with a desire to remain "under the radar" due to their history of conflict:

> I ripped up the carpets and finished my floor and concrete and did plaster walls, and updated cupboards. I updated my bathrooms, I changed the sinks, I put in new shower stalls, took out the old disgusting ones . . . put in a washer dryer—I actually rewired it for a washer dryer in the closet. I mean they used my apartment to see what could be done [with the other apartments] when I updated it.

A few participants have been able to share the costs of basic maintenance with landlords and, in the process, upgrade items to suit their aesthetic tastes. Dave has lived in his home for twenty years, and like Vanessa, has the skills to do renovation work himself. He's made extensive modifications to his home over the years, including removing the ceiling in the living room to create a loft, adding wood paneling to the back room, installing hardwood floors, and constructing a porch. His bungalow had a lot of deferred maintenance when he first moved in, which presented an opportunity to make repairs while also personalizing the space. He was able to work out a deal with the landlord where he would perform the needed work for free, and the owner would take the cost of materials off the rent:

> I kind of made a deal with the landlord saying like, "I like this place, I could really fix it up." Like I have the technical skills to improve upon it, because it was in bad shape. So that led me to getting it and then also you know they were very upfront about saying any work you put into it I will pay for your supplies, you can take it off the rent, and that made it a comfortable transition.

Spatial appropriation can take the form of everything from caretaking practices like decorating or landscaping to major modifications to the space. Korosec-Serfaty expands on the concept of spatial appropriation as a means of joining the residents with their environment. She describes the dweller as an "active subject who confers meaning upon the world but also as an individual who is acted upon by the world of which she or he is a part."[12] Korosec-Serfaty cites ornamentation, maintenance, and housework as examples of appropriation activities. She draws an important distinction about what is actually being appropriated, which is not the physical space itself but the *meanings* and types of *relationships* one establishes with the space. In other words, it is the process by which an apartment shifts from being a rented "unit" of housing in which to perform biological needs to a home.

For others, given the combination of constrained mobility within Santa Monica and their ability to save money due to paying under market rents (especially for long-term tenants), a willingness to invest in improving the home is pragmatic.* This is the case for both participants who never plan to move and those who hope to or are open to it eventually. Despite her ambivalence about her living situation, when Amy inherited some money after a parent passed away, she invested it in improvements to her kitchen and bathroom. Sharon replaced the carpeted floor with hardwood flooring at her own expense. For Amy and Sharon—both long-term tenants—residence in Santa Monica is dependent on retaining their current housing. This incentivizes investments in the home environment beyond what might be expected in a rental dwelling. This finding complicates one of the primary critiques of rent control, that it disincentivizes landlord maintenance and leads to a decline in the quality of the housing stock.†

Relationships with the Neighborhood

Nearly one-third of participants expressed attachment to their neighborhoods. Rena loves Sunset Park, explaining that there's no other neighborhood where she would want to live within the city. In particular, she appreciates the variety of trees and the proximity to Santa Monica College, with all it has to offer. Her attachment is mainly practical and based on how the neighborhood meets her needs. For Nate, Sunset Park is the perfect balance between the suburbs of Miami where he grew up and some of the more urban areas where he lived when he first moved to Los Angeles. His neighborhood now feels like home. Although he and his family plan on upgrading their housing at some point in the future, "It feels like a neighborhood and a place where, if we're here for a long time, we would be content." If they do stay in their home throughout their son's school-age years all of the public schools he would attend are within a half mile. Nate's attachment to the neighborhood is partially connected to the atmosphere, but it also centers on the ways in which its amenities and resources support his family, and, particularly, his young son.

---

* Cosmetic improvements are different from basic maintenance that the landlord should be performing, such as replacing old carpet or linoleum. This type of work is discussed in Chapter 5.

† Structural maintenance is generally beyond the scope of what residents are willing or able to address, so elements like electrical wiring, plumbing infrastructure, and seismic retrofitting don't benefit from a tenant's willingness to invest in home improvements.

In addition to practical aspects that facilitate attachment, time plays a significant role. This is true through both the repetition of routines associated with daily life over time* [13] and the function of places as conduits between the past and the present as sites of memorable events.† [14] Raquel is in her late sixties, grew up in Santa Monica, and has lived in her current home in the Pico Neighborhood for around twenty-five years, where she raised her children and is now raising her grandchildren. Her attachment to the neighborhood is rooted in biographical associations. In addition to being able to walk to the market or church, she likes being close to the house where she grew up and how when she walks up her former street she is reminded of families she has known in the past. Mariana—also a lifetime resident of the Pico Neighborhood—feels similarly. "This is the neighborhood that I grew up in, and this is a neighborhood that my son grew up in, and this is the neighborhood that I still live in," she explained. "I have so many memories of different things."

When asked to describe the neighborhood, participants' opinions were overwhelmingly positive. Standout attributes were character and sense of place, how people are (e.g., friendly), location within the city, and having social ties. A follow-up question about the best features (if not already shared in reply to the previous question) pointed again to how people are, in addition to walkability and amenities. Responses to "what could be better?" included affordability (both housing and general cost of living), improved public transit and mobility, and people being more considerate or "down to earth." When asked how the neighborhood has changed over the years participants pointed to the built environment, the character of commercial areas, and the socioeconomic composition of residents as well as increases in homelessness, crime, and traffic that are occurring citywide. Some had unambiguously negative opinions about these changes, while others described them without sharing their orientation. Not surprisingly, negative opinions were mostly expressed by long-term tenants, whereas neutral descriptions were spread across the spectrum of tenure length.

---

* Geographer David Seamon developed the concept of "time-space routines" or "place ballet" to describe the way in which daily routines create the foundation for the relationship between a person and a place they inhabit—be it residence, work or leisure.

† Personal memories connected to places produce what environmental gerontologist Graham Rowles describes as "autobiographical insideness." This manifests in the type of nostalgic anecdotes that most longtime residents can share while taking a walk through their neighborhood. These recollections and associations—which Lewicka calls "episodic declarative memory"—are important for personal identity and continuity. Illustrating the importance of long-term tenure, these memories fuse time and space together to create place meanings that support attachment.

Social Fabric and Sense of Community

When asked if there's a sense of community in their neighborhood, about half of participants responded affirmatively, several reported some sense of community, and a few described an absence of community. As illustrated earlier, longevity of tenure deepens social bonds on the neighborhood scale. Part of what makes Estelle feel at home in her neighborhood is the social knowledge of place she has developed over the nearly four decades she has resided there. Ocean Park is a place where, among longtime residents, "most of us like each other, we know each other, and you know—we appreciate each other." Estelle knows the history of who has lived in the buildings around her and explained, "We have relationships, we have experiences, we have stories. . . . It's more than just my apartment it's my community." This sentiment exists alongside other aspects of place alienation and residential alienation that Estelle described, including being the only study participant who doesn't feel at home in her residence, illustrating the complex and sometimes contradictory nature of the person-place relationship.

Heather described a similar experience in her forty-three years as an Ocean Park resident, citing a recent study that scored the neighborhood at three times the national average on feelings of trust. She theorized that the elevated level is due to "a lot of us aging hippies who still live around here that I've known all the time, and we all help each other out." Mariana described social ties with her longtime neighbors in the Pico Neighborhood as being "like family." They have a neighborhood watch program, and they "all take care of each other" by being mindful of people who look potentially suspicious and are loitering. Mariana highly values the community feel in the Pico Neighborhood, which she would miss if she had to move out of her home and neighborhood:

> After being there for as long as I've been, it's like a family. I know all of my neighbors. . . . We all talk, we get together, and we have little block parties. We've done this for years, you know. So it's a very enriched community feeling. I feel safe there. . . . I know when someone's outside, they're keeping an eye out on everyone.

Heather, Estelle, and Mariana's similar descriptions of their neighborhoods' social character align with what Capek and Gilderbloom[15] depicted in their seminal case study on Santa Monica, which emphasizes the tight-knit social fabric of Ocean Park and the Pico Neighborhood. This social fabric was key in facilitating Ocean Park's role as the hub of the rent control movement, in the late 1970s and early 1980s, and decades of community activism in the Pico Neighborhood.

For other participants, casual familiarity with people in the neighbor-hood—both residents and business employees—is an integral component of a sense of community. Selena described how the staff at her two local grocery stores know her because she has been a customer for years. Joyce character-ized sense of community in Wilmont as a "villagey" atmosphere, where she is able to walk around the neighborhood to various businesses, walk her dog, and see the same people every day. This familiarity has cultivated feelings of solidar-ity: "I know who lives where and stuff like that. And even the shop owners . . . you know, when you see people every day, even though you're not tight with them, if there was a problem you would instinctively help." Mariana described a similar experience of forming relationships of familiarity with people who live or work in the vicinity of her home through repeated interactions:

> There are people who live within a certain radius who I see frequent-ly. And even though I may not know them by name, there is a friend-ly, like, sense that they know who I am, where I live. I know who they are. I know where they live. We kind of have this feeling of watching out for each other. We're always cordial and polite and say hello.

Nate described how chance encounters in the neighborhood with other par-ents and children from the school his son attends have created a sense of community. He compared this with his experience living in Burbank, where "you never bump into somebody else [you] know." He credits rent control with creating housing stability for his family, especially during the financial uncertainties of both the pandemic and freelancing. This stability has, in turn, given them a sense of community and belonging through these re-peated encounters and activities:

> I didn't really feel it until we had our son—but when we go out for walks, we go to the park, go to the store, we bump into people that we know, and I think that's really what makes it to me—has made it re-ally feel like community. . . . I feel like it happens quite a bit here where we'll be at the playground and somebody we hadn't intended to have a playdate with, we'd bump into them and then the kids play together and I talk to the parents. Or going into the store, driving down the street and yeah, I've seen somebody I know and just waved. Like that kind of familiarity is really what makes it to me feel like a community.

Character and Sense of Place

Descriptions of neighborhood character and sense of place were composed of an array of elements, including the natural environment, geographic location, historical narratives, the built environment, and the social climate. Not surprisingly, the sense of place differed across neighborhoods. In the Pico Neighborhood the social element is of particular importance. It is known for its strong sense of community, racial and ethnic diversity, and affordability. Mariana, Christina, Raquel, and Ricky are all Latino, and share similar perceptions of the neighborhood. For Mariana, her lifelong residency has created a social fabric that is tangible when she is out in the community. She attributes that stability in part to rent control:

> There's still a lot of people that live there that have lived there almost as long as I have. And I don't know other neighborhoods like that. It's not the only rent control building in our little neighborhood. So I think that's another reason why many people are still there that have been there since I was a kid. . . . Plus, you know, because we are very community oriented. . . . There are people who live within a certain radius who I see frequently. And even though I may not know them by name, there is a friendly sense that they know who I am, where I live. I know who they are. I know where they live. We kind of have this feeling of watching out for each other. We're always cordial and polite and say hello. And, you know, sometimes we stop and have a little chit chat.

Ramona also grew up in the neighborhood, is in her early sixties, and has lived in her duplex home with her husband, children, and niece for twelve years. She knows pretty much all her neighbors and describes the neighborhood's longtime residents as low-income families who are living "day by day" financially and are generally "loving" and "nurturing." This contrasts with newer residents, who in her observation tend to not have children, as indicated by a recent lack of trick-or-treaters on Halloween. For Ricky, a Santa Monica native in his early thirties, it's "probably the most interesting part" of the city, with "the most character of any part of the city in terms of diversity and people coming and going." He illustrates this characterization by pointing out that it is the only place in Santa Monica where one can find a vendor who sells elote, a classic Mexican street food. The neighborhood is known as the heart of Santa Monica's Latino community, and Ricky also referenced the urban renewal that shaped the neighborhood in the late 1960s, by placing the 10 freeway through what was at the time the city's Black community:

> It was predominantly Black and brown folks living here but that's why the freeway ended up going through this neighborhood. A lot of Black and brown folks were displaced by that and it cut the

neighborhood in half, the city in half, and like, decimated the Pico Neighborhood.

Neighborhood change was a common theme for residents of the Pico Neighborhood. Raquel described its shift from a working-class neighborhood shared by Black, Latino, Asian, and white households to its current incarnation, as a gentrified space with white families and young professionals moving in. She observed a trend of these families who are "maybe young couples just out of college . . . buying the cheaper homes" and renovating them. This demographic shift has catalyzed the transformation of the neighborhood's small business landscape, with Latino specialty stores, drug stores, and little markets closing. Amy—who is white, is not originally from Santa Monica and does not have the same attachment to the neighborhood's social character— also noted the changing nature of the commercial strips, where "fancy" restaurants have recently emerged. As a result of these social changes, Christina described the neighborhood as a "divided community," where Black and brown residents feel united and newer residents passing through the park sometimes regard them with nervous looks. Changes over the years of what type of person is able to afford to live in one's neighborhood—especially when it's along racial or ethnic lines—inevitably impact long-term tenants, as they experience the often painful feelings of their social fabric disintegrating.

Patrick, who moved to the neighborhood four decades ago from Orange County and is white, offered a counterpoint. He recalled how it was "not the most sought-after part of town to live in," at the time, and would have been considered "the other side of the tracks." Since then it has gentrified and crime has decreased, but it has remained a diverse neighborhood where people are "cordial—everybody gets along or maybe you know, looks out for each other and you know, [is] respectful." Ricky also pointed out some positive aspects of neighborhood change, and how the city has taken the initiative to preserve the social fabric that is so intrinsic to the neighborhood's sense of place:

> There's been more city investments. You know, the park didn't used to have a library. The affordable housing that I'm talking about across the street from me used to be a row of abandoned homes and condemned homes that—it actually used to be a lot of gang activity there, and . . . there was just a lack of investment in this part of the city in the past. I think it's gotten better in that the City has made concerted efforts to be wary of displacement.

Residents of the Wilmont, Mid-City, and Sunset Park neighborhoods conveyed a very different sense of place in their neighborhoods. Aspects like flora and fauna, architecture, quietness, proximity of amenities (e.g., grocery stores, restaurants), safety, and walkability were identified as positive elements in all three locations. For Daphne, who was working from home during the early stages of the pandemic, Wilmont's natural elements offered a respite from the monotony:

> Even though it's built up, [there are] lots of trees, you can see the sky, you can hear the birds. And became more aware of that when last March we were all sent home from work. I had to work from home . . . so I could sit with the door open and the windows open and have a breeze, and you could hear nature. Like wow, what a treat rather than being stuck in a high rise.

The name "Wilmont" is a portmanteau of Wilshire and Montana, which are two major thoroughfares that run west to east through the city. Wilshire Boulevard stretches roughly sixteen miles to downtown Los Angeles, while Montana Avenue terminates shortly after Santa Monica's border. Wilshire Boulevard is a major commercial strip containing car dealerships, drug and grocery stores, and other businesses that serve a wide clientele. Montana Avenue has a distinctively different feel. It is a narrow street with smaller buildings, and higher-end restaurants and boutiques. Montana borders the neighborhood to the north and Wilshire delineates the southern edge. Between the two streets there is a large concentration of multifamily housing, while north of Montana is almost entirely single-family homes valued in the multimillions of dollars. In this sense, the Wilmont neighborhood, and its commercial districts and amenities, is an interstitial zone shared by Santa Monica's renter households and its wealthiest residents.

Several participants were cognizant of the different socioeconomic populations that the two streets serve and pointed to the social tensions therein as a negative aspect of neighborhood character. Daphne recalled feeling uncomfortable in "snobby" Montana Avenue shops, where the staff "eye you up and down." She described the difference between the two parts of the neighborhood:

> You can just tell when you go south, Wilshire is a little bit more lived in; when you go north of Wilshire it's more manicured lawns. People have more of an attitude. . . . And I've definitely noticed there's been a change over the years. The people that I've known since I moved in here are all very down to earth, but I've noticed over time, the people that have moved into the area are very entitled.

Luis grew up in Venice and the Ocean Park neighborhood of Santa Monica and has lived in Wilmont for almost ten years. He described the neighborhood as "posh suburban" and very "bougie," with a lot of "soccer moms" picking up their kids in expensive cars. While he enjoys some of the amenities on Montana Avenue and the walkability of the neighborhood, he would like to see people be "a little bit less uptight" and more "down to earth." These experiences in Wilmont illustrate the social tension of an economically diverse neighborhood with an upscale commercial district, where low- and moderate-income households are primarily able to remain only by virtue of their rent-controlled housing.*

Relationships with the City of Santa Monica

Twice as many participants expressed strong attachments to Santa Monica as to their neighborhoods. The strength of feeling around the city versus the neighborhood may be due to Santa Monica's small footprint. In contrast to Los Angeles—where the neighboring Venice area feels like a small city unto itself—Santa Monica's diminutive size makes the whole city fairly accessible to most residents and may result in less of a distinction between neighborhoods. Additionally, the city's identity and branding make it a more cohesive entity than its individual neighborhoods. Some participants were even unsure what their neighborhood is called.

While some people used the word "attached," others expressed how emotionally difficult it would be to move out of the city. Ramona, who is being displaced from her duplex by the new owner's family member,† considered her housing options. Faced with the reality that she cannot afford to buy a home in Santa Monica, she wonders how close she would be able to stay: "I wouldn't be able to move too far because I would miss all the community. I would miss my neighbors. And because my heart is here in Santa Monica." Other participants who grew up in the city expressed similar sentiments. Mariana has nightmares about leaving Santa Monica. She describes herself as being "deeply rooted," to the extent that she doesn't know what she would miss about it unless she were to actually leave. Though she has considered moving "100 million times," she can't envision being as happy anywhere else. Christina has mixed feelings about the city, explaining that "I hate it, but it's home. . . . I don't know where else I would be as comfortable

---

* My dad lived in the Wilmont neighborhood for over thirty years. However, since his apartment was closer to the Third Street Promenade and further away from where the Montana Avenue shopping district started, it had a slightly different feel than what these participants describe.

† This is one of several allowable reasons for landlords to terminate a lease under Santa Monica's rent control law.

as I am here." Ricky—who is heavily involved in and informed about local politics—shared critiques of city leadership and other local actors through-out the interview. Even given these elements, he explained:

> Man, look I love this place. I live here and. . . . I say these criticisms very much in that way that I would—I feel like I'm talking about myself in many ways. I feel like I can be critical because Santa Monica, for better or worse, is in my soul. It's where I grew up. I grew up a working-class kid in the city. And it gave me a chip on my shoulder, but it also gave me the tools that I have to be successful.

Growing up in a military family, Heather moved around frequently before settling in her home four decades ago. With the exception of Santa Monica, she never had the desire to stay long term: "I never felt attached to any part of the country in America that I would even really consider staying. . . . That's why it's like a great feeling—it's like 'gee I belong here.'" It means a lot to her to feel at home here because she "never felt at home anywhere." This attachment led her to pass up a promising career opportunity years ago that would have required her to move out of state for several years.

Joyce has moved all over the country for work and feels lucky to live in Santa Monica. She would be "hard pressed" to find another place where she would feel more at home. "I feel like I belong here," she explained. Despite Amy's tempestuous relationship with her landlord, she loves Santa Monica and has determined that it's worth dealing with those stresses to continue living there: "I love Santa Monica, I love the weather, I love being able to swim. I would not be able to live here if I were not in this apartment. So there's a cost that comes with it, which I've determined at this point is worth it." Gina has lived in Santa Monica for most of her adult life, and experiences deep anxiety about being displaced from an environment that has become familiar and the city that has become home. If she were to lose her rent-controlled apartment she would only be able to remain in Santa Monica if she was able to access affordable housing. Patrick listed the city's many amenities, describing it as an "idyllic place to live," adding that he is "blessed" to be living there.

Most participants expressed strong opinions about the city, to a much greater extent than the neighborhood. This is consistent with the presence of stronger attachments at the city than at the neighborhood level. The semi-structured participant-led nature of these interviews enabled participants to expand sections of interest into in-depth discussion, which was often the case with this topic. Participants also found it relatively easy to describe the characteristics of their neighborhoods, whereas the prompt to describe Santa Monica frequently elicited reactions of laughter or contemplative silence followed by in-depth discussion. Those who have grown up in the city or lived there for decades sometimes conveyed the difficulty of describing something so familiar, while newer residents seemed more able to respond. This phenomenon evokes the sociologist David Hummon's concept of two types of "rootedness," where longtime residents have a less self-conscious sense of place, whereas people who have lived in multiple locales are often better able to articulate a sense of place.[16]

Opinions on the city were mixed: negative views were expressed exclusively by long-term residents with tenures over twenty years, while positive opinions were shared by participants across the tenure spectrum. There was some overlap between people who expressed both. Prevalent negative aspects were general change, loss of character and sense of place, and shifting socioeconomic characteristics. Standout positive qualities were amenities and location, and character and sense of place. Elements of amenities and location were the beach, the climate, bicycle infrastructure, public transit, high-quality public schools, access to natural areas, cultural resources, dining and entertainment, and community resources like Santa Monica College. There was no apparent relationship between length of tenure and appreciation of these features.

Participants had overwhelmingly negative feelings about change at the city level. These opinions were expressed both throughout the conversation and when questioned directly about how the city has changed over time. Negative views about change were primarily expressed by residents with tenures over twenty years and by a few in the ten- to twenty-year range. As with feelings about change on the neighborhood level, this suggests a difference in perception and satisfaction related to length of residency, which is likely based on which version of the city feels like the "real" Santa Monica. Over the course of the interview, participants across the tenure length spectrum also expressed high levels of concern about city issues like homelessness, housing costs, overdevelopment, crowds and traffic, and safety and property crime. Participants often offered their analyses of these issues, connecting them to political dynamics within the city. Discontent arising from quality-of-life issues and change that threatens place meanings and social fabric is an element of place alienation, a phenomenon where long-term place-attached residents experience their communities as something alien with which they struggle to identify.* [17]

---

* Hummon coined the term "place alienation" to describe a deficit in an individual's attachment to place. Later, Tuttle developed a similarly named construct called "alienation from place." This describes both a process and an outcome wherein longtime residents experience their communities as something alien to them. Unlike Hummon's place alienation, Tuttle's construct is predicated on the continuing existence of place attachment, theorizing that concurrent place attachment and alienation interact as "a dynamic response to neighbor-

Social Fabric and Sense of Community

It was difficult at times for participants to differentiate between a sense of community on the city and neighborhood scales, again possibly because Santa Monica is so small geographically. When discussing one scale there was often a drift into the other. Overall, almost two-thirds of the participants experience a sense of community, a few experience *some* sense of community, and several feel that there was no sense of community at the city level. Most of this latter group *does* experience a sense of community in their neighborhood but explained that the city is too socially fragmented to feel like part of a community on a larger scale. According to Christina, who grew up in the area:

> It's kind of too big. I think it's too diverse now to really have that community feel. . . . I think Santa Monica used to have a very even keeled vibe through the whole city. . . . I think there was an underlying, like, we're all the same, and I don't think that's here anymore.

Gina attributed a lack of community to the influx of people in their early thirties who are single (and presumably childless), have high-paying jobs, and are moving to the city but do not actually care about it.

Two themes emerged in how a sense of community is experienced at the city level. Almost one-third of participants mentioned how social media platforms like Facebook and Nextdoor have facilitated community building through mutual support, especially during the early days of the pandemic. For some, interactions on those sites have been their main source of citywide community, both before and during the pandemic. The Facebook groups *Ask, Borrow, Give* and *Buy Nothing*, in particular, were identified as virtual spaces where community is experienced. Katya identified positive and negative aspects of these platforms for community discourse. While there is a level of volatility in some social media interactions, she has also seen "a lot of folks really come together to help provide support for people who really need it." On the *Ask, Borrow, Give* Facebook page, group members can share unwanted items with other members, or request items that they need. She described how on two occasions, someone was simply having a bad day and asked if there was anyone they could talk to. In response, "sixty people were like, you can talk to me just DM me, here's my phone number. . . . I'm almost crying because it's really beautiful to see a community that may not always

---

hood conditions and transformations" (p. 3). In this conceptualization, "alienation from place" cannot exist without a high degree of place attachment. For the sake of consistency with residential alienation, I use place alienation to describe Tuttle's concept.

agree with each other kind of come together to support everyone, no matter what."

Amy shared a similar experience with her local *Buy Nothing* Facebook group, which is her primary community space. In the course of her engagement with the group, she's observed how members "kind of rally around, like if someone's sick [they'll] drop off food . . . and there's definitely some people who are ill that need help and put it out there and people step right up." Participation in the group has acquainted her with people she would not have otherwise known, which has been "really lovely." Karli described these Facebook groups as a positive asset for the community as a whole. The interactions she observes give her "that sense of community where like, people are there for each other if you need them to be." For Georgia, *Ask, Borrow, Give* is her main source of community aside from her friends. Sarah described *Ask, Borrow, Give* as a space where "everybody is so friendly, and so nice, and so thoughtful and just so giving. . . . You can tell this is like a tight-knit community group." In this sense, networks of mutual reliance that may have formed through other means before the advent of social media platforms have found a thriving home in the virtual world.

A culture of civic engagement is another way some participants experience a sense of community in Santa Monica. For those who already have a high level of civic engagement, participation in various nonprofit, grassroots, and city groups is an opportunity to be in community with other Santa Monicans. Vanessa doesn't feel like a part of her neighborhood community due to the perceived pervasiveness of the NIMBY ideology. Instead, she feels a sense of community with the city staff and activists she interacts with in the course of her work to improve the city's multimodal transportation and sustainability initiatives. Rena, another longtime resident who has been highly active in community groups for decades, described similar experiences: "Even if we don't agree about political issues, people are at the [various city] meetings." While he does not participate in any place-based groups or community forums, Luis agreed that there is a sense of community citywide and connected it to civic engagement. Conversely, he does not experience a sense of community in his Wilmont neighborhood for reasons previously explored.

Selena shared a more tangible example of civic engagement, remembering how Santa Monicans came together spontaneously after the mass looting event of May 31, 2020, to clean up the streets:

> After the George Floyd murder there was some, you know, vandalism in the city of Santa Monica and the next day—I was out there about I don't know 11 o'clock or something—and the streets were

filled with people. I mean, I had my broom and my dustpan. People had, within a couple of hours, cleaned it up, cleaned up the Santa Monica Place, cleaned up all the glass. Just, the community did that—it wasn't the City, it was the community.

Nearly one-third of participants perceived a deepening sense of community during the pandemic. An increase in mutual aid networks, where community members offer support in a peer-to-peer model, mirrored a nationwide phenomenon. Heather described how her sense of community increased during the pandemic through hearing about various mutual aid networks, along with "the awareness that you need the people around you." Katya has "seen a lot of folks really come together to provide support for people who need it" on her local *Ask, Borrow, Give* Facebook group. Heather and Diane have seen this behavior on Nextdoor, with some of the neighborhood's younger residents offering to grocery shop for older residents. Ramona explained that "a lot of people, they go out of their way to check in on those who are homebound and they take them food."

While a sense of community and/or place attachment do not *predict* participation in the community, they are generally a precondition of it.[18] Neighborhood associations were not a primary method of participation, as illustrated by participants' experiences with the Wilmont Neighborhood Association and the perception that their agenda centers on the concerns of affluent homeowners. This is not a surprising finding in that neighborhood, given the socioeconomic divide, and is also supported by research on neighborhood associations and their orientation toward homeowner priorities.[19] One participant has attended Wilmont Neighborhood Association meetings but describes them as "a lot of talking" where nothing is accomplished. However, several other people participate in their neighborhood associations in Ocean Park and the Pico Neighborhood, which have a history of community activism that includes renters.

Participants have engaged in a wide variety of other community groups and activities. Almost all have participated in some kind of civic or volunteer group or activity, including citywide groups, neighborhood groups, regional or national organizations, and community events. Christina sets up a "community giving table" once a week in her complex's courtyard where people come to pick up groceries and prepared meals, Gina volunteers with a local rabbit rescue organization, Ramona hosts a Christmas party with a live nativity scene for the neighborhood, and Nate coaches youth sports. The time these tenants invest in their communities challenges the stereotype of renters as disengaged and the conventional wisdom that homeownership contains a special quality that promotes investing time in one's community.

Character and Sense of Place

The amenities participants listed as positive attributes of living in the city were often components of a more holistic vision of Santa Monica's identity and how it feels to live there. Participants frequently used "beach" as a descriptor before "city" or "town," underscoring the role the city's geographic location plays in shaping its character and identity. Two participants—both of whom moved to Santa Monica in the past five years but are decades apart in age—described it as a "friendly beach city." Terms like "laid back" or "casual" were also common, though several people who used that language also said it was changing. Vanessa appreciates the feeling of being a small town in a large urban environment, with proximity to a wide range of natural areas. Karli echoed this sentiment, stating that "there's everything that you would want from a city," with the added advantage of being close to the beach and hiking areas. Selena painted a picture by evoking the city's built environment, natural features, and atmosphere:

> The beach, the weather, the air, the palm trees, the pier—you know, even though we can't go there because it's so crowded. But just seeing the pier, driving down PCH [the Pacific Coast Highway] and seeing the pier lit up you know the Ferris wheel lit up. . . . I like the beach atmosphere, you know? Everyone's very casual and that's really what I like.

In contrast to this urban imaginary of the "laid-back beach town," several participants mentioned the affluence of the city's residents and the cost of things in general, in addition to the city's identity as an international tourist destination. Nate explained:

> It kind of feels kind of like a theme park. . . . It feels like sometimes there's two halves of Santa Monica. There's Santa Monica on like a morning with the marine layer before like nine o'clock when I go down to the beach and run or surf or ride my bike. And then it still feels like a small town.

City leadership's initiative to attract and sustain tourism can sometimes clash with this laid-back beach town vibe of Santa Monica that residents appreciate. Nate contrasted this peaceful vignette with a statistic he heard that estimates the population expands from about ninety thousand to nine hundred thousand during the day, with tourists and workers from other parts of the Los Angeles area. While that is not ideal in some ways because "it does feel like you're living in someone else's vacation destination," he also understands that the tax revenue from these visitors is what facilitates "all the things that make it great to live in Santa Monica," such as city resources that some participants consider superior to those of neighboring jurisdictions.

Duality is a common theme in descriptions of the city. Katya evoked Santa Monica's poetic motto to describe its identity, which she characterized as the tension between its idyllic natural setting and climate and the inaccessibility of affordable housing:

> Santa Monica's motto is the most accurate motto for a city I have ever heard. It is "fortunate people in a fortunate land." . . . It is a place where you can go to the beach and breathe in the amazing ocean air. It's not too hot, it's not too cold, it's the Goldilocks of cities. Or it would be if it had enough housing.

The social dimension is a significant component of many participants' feelings and opinions about the city. Surprisingly, given the demographics as compared to neighboring Los Angeles, a number of participants described Santa Monica as "diverse." The majority of these participants identify as Latino or mixed race. The only person who described it as "very white" moved to the city recently from Washington, DC, and would likely have a different perspective on racial and ethnic diversity due to the demographics of that city. Several participants described Santa Monica as economically diverse—including longtime resident Rena—who attributed the continuing tenure of artists and seniors to rent control. Dave, an artist and art instructor, recalled reactions of surprise when he tells people in other parts of Los Angeles that he lives in Santa Monica, based on their assumption that it's an expensive city where only the wealthy can afford to live.

Returning to the theme of duality, the dichotomy between liberal/conservative, wealthy/working class, and renter/homeowner was the most common observation about the sociocultural and socioeconomic character of contemporary Santa Monica. These divisions have been experienced in online forums and in neighborhood association and city council meetings as well as in the changing character of the city's commercial areas. Sharon described the conflicting priorities between renters and homeowners, with the latter exhibiting a sense of entitlement and a "conservative bent":

> I think it's also quite segregated in some ways. I don't mean racially segregated although that's probably part of it. But there are, you know—there's a lot of conflict between what renters want and what homeowners want in the town or where they think the priorities lie. I mean listen to any City Council meeting which I used to do a lot. You know there're just a lot of conflicting priorities in the town.

Nextdoor, in particular, emerged as a platform for a certain type of discourse. Sharon joined the site after the looting of May 31, 2020, and left soon thereafter. She was surprised and upset by the "level of regressive thought that occupied this town" and decided she was "just really horrified" and did not want to participate in discussions on the site. Selena also observed this behavior on Nextdoor, with a lot of complaining about rent control and people experiencing homelessness. In general, she's selective about when to mention her status as a longtime resident of a rent-controlled home, explaining that "you could just feel that chill and that anger coming from some people, because they tend to be wealthier people who own property." At the same time, she echoed Dave's observation that people sometimes assume she is wealthy because of where she lives.

Katya has also observed "toxicity" in some of the conversations online, though she acknowledges this is also a wider issue with social media and divisive rhetoric on national level. She has a high level of civic engagement and participation and has observed the "north side-versus-south side" dynamic described previously in relation to the social significance of Montana Avenue as a dividing line. She characterizes this divide as existing between residents of single-family homes and residents of multifamily housing, including condominium owners. Daphne experienced this at a Wilshire-Montana Neighborhood Coalition meeting. She quickly realized that, when people say Wilmont, "they don't actually mean my side of the street," they mean north of Montana where wealthy homeowners live. Daphne felt that meeting attendees seemed to wonder why a renter would be in attendance.

This social dichotomy has discouraged Wilmont resident Nicholas from participating in his neighborhood association. While he didn't experience the divisiveness that several other participants identified, he perceives the neighborhood association as serving the interests of wealthy homeowners north of Montana.* He described Santa Monica as a "cross between sort of a lot of liberal ideology and I think now a lot of hardcore conservatives." He illustrated this assessment with *Los Angeles Times* data showing that voters in the Democratic primary voted overwhelmingly for Bernie Sanders and other progressive candidates throughout most of the city, with the notable exception of north of Montana, where Michael Bloomberg carried the vote. That a centrist Democratic candidate could be described as "hardcore conservative" is a testament to Santa Monica's four plus decades of strong progressive culture and identity.

---

* Though both Daphne and Nicholas describe Wilmont as including the neighborhood north of Montana, that area has a separate neighborhood organization called North of Montana Association. Perhaps homeowners from north of Montana attend the Wilshire-Montana Neighborhood Coalition meetings because issues occurring in the adjacent neighborhood impact them.

Issues at the City Level

Every city faces challenges, and Santa Monica is no exception. The pandemic undoubtedly put added pressure on existing stress points, which was evident in cities across the United States in this relatively early pandemic era. Still, the level of discontent (mixed with attachment) at the city level is notable. Issues don't spring up overnight, and most of what participants described has roots in prepandemic life. These elements of place alienation complicate resident relationships with their home environment, leading some to question their continued tenure in Santa Monica. For longtime low-income tenants paying rents well below market rates, this decision would be especially difficult to make, as the departure from the city would most likely be a permanent one.

Socioeconomic and sociocultural changes go hand in hand, and participants often connected these to the city's recent identity as "Silicon Beach," and the influx of capital that came with it. Nicholas described how the city he originally moved to, a little over a decade ago, was much more laid back and more of an artist, film industry, surfer, and skater community. Though some of that culture is still intact, the only people who can afford to move to Santa Monica are tech industry workers who seem to have "bottomless pockets." Some of the participants who grew up in the area have particularly strong feelings about social change. Luis also pointed to tech companies as a driver of cultural change: "You have a lot of young, upwardly mobile individuals that are, you know, from all over the country. And I just feel like they're trying so hard to be cool." He echoed other participants who grew up in the city and articulated a fundamental shift in sense of place:

> I feel like the Santa Monica I grew up with and the Santa Monica now are almost two different places. Santa Monica always had a significant amount of wealth, at least on the north side of Santa Monica. But it was really just kind of like a beachy, laid-back, creative, kind of artistic community. A little bit bohemian, a little bit touristy. I don't know, it was unique. And now it just feels kind of overrun with wealth and gentrification. And I think it's lost a lot of its character. But it's definitely still all of those things. So it's definitely still touristy and it has, you know, some eclectic people and creative people and you know, people from like, different walks of life and there is still poor neighborhoods in Santa Monica. But it has become more corporate and more gentrified.

Raquel is almost two decades older than Luis, yet she shared many of the same observations having grown up in the city. Housing costs are the main thing she would change if she could change anything, which she theorized are inflated due to the presence of the tech industry. When asked how she would describe Santa Monica, she emphatically replied, "Snobby, because it's not the Santa Monica that I grew up in. So it's changed I don't know, probably because of the tech companies that have sort of settled so you've got . . . all the techie people." Christina grew up in adjacent parts of West Los Angeles but has spent time in Santa Monica throughout her life. She also pointed to the role of capital in corrosively changing the city's culture. She described how Santa Monica went from being a friendly place with a laid-back surfer vibe to being a place where "now you got to drive a Maserati and, you know, be able to, you know, shop at the high end, you know restaurants and it's just, it's different. It's more a Beverly Hills vibe."

The tension between tourism as an economic development strategy and the impact that it can have on the city's sense of place was prevalent in negative sentiments about Santa Monica and, in particular, in descriptions of change at the city level. Though two participants noted that the revenue from tourist taxes is what enables Santa Monica to have city resources (e.g., schools, parks) that are superior to neighboring Los Angeles, a greater number of participants felt that the city's tourist orientation is an existential threat to its identity and livability. After nearly four decades in her home, Estelle has become disillusioned with the city for a number of reasons. She cited evidence of how "the community culture has been changed dramatically . . . by the so-called economic development plans of the city," tracing the beginning of this plan back to the late 1980s or early 1990s, when the "so-called planning department" began to "convert Santa Monica into a regional shopping destination and an international tourist destination."

Several participants connected tourism with a loss of character and a host of other problems, including an increase in traffic and general crowding as well as the demolition of beloved "third places"* [20] like diners. The extension of the Metro E Line light rail into downtown Santa Monica is also perceived as playing a role in this issue. Claire described how tourists from other parts of Los Angeles come in on the weekends and "trash the place." Mariana attributes the loss of the twenty-four-hour Norms and Denny's diners—and with them a certain era of Santa Monica—to the Metro. Both restaurants were demolished to build large transit-oriented housing developments. Mariana explained:

---

* First used by sociologist Ray Oldenburg (1989), a "third place" is a gathering place for social interaction such as a coffee shop, bar, or park. The home is theorized as the "first place" while the work site is the "second place."

Before the Metro existed . . . there were some parts of Santa Monica that still felt very . . . we had the Norms, and we had the Denny's, and we had these old school places that were very kind of classic Santa Monica. And when they put in that Metro they took out a lot of things.

Patrick expanded on this perception that planning and development in Santa Monica is oriented toward "outsiders" at residents' expense:

When I first moved in here we had businesses that catered to the local people, you know mom and pop things . . . things that were local that were owned by people in the neighborhood and catered to people in the neighborhood. And Santa Monica has totally gotten rid of that. The government, they've gone for the tourist industry. . . . Everything has been catered toward outsiders, and they don't really care about their citizens that much anymore. They really don't, and that has been very, very bad for Santa Monica.

Daphne shared a similar sentiment, explaining that "it used to be a sleepy little beachside town, which was what attracted me to it, many years ago. It was funky, it was quaint." Now it is "too tourist," with too many cars and large-scale developments. Evoking Mariana's memories of Norms and Denny's, she describes the memory of what Santa Monica used to be like through a vignette of going out to eat at an all-night diner with friends after a night on the town:

The places that we all used to go to at one o'clock in the morning for something to eat aren't there. They've all gone, they've been pulled down and an apartment building is being put in its place. It's lost so much of its character and . . . when I go down to Santa Monica I think "oh my God I don't even recognize it."

Many participants also expressed a negative opinion of downtown Santa Monica, and the Third Street Promenade and Santa Monica Place shopping mall, in particular. The Promenade—a three-block open-air shopping center—was redeveloped in the late 1980s and quickly gained popularity with Santa Monica residents before eventually becoming one of the top tourist destinations in Southern California. The main reasons participants cited for their disillusionment were the increasing presence of unhoused people and crime (which some connected with the advent of the pandemic) and the gradual shift to almost exclusively chain stores, whereas the Promenade used to be filled with small businesses like bookstores and vintage clothing shops.* This latter sentiment was not surprisingly correlated with longtime residence in the city or area.

Raquel, who is from Santa Monica, has felt "very uncomfortable" at the Promenade in recent years, which she connects to socioeconomic changes brought on by tech companies. "It's not the same homey neighborhood when I was growing up," she explained. "I would describe it as snobby." Sharon also grew up in Santa Monica and avoids the Promenade as a rule despite living close by:

> I tend to stay as far away as possible from the Promenade as I can except for farmers market runs and errands like midweek on an evening when it's not crowded. My gym used to be down there. I haven't been there in a long time. It's funny, the places that I tend to go are not right in my neighborhood.

The Santa Monica Place mall (adjacent to the Promenade) is similarly perceived as being oriented toward tourists. Mariana, who is a lifelong Santa Monica resident, complained that, when the mall was renovated recently, stores like Tiffany's completely changed their character:

> There are places that I no longer go to. Because it's not for me. It's for everyone else who comes to Santa Monica. You know what I mean? Like, all of those changes aren't for the locals. Like the locals didn't want any of that. . . . If we wanted to go shop at Louis Vuitton we would have gladly gone to Beverly Hills.

Two-thirds of participants identified homelessness as a major issue in the city. Concerns ranged from safety of housed residents to the well-being of unhoused individuals, and several people expressed a deep frustration with the city for its inadequate response to the issue. According to Daphne, "Most people in Santa Monica, if you asked them 'what are your biggest concerns,' it's going to be the homeless situation and the overdevelopment of the city." For Heather, the homelessness crisis includes a "danger factor," due to the perception that a large percentage of unhoused individuals have mental illness. She cited incidents of violence perpetrated by houseless people, including punching or stabbing people in the face.† Lisa also described "more

---

* Several months after these interviews were conducted the city council adopted a new plan for the Promenade that expands the type of business allowed in an effort to reposition it toward residents.

† Right after I completed the interviews several violent crimes, allegedly perpetrated by unhoused individuals, were reported in the Santa Monica *Daily Press*.

aggressive homeless" in the area than in previous years. Claire avoids going to the park across the street from the church she attends out of fear for her safety due to an increased number of houseless people. Selena theorized that the City has a containment strategy at this particular park, recalling a time when she set up a tent at another park to photograph for a Craigslist post, and the police arrived within minutes. Joyce attributes the increase in homelessness to the Metro and described a humanitarian crisis on the city's streets:

> We are inundated with homeless and mentally ill like I've never seen. We have people dying. You know, Timmy died in his wheelchair in front of Wells Fargo. I mean, people are laying on the sidewalk, laying there, languishing, mentally ill. It's just horrifying, horrifying . . .

Diane connected homelessness with a lack of housing options, explaining that the city council is "more inclined to support real estate developers that want to build condos and expensive homes." Because of these priorities, "we're always in a struggle with the City Council to try to make housing for the homeless and also for low-income people." Karli, a relatively new resident, would like the city government to do something to "improve the quality of life" for unhoused people, explaining that it is unpleasant to see an encampment close to one's home. Sarah—also a somewhat newer resident—noted that the cost of living in Santa Monica has increased and speculated that the homelessness crisis may be related.

Distrust of the city government, elected officials, and their priorities is a major theme in the place alienation some participants experience. This distrust stems from issues outlined earlier: overdevelopment, touristification, and the response to the homelessness crisis. Observation of a dysfunctional dynamic and an ineffectiveness in addressing these problems was the prevalent theme in discussion of the city's political atmosphere. While some participants attributed these problems to city administration or former council members, others expressed distrust of newly elected council members, who they described as "regressive" NIMBYs. At times it was difficult to keep track of which agenda each politician supported, as occasionally different participants had contradictory analyses about the same person. Some had overlapping concerns but different ideas about how development, density, and housing should be addressed. Additionally, some participants who had virtually identical perspectives on key issues voted for different candidates in the most recent city council race, illustrating just how nuanced the political discourse had become in a city where most, if not all, politicians identify as progressives.

Mariana used to regularly attend community meetings and summarized the exhaustion and disillusionment many participants seem to feel:

> You can only go to so many meetings where the topics are the same, but the solutions are never different. So at some point, you just kind of like. . . . I know what this meeting is gonna be about. It's more about how we can sell properties and make more money and build certain things that really nobody wants. But we're gonna do it anyway. So you're just kind of like, okay, well, I don't need to go to that one. And then, you know, you just don't. And then the reality is you just don't want to make time for it. And I don't: I'm done.

Christina similarly feels the discourse is not productive. She described an atmosphere of name calling that evokes junior high school dynamics. "I don't follow politics a ton to begin with," she said, "but yeah, it just seems like everybody's just picking on each other. Nothing's ever really got done. Everybody's just pointing the finger at other people."

The core of many participants' critique is the perception that various incarnations of the city council over the past two decades have been allied with corporations and developers over the interests of Santa Monicans. And because SMRR candidates have held a majority on the city council since the early 1980s, this perceived prioritization of development is interpreted by some as being part of SMRR's hidden (or not so hidden) agenda. Diane, a renter in her eighties who had been a longtime SMRR supporter, stopped going to their meetings because "over the years they've become more pro-real estate than pro-consumer." She expressed hope that the new council would bring change. Heather agrees with Diane, stating that the City is "giving away the store to developers." Daphne explained that the three SMRR-backed incumbents who were voted out in the 2020 election lost their seats because they were only interested in "lining their coffers over development." Similarly, Nicholas speculated that voters ousted the three incumbents because they had had enough of corporations going "ramshod over the city."

This sentiment was echoed by Selena, who said, "the city is completely sold out to developers at this point," and Patrick, who feels that the city is "tailor[ed] to the developers" who tear down low-rise buildings and build high rises. When asked if she gets the sense that people in city government care about the interests of renters, Christina emphatically answered "No, they care about big developers." She expanded on this to clarify that they care about affluent renters who will live in the new developments, but not long-term "renters like us." Luis responded to this question similarly, stating "No, I feel like they care about developers." When asked for evidence of this agenda, he readily provided a long list of ways the city's built environment has been transformed over recent years:

> All the new high-rise apartments going up all over Santa Monica, you know, they'll tear down an older style home or maybe like two lots with two homes on it. And they'll build like a six story apartment [or] condo with mixed-use on the bottom. And that's happening everywhere in Santa Monica. And I think the biggest developments right now are on Lincoln. They tore down Norms, and Denny's and . . . they're gonna tear down the supermarket, the Vons. And they're all becoming like this, these massive apartment block complexes that literally take up like the whole block and are seven or eight stories and close proximity to the new train.

Luis's next comment brings nuance to the tension between the need for more affordable housing and the desire to preserve the city's low-density character, which Ricky and Christina pointed to in their anti-NIMBY political analysis. He explained that the income-based housing generated in market development by the city's inclusionary zoning requirement is inadequate:

> They're supposed to have a minimum number of affordable housing units for each new complex they build. But typically, the affordable housing units are like tiny, tiny boxes, that . . . the developers have set aside for affordable housing. And then the rest of the units are much larger, and they can charge a lot more for. So they're just doing the bare minimum to meet the requirements.

Nicholas has toured several of these new income-restricted apartments and his impression was not favorable. The apartments were "the size of a shoe box," with ADA-compliant bathrooms bigger than the living rooms. According to what he has heard from other city residents, a new building's designated affordable units are often composed of "leftovers," resulting in tiny apartments with odd layouts. In his estimation, "You're living in the breadcrumbs and paying." Additionally, even with the affordability covenant, all the apartments that he viewed cost more than what he pays for his current home. In terms of the income ceiling for these apartments, Heather argued that "affordable housing is a joke, because what the developers are talking about for affordable housing, I could not even afford with my corporate salary." This belief that the City as an entity—and for some SMRR as a political party—cares most about tax generation from tourism and kickbacks from corporate developers has resulted in discontent and a loss of trust.

Gina is a low-income professional in her midthirties who has lived in her apartment for just over a decade. Though she didn't grow up in the area and has lived in the city for much less time than many other participants, she expressed anxiety and sadness when discussing changes she's noticed in her neighborhood and the city as a whole. With big expensive apartment buildings, fancy cars, and chain stores replacing the city's "small town charm" and laid-back beach town atmosphere, "things are ebbing away." At the same time, Gina recognizes that some of those large new developments include affordable housing that might be a lifeline were she to lose her current home, which is a concern. Her analysis of the feasibility of living in Santa Monica long term, and what trade-offs must be made at the city level to enable rental affordability, balanced her personal feelings about the changing sense of place with economic realities:

> From what I understand, with all of these big apartment buildings that are being built, they're being built with affordable housing which counts for that below-market housing list. And so I'm so torn on it. Because it's not the Santa Monica that I chose to move to, but one day I may have to live in one of those places. And if they're building new ones, that means I won't be moving into a really old apartment that's falling apart. So I really am of many sides, like I can't decide how I feel about them. I don't like them, but I may have to like them.

Overall, study participants were highly cognizant of the political economy of the place they call home. Knowledge of the cost of housing, commercial and residential gentrification, homelessness and the socioeconomic shifts that accompany these changes was pervasive. Place attachment binds them to their home environment, while levels of place alienation complicate their relationship with their neighborhoods and city.

Conclusion

Though participants expressed strong feelings about issues at the city level and change at the neighborhood and city levels, they also overwhelmingly expressed attachment, sense of community, rootedness, and other sentiments that evidence a strong dwelling relationship with their home environment. Most plan to stay in their homes for the foreseeable future, while some hope to stay forever. Only a few participants were actively considering moving out of the city at some point in the next several years. This portrait of thirty Santa Monica renters challenges the popular conception of tenants as intrinsically transient, moving from unit to unit to realize the Pareto optimal allocation of housing attributes until they can afford to purchase property. Instead, these residents prioritize their emotional *and* practical attachments to their homes, neighbors, neighborhoods, communities, and city in making decisions about where to live.

At the same time, most participants' housing options within Santa Monica are constrained by the economic realities of the housing market, which is part of the globalized landscape of real estate investment. That these participants—some of whom are moderate-income, young and upwardly mobile—continue to find the trade-offs worth it illustrates that home truly is more than the sum of its parts. Santa Monica's rent control and other tenant protections and resources support their choice to remain.

5

Security, Insecurity, and
the Residential Experience

D espite some feelings of discontent around the city and neighborhood
and some issues with their homes, almost all thirty of these Santa
Monica renters who participated in the study experience place attachment and dwelling in their residences and wider home environments. For
this reason, the stakes of maintaining their housing are high: most would
face displacement from the city if they lost their rent-controlled homes. The
impact of this loss would be not only material but social and emotional.

Housing quality issues and feelings of precarity related to the landlord-
tenant relationship, legal loopholes, and the real estate market are elements
of what urban planner Peter Marcuse described as "residential alienation."[1]
At its most basic, this term refers to the experience of feeling "not-at-home"
in one's residence. In this sense, it's essentially the opposite of dwelling. His
original concept focused on the level of control the resident exerts over their
home: from decoration and design to rules to the right to remain as long as
they wish. In their recent book, *In Defense of Housing*, Marcuse and David
Madden define contemporary residential alienation as encompassing experiences of precarity, insecurity, and disempowerment. They argue if we want
to understand the consequences of the hypercommodification of housing*

---

* The authors define "hypercommodification" as a condition produced by deregulation,
globalization of capital flows, and financialization (e.g., private equity funds). To be sure,
these aspects exacerbate residential alienation, but they are not exclusive to large corporate
landlords. I've heard about experiences of residential alienation—both in this research and
in my work as a tenant organizer—in housing owned by local small and medium landlords.

of the recent decades, "we need to understand the alienated psychosocial experience—the stress, anxiety and disempowerment—that the current housing system produces." This new definition expands on the original to include additional elements like overcrowding, forced mobility, and homelessness. At its heart, residential alienation is the severance of one of the most basic human impulses—to make a home—from the ability to do so. It represents "the painful, at times traumatic, experience of a divergence between home and housing."[2]

This chapter explores three key aspects that shape the residential experience. I then examine how these experiences inform security and insecurity and some of the coping behaviors participants adopt to mitigate these conditions, including engagement with tenant resources. Finally, I examine how these experiences and perceptions relate to behavior and decisions. Ultimately, while only one of these renters experiences *absolute* residential alienation, components of residential alienation, like precarity of tenure and maintenance issues, undermine the intended effect of rent control and other tenant protections, to some extent for some participants. At the same time, as compared to unregulated private market rental housing in other homeowner societies, Santa Monica's tenant protections and resources offer a significant buffer against these elements. There is clear evidence that tenant protections and available resources contribute both to feelings of security that come with perceived stability and to actual stability as realized through longevity of tenure for both the household and neighbors.

The Role of the Rental and Real Estate Market

It would be impossible to live in Santa Monica and have no awareness of the city's astronomical rents and housing prices. The city's high cost of living is also well known in neighboring cities, where it has a reputation as an expensive area accessible only to the rich or those lucky enough to hang on to their rent-controlled apartment. This material reality unavoidably impacts renters' sense of security and informs their housing choice and mobility or lack thereof. In addition to rents and the cost of homeownership, trending multifamily housing industry practices are also shared among renters, as landlord investors evolve their tactics and business models to adjust to the financial and policy landscape. As illustrated in Chapter 2, this often takes the shape of a prolonged dance between the city and the industry, with each trying to outmaneuver each other.

Several of my study participants with the most egregious issues living in buildings owned by "mom-and-pop landlords."

Homeownership, Constrained Mobility, and Trade-Offs

Homeownership is a cornerstone of the American dream and is synonymous with full stakeholder or citizen status. Yet, home prices in Santa Monica are some of the highest in the Los Angeles area, and many of Santa Monica's roughly sixty-five thousand renters are faced with the reality that they will never own a home in the city. This market condition plays a fundamental role in the cognitions, behaviors, and decisions of renter households. When asked about their aspirations of owning a home at some point in the future, responses fell into three categories with some overlap. Nearly two-thirds of participants reported that homeownership is out of reach in their preferred location (Santa Monica or the Los Angeles area) and they have no desire to relocate, about a quarter hope to eventually own a home somewhere outside of the area or are already looking into it, and several have no desire to own a home. A few own or have previously owned property outside the area. No one was hopeful about the prospects of buying a home in Santa Monica, West Los Angeles, or anywhere in the metro area aside from possibly the furthest suburban fringe.

For many longtime tenants, the window of opportunity to buy a home in Santa Monica closed years ago. Selena reflected, "When I look back I should have bought a couple of condos in my neighborhood because I had those opportunities, but I didn't because I didn't know any better."

Amy grew up in a conservative environment and thought it best to wait until marriage to buy a home. Around 1999, she decided to start the process even though she still wasn't married, but she began her search "just as the market took off." At that point, it became "too expensive and too overwhelming," and she eventually ended up buying a home out of state several years later as an investment and "plan b," in the event she is eventually displaced from her Santa Monica apartment.

For others, it was never really a possibility due to financial constraints and life circumstances. Sharon had a large financial settlement from her divorce when she first moved back to Santa Monica—where she's from—and was interested in buying a home. But she was unemployed at the time and the difficulty of getting a mortgage without a job prevented it, even though she had enough money for a large down payment. "I just sort of gave up on the idea of buying a place," she remembered, "which now of course it's like . . . ugh . . . would have been a really good thing to have done. . . . And then the rents started to really escalate," and eventually it was no longer an option at all.

When Raquel inherited some money from her mother, she considered buying a home but was worried that she would have to make balloon payments and would potentially lose the house to foreclosure on a single income. Lisa's sister had a condominium she was selling when Lisa first arrived in Santa Monica, but Lisa didn't have the funds to purchase it. Georgia started her career late and was never able to save enough to keep up with the housing market and purchase a home. For Estelle, it was a "moving target," where she never had the combination of enough for the down payment and the ability to get financing.

For younger participants with shorter tenancies, there has never been a time when the housing market in Santa Monica was accessible. Ricky doesn't have the generational wealth that would be necessary—in his analysis—to purchase a home there. Bonnie is a relatively recent arrival in the city. She would love to buy a house with a yard, but "it feels so unattainable anywhere that I don't know if it would actually happen." Based on what she has heard about the market, she doubts she would be able to afford anything within Los Angeles, let alone Santa Monica. Similarly, Gina dreams of buying a small Santa Monica bungalow but knows that she will never own a home as long as she remains in the Los Angeles area. Karli and her partner are interested in exploring the idea of buying a home at some point, but only if it makes more sense financially than renting. She feels like buying in Santa Monica is probably out of reach and potentially in Los Angeles as well.

A small subset of participants are not interested in owning a home. With the exception of Nicholas, they are all retired. Olivia is in her seventies, sold her house in another state after her husband passed away, and rents an apartment in Santa Monica to be close to her daughter and grandchild. She has lived in her home for four years and anticipates remaining there indefinitely. Patrick appreciates not having to worry about maintenance and has never considered being a homeowner. Selena owned a home out of state for a period and it required a lot of upkeep. Between those expenses, the mortgage, and the property taxes, she questions whether a homeowner actually owns their home. Ultimately, she prefers not to waste money on housing and be "house poor." Nicholas feels similarly, explaining that the financial burden of ownership can outweigh the benefits. He wonders, "What's the point of owning, really, if you're happy with where you're living in this apartment?" Diane has never been married and has simply never felt that she needed to own her home:

> I just needed an apartment with lots of space. I lived with roommates for a long time and had no problems, and I like renting . . . most people will say, "I want to buy a house, I want to buy a house, it's mine, it's mine" but I never felt that.

For many of the study's participants, achieving housing stability in the location of their choice is a more realistic goal than homeownership—a new kind of American dream.

The construct of "constrained mobility" is sometimes attributed to rent control in literature that examines the policy's impacts. It describes a condition in which a renter who is paying way below market rents is dependent on retaining their current housing because they cannot afford market rents and thus don't have the financial means to choose housing that meets evolving needs for space, location, and other aspects. One-third of participants touched on the lack of housing options in Santa Monica—and for some in the greater LA area—which underscored the importance of retaining their rent-controlled home. This was generally portrayed as a factor that limited their housing options. For some of the long-term tenants, the only option if they were displaced from their home would be to move out of the city, and possibly the county and state. For others, having to find new housing in Santa Monica is a possibility, but their analysis of the cost/benefit relationship doesn't favor it.*

Sharon and Amy are both long-term tenants in their fifties who do freelance work and rely on their rent-controlled apartments for financial sustainability. Sharon has been living in her home for over three decades and would not be able to afford a market rent in the area. She grew up in Santa Monica, is attached to it, and does not want to move in the near future, but she is open to relocating out of state eventually. Though Amy has a difficult relationship with her landlord/manager, she recognizes that remaining in her apartment is the only way she can continue to live in Santa Monica, which is a worthwhile trade-off. She explained, "There's so many wonderful things that outweigh the negatives, but it's like, you have to be diligent."

Gina and Luis have tenures that are shorter, at just over ten years, and are in their midthirties and early forties, respectively. Though they are in a different life stage than Sharon and Amy, they are also limited in their ability to move within Santa Monica. Gina, who is working at her "dream job" but makes about 40% of the area median income, cannot afford to pay a market rent in Santa Monica at all. She recalled reading a conversation on social media where someone complaining about noise in their apartment was advised to simply find a more suitable living arrangement. These comments struck her as insensitive to the economic reality of housing constraints for many in the city:

> The number of people that commented "well if you don't like apartment noise, then you should just move to a house," or like "if you don't like apartment noise figure out a different, like different situation—like if you live in an apartment you should just be used to that." So I'm like, where am I supposed to go?!

---

* See the data chart on rental affordability in Chapter 2.

Luis is an upwardly mobile professional working in the creative sector. Unlike Gina, Sharon, and Amy, he might be able to afford a market rate rent in Santa Monica, but the sacrifice would be impactful. Much more of his income would go toward rent, leaving little funds available for travel and other things he enjoys. "At that point, I would probably reevaluate and think about places throughout the country that I've enjoyed visiting or staying and, you know, see if maybe I could live there." He also would not want to move into an apartment without the tenant protections he currently has, where rent would potentially increase with market conditions. In this sense rent control is "like a double-edged sword. It's offered a lot of protection, but maybe it's hindered me from growing or moving into a larger space, because I'm so secure."

Nicholas is similarly situated in terms of finances and life stage. Though he would potentially be able to afford to move within the city he would most likely leave the area if he lost his current housing. He has looked at other apartments and found that the "give and take on the amenities has not been that favorable." Dave has come to a similar conclusion. He explained, "Most people would live somewhere and they would always be looking for maybe an upgrade in their same city. I kind of gave up on an upgrade here or proximity to where I work."

Participants were also asked about their future housing plans. About a third reported that they never want to move out of their current home, a little over a third plan to stay for at least the foreseeable future, several indicated that they would like to move eventually, and one person has to move in the near future for financial reasons. There was some overlap between these, with several participants expressing multiple sentiments, and several others who weren't sure how to answer. Diane, who is retired and has lived in her home for over three decades, plans to live in her apartment for the rest of her life. Joyce can also see herself dying in her apartment because "where would I go that would be better? . . . I'd be hard pressed to find some place where I feel more at home." Patrick plans on remaining in his home "for the duration," meaning for the rest of his life. While the majority of participants who never want to move are over sixty, there were two people in their forties and fifties who expressed a desire to stay in their apartment as long as possible. Though some have ongoing tension or conflict with their landlord or manager, these participants were mostly satisfied with their living arrangements.

Relationship status and life stage are relevant for those who indicated they had a more open plan that accounted for changing life circumstances. Katya is in her early thirties and has been dating her boyfriend for a short time. Were they to move in together, her apartment would not have enough room for both of their things. Though Katya is happy in her home, is attached to it, and feels that it meets her needs, there are two conditions in which she would consider moving:

> I'm not really planning or considering moving out anytime in the near future. Given how good of a deal it is, all things considered, and the space I have for the price in the location . . . that calculation of the three variables kind of makes me not ever want to move, unless I win the lottery or get married—basically those are the two.

Karli is a young professional in her early thirties who lives with her partner. She's mostly satisfied with her current home and plans to stay "until we can either upgrade to a better rental or if we can ever afford to buy somewhere in LA." Nate is also a young professional in a dual-earner household and is open to moving, eventually, but wouldn't consider leaving the neighborhood while his young son is in school. In the meantime, he doesn't anticipate finding a better housing option. He explained that "in some ways it's been like a blessing and a curse because it's so much space for the price we pay . . . we can't find anywhere with as much space as we have that is, you know, for this value." Gina is in her midthirties and would like to stay in her home for as long as possible but is also open to moving if a better opportunity presents itself, such as purchasing a home with friends or a partner.

In addition to the cost/benefit analyses described earlier, there were other trade-offs that factored into participants' housing choices. Having cheap rent in Santa Monica was generally considered worth dealing with landlords who do only the bare minimum in maintenance, older housing, and even the inherent instability of renting. Several people described a favorable trade-off with a landlord who has a laissez-faire approach to management. While there may be deferred maintenance and minimal repairs, the resident also enjoys autonomy in their home, minimal contact with the landlord or manager, and affordable rent. In contrast with her previous Santa Monica apartment, Daphne's landlord/manager never enters her home without asking, is rarely seen, and allows her to modify her apartment. This situation—combined with the rent—outweighs the inconvenience of a faulty heater and an outdated kitchen with cabinets that are slightly crooked.

Joyce's first apartment manager "didn't care [what the tenants did] as long as he got the money, which is pretty unusual, because there were a lot of rules [at other apartment buildings in the area]." At the same time, her apartment had windows that were falling out of their frames, which the manager refused to replace (in violation of housing code), but it was worth it because "the location is magnificent." Ricky is also content to live with a manager who is "a little bit of a skinflint" but is also not a "super hands-on person." This makes him feel like he has autonomy in the space, without the micromanagement some renters experience.

Dave lives in an older bungalow-style home owned by a landlord who maintains the property at the bare minimum. He described a trade-off between cheap rent and a lack of "modern convenience living in an older house," such as having "normal heat," and he also does whatever maintenance he can. Christina has a similar understanding and doesn't mind doing her own maintenance and repairs when she can: "I really think that the biggest trade-off is just kind of knowing that there's gonna be issues in your apartment, and you're gonna either take care of them yourself or just have issues." Raquel also weighed the pros and cons of living in a rent-controlled apartment. While she appreciates that her rent increases by a nominal amount each year, she also understands—possibly because she works for a property management company—that the owner is not going to invest more than what is necessary in the upkeep until a long-term tenant moves out.

Several participants pointed out the benefits of renting versus owning. Patrick appreciates being able to call the landlord when something major happens, like a pipe break. Joyce understands that her home is not an investment but feels that it is also less of a "burden" than a home that one owns. On one hand, Ricky would "love to put money into turning this into like a weird little condo," but he recognizes the downside is that the building is old and has many issues. In his current tenure as a renter, he can call the landlord when a drain is clogged or there is another issue, whereas if he owned it, he would be responsible for all those costs. Lisa has had more positive experiences with maintenance and repairs than these participants and also enjoys not having to worry about these issues. These individuals are making savvy decisions based on the extreme constraints of Santa Monica's housing market, forgoing the status and equity building of homeownership for continued residence in their preferred location.

Market Conditions and Social Fabric

As outlined previously, participants value living in buildings with neighbors who have longer tenures. The presence of longtime residents was described as a desirable feature of the apartment building's social fabric, which is an important component of the residential experience. Participants who mentioned turnover in their buildings often offered theories or critiques that addressed its root causes. High rents were the top reason cited, with several long-term tenants directly connecting this to the passage of Costa-Hawkins and the end of vacancy control in 1999. As one person speculated, there is little incentive to stay in an apartment long term when you are paying Santa Monica's market rents. Another explained that some high-income households rent temporarily while they are searching for a home to purchase. One participant theorized that the young people who cannot afford the rent simply move out of Santa Monica, while several others believe that it is *mostly* young professionals who can afford the high market rents.

Participants connected an influx of new tenants with several negative outcomes, including a change in the building's socioeconomic character and an increase in partying behavior and other noise issues. Sometimes these overlap:

> We get a lot of young people with high discretionary income to move in for a year or two or three and then they're gone. So the sociocultural quality within the community changes. . . . They're either party types or they feel, I would say, entitled because they're paying so much rent.
>
> There are three units in the building that have been pretty much in a chronic state of turnover and not to the benefit of the rest of us. . . . They're mostly young. And loud. That's all I can say. I mean that's pretty much been the case in those units where it's just sort of like . . . Okay you're not still in a sorority and there are other people who live here.

Several participants speculated about landlords' business models and how they serve to intentionally increase turnover. Daphne shared a story she heard from her hairdresser about their rent-controlled apartment that had been flipped using cash for keys and vacancy decontrol:

> Every tenant was offered a few thousand to move—some did, some didn't. And then there was the bartering going on or the negotiating going back and forth. And ultimately, nearly every tenant moved, with the exception—I think it was about four because . . . their relocation allowance that they wanted was too much. So the new owners came along, they filled in the pool so now they don't have to—there's no upkeep there and they put laminate down in all the units. . . . And the rents went from probably $1,500 to two up to starting at $3,000 and up. So you're now seven blocks from the beach and it's a revolving door. It's month-to-month, you don't have to sign a one-year lease. . . . And people stay six months, they move out, the rent goes up. Somebody else is in for six months, they leave, the rent goes up.

Several participants mentioned this business model of a "revolving door"— an industry practice evident in the market language section of Chapter 3— in which landlords seek to maximize rents in rent-controlled buildings through intentional turnover. Amy, who lives near Santa Monica College, reported that her landlord only rents to students and usually to international students who will not be able to continue to live in the building after their studies conclude and their visas expire. As an added bonus for her unscrupulous landlord/manager, these students aren't familiar with tenant rights laws and often have limited English proficiency, making it unlikely they will advocate for themselves. At the time of the interview, ten of the sixteen apartments in Amy's building were empty, and she theorized that the landlord was holding out for in-person studies to resume so he could continue this practice.*

Mariana's landlord's business model has changed over the more than four decades she has lived in the building. For the two apartments that don't have longer-term residents, the landlord leases each bedroom separately, rather than offering one lease for the entire household. This enables households—which are composed of "college kids"—some flexibility in moving in and out. Mariana theorizes this frequent turnover also means that new residents are "sold on" the building's desirable location without knowing about its deferred maintenance, and they don't stay around long enough to take action to remedy it.

Nicholas shared strong views about Santa Monica's housing market and affordable housing crisis. He values the stability and longevity of the tenancies in his building and, in particular, knowing who his neighbors are. He connected high market rents and the resulting transience of residency with the inability to form community or a personal connection with the home:

> Nothing can stay long enough to grow. You know . . . if you think about it a community is like a plant, if you're constantly repotting the plant and putting in a new plant and then you never have a fully blossoming flower because you're constantly pulling it out, and it's constantly just a bud. You never have a plant, just have a pot. And that's what I feel like the city is.

In conclusion, knowledge of the rental and housing market plays a key role in renters' housing choices, interpretation of landlord behavior, and experiences of community in their buildings. The lack of housing options—combined with this knowledge—creates feelings of precarity for some tenants. For others, putting up with inconveniences like deferred maintenance and forgoing the equity-building of homeownership are a calculated trade-off.

---

* These interviews were conducted in the spring of 2021, and Santa Monica College resumed in-person classes in the fall, later that year.

The Role of the Landlord or Property Manager

The relationship with the landlord or property manager is one of the primary elements that shapes experiences of residential alienation in a rental home.[3] Participants described a range of relationships and interactions with their landlords and managers, from friendship to a strategy of total avoidance whenever possible. Several have pursued private legal action or remedies through the City's various departments. Some participants shared more than one opinion of their landlord throughout the course of the discussion, pertaining to different aspects or interactions. Overall, positive impressions were more common about landlords than about property managers.

Those who have positive opinions about their landlord or manager cited responsiveness to maintenance issues, aesthetic improvements to the property, capital improvements, working with tenants who lost income during the pandemic, flexibility (e.g., having an understanding about the tenant personalizing the space), accessibility, and a friendly demeanor. When asked if she has ever had an issue with her landlord or manager over the four decades she's lived in her home, Diane replied, "Never. I'm very lucky because . . . we have a washer and dryer in the building and if one of them breaks down the next day someone comes and repairs [it]. It's just amazing. We're very lucky."

Nicholas has a positive view of his landlord, who has owned the building since the 1970s. As a result of his feelings about the relationship, he hasn't looked into his rights as a tenant in a while. Unlike most participants, his landlord has made improvements to his apartment during his tenancy. He also appreciates that she lives on-site.

> It's also nice that my landlord is an actual human being as opposed to a company. She actually lives in the building up in the front unit. So it's a situation where if there's an issue, she's already aware of building wide issues, as opposed to someone not having any connection at all to the building or understanding the significance of, you know, the washer dryer being out, or, you know, the water heater not functioning properly, and so forth. So, those things are usually taken care of pretty quickly.

Selena has become close to the family who owns her building, who are the second-generation owner/managers and live on-site. She expressed gratitude that the owner has permitted her to make so many creative choices in renovating and personalizing her apartment. She calls it the "magic building." Though the owners are very responsive to maintenance requests, Selena is also happy to pitch in when possible. She explained, "I've been here a long time and I'm very handy so I fix a lot and plus I help whenever I can around the building, I feel you know. . . . It's just part of saying thank you. For just being wonderful."

Several participants with positive opinions of their landlords framed their experiences in comparison to other renters they know. Rena commented that her landlord is "definitely not looking to push us out," unlike a lot of her friends in rent-controlled housing who have experienced forms of harassment from their landlords or management, ostensibly intended to encourage them to terminate their below-market tenancies. In contrast, her landlord is a "very nice guy" and a Christian, even though she has some critique of his quality of work in maintaining the building. Karli described her relationship with her landlord as "pretty good compared to other people that interact with property landlords or property managers." Nicholas compared his situation to friends in Santa Monica who have had conflicts with their landlords and have experienced "all kinds of things that the landlords have done to make living there unpleasant or trying to make them move out."

The impact of an uneventful relationship with one's landlord/manager can be best summarized as "out of sight, out of mind": not so much a bonus as one less thing to worry about in life. Conversely, a fraught relationship with the landlord or manager may not only impact the residential experience but also become a source of general stress or feelings of instability. Several participants have had more than one landlord at the same home over the years and compared conditions under different regimes. Estelle has lived in her apartment for almost four decades and had a generally positive experience with management until a new owner took over the property some years ago. The weight of her negative experience is illustrated by how quickly she reviewed her impressions of previous management experiences, compared to the amount of time devoted to discussing the present management. She described the beginning of the current management's tenure as "like the Gestapo . . . basically imposing control over us and it became hellacious." In addition to covering decorative exterior painting that gave the building character and dramatically pruning a rose bush she had planted, the social atmosphere also became constrained by what she described as "martial law." Estelle feels that she is being harassed and targeted. Notably, she's the one participant who said she doesn't feel at home at all: "Late at night I wake up in the middle of the night crying sometimes."

Patrick is another longtime tenant who has had a range of experiences with his four landlords over the years. He lives in a small complex and the various owners have also been the property managers. Whereas he described his original landlord as a laid-back person who charged under market rents, the current landlord is always looking for reasons to end his tenancy:

The other guy you could talk to, and you know, have a conversation with. This guy is just . . . I don't really interact with him that much to be honest with you. The less I have to deal with him the better off I am. It just ends up in a shouting match.

Tenants who have negative impressions of their landlords or manager most commonly described feeling that they don't really care about the building or its tenants and/or that they're not appropriately responsive to maintenance issues. Ramona grew up in Santa Monica and has lived in the city for her entire life, during which time she has lived in several rent-controlled homes. The house her family rented prior to her current residence had a hole in the floor, which the landlord only repaired after she escalated the situation by sending a formal demand letter. She explained that, in general, "the owners of the property that [is] under rent control, they really don't care about the tenants at all." The feeling that the landlord or manager of a rent-controlled home will only fix a serious problem like a hole in the floor after repeated requests creates a stressful relationship and unsafe living conditions—both of which are conditions of residential alienation.

Several others described these types of issues with landlords or managers that also have difficult personalities or unethical business practices. Amy's experience with her longtime landlord/manager involves a dysfunctional pattern of deferred and incorrectly performed maintenance, harassment, verbal threats, attempted wrongful eviction, illegally taking away her parking spot, and lying to city officials. She recounted a lengthy saga where the owner tried to evict her neighbor, Jim—the only other long-term tenant in the building—through various underhanded tactics. After she became involved, the city attorney's office opened a harassment complaint and the owner was ordered to pay fees for violating the harassment ordinance. She has also seen the owners use tactics like posting a termination notice on a tenant's door, photographing it for documentation, and then removing it immediately so the tenant is not aware of it and thus unable to respond. Amy's strategy is to meticulously document every single interaction and be "on guard," for both herself and her neighbor, but these experiences have left her exhausted and ambivalent about feeling at home in her apartment.

Negative impressions of some of the property managers who are not landlords involved similar issues of unresponsiveness and incompetence. Raquel's building was recently sold, and, since then, she's experienced some difficulty getting the management to respond to maintenance requests. When her toilet had a major leak, she called the management office and they asked her to take photos of it, though she explained that it was an emergency that required immediate attention from a professional. She had to wait until the next day for a maintenance worker to reposition the toilet, and then the incident occurred twice more, with water running down the hallway the second time until maintenance came out to respond. Finally, on the fourth occasion, she paid a friend $180 to fix it.

Self-advocacy can sometimes result in being treated differently than other residents. In Luis's case an initial exchange with his manager at the beginning of the relationship strained the dynamic permanently. In addition to issues of general incompetence, Luis has also experienced "an attitude" from the manager whenever he reports that maintenance is needed. He described calling the manager about a faulty water heater and being asked, "Why is it always you? Why are *you* always reporting it?" though Luis had previously confirmed with some of this neighbors that they had also reported the problem.

Luis and Raquel's issues are minor compared to four longtime tenants who detailed lengthy and turbulent histories with their property managers. Heather described her building manager as a "piece of work" and the most challenging to deal with out of a series of managers over her forty-three years of residency. Before his tenure, she had the autonomy to paint and make other modifications, but he "is always looking for something to kick me out at any moment," she explained, sharing a long list of incidents to illustrate her prolonged struggles with him over the years. "They want you to be as kind of miserable as you can in hopes that you'll move." As a result, she tries to avoid doing anything that will upset him.

> He's extremely intimidating. And I have people that I've talked to that are older, living in buildings he manages that actually have PTSD because of him. . . . Because he can be so unpleasant and it's your security, it's your house.

Vanessa has a similar opinion of her longtime property manager and also described him as a "piece of work." His problematic behavior began when the building was converted to condominiums under TORCA, and he successfully pressured most of the tenants to move out, rather than exercise their right under the policy to continue renting. Over the years since then, he has initiated a number of conflicts with her. Fortunately, the homeowners' association has tempered his antics, but "I just never know when he's gonna pull something else," she explained, and then "with a sweep of the hand I feel like I have no voice." These experiences of stress, power struggle, and lack of control may produce feelings of residential alienation.

Struggles over maintenance issues are impactful not only because they compromise the quality of life within the dwelling but also because they have the potential to evoke the uneven power dynamic between landlord and tenant. One way to address this stress point is for the tenant to handle the problem themselves. While this strategy is sometimes motivated by feelings of precarity, for others, it's understood that tenants are responsible for their own basic maintenance in a rent-controlled apartment. Daphne and Diane have both lived in their homes for several decades. During this time, Daphne has repainted on multiple occasions and resurfaced the kitchen floor and is considering paying for the porcelain bathtub to be reglazed. She explained, "Having been here for so long after a while things start to look a bit tatty, and so I do need to do my kitchen floor again because . . . the linoleum is beginning to peel up." Diane agrees that it is just part of apartment life in a rent-controlled Santa Monica home: "Oh yeah, for the rent control apartments you have to do it yourself. So maybe every ten years I've recarpeted and repainted the walls." This acceptance of a tacit maintenance partnership is part of the trade-off analysis discussed previously.

Half of the participants have paid for and/or performed maintenance and repair tasks in their homes.* Painting walls and replacing floor coverings are the most common type of work tenants take on. Raquel used one of her COVID-19 stimulus checks to replace a fifteen-year-old carpet due to ongoing sinus infections. Neither state nor local law includes a "life expectancy" metric for paint or floor coverings, which would specify the point at which the landlord would be expected to replace them. However, the Rent Control Charter stipulates that the rental home be maintained in habitable condition and offers tenants the option of filing a decrease petition for flooring if it is "damaged or missing" and for paint if it is "damaged." Since these descriptions are subject to interpretation—and because "damage" may not describe a carpet that is fifteen years old—it's not surprising that many tenants choose to perform this maintenance themselves. Additionally, the process of sending the landlord a "demand letter" and then filing a petition if they don't respond favorably comes with the possibility of straining the relationship.

Almost two-thirds of the participants experience deferred maintenance on some level. Just over one-third live in buildings where essential maintenance/repairs are always done on time (which does not preclude larger structural work or nonessential maintenance/repairs being deferred), one-third live in buildings where maintenance is not timely, and almost one-third reported that maintenance may or may not be done promptly, but it is not done *correctly*. Several participants do what maintenance tasks they can to avoid the potential hassle and delay when submitting a request to the owner or manager. Others consider themselves to be "handy" and find it easier or reasonable to just do what they can themselves. Fear of straining

---

* This work is not the same as modifications and improvements, which are aesthetic expressions of the tenant's personal preferences and are thus components of dwelling.

the relationship with the landlord or manager was also a motivation in some cases, which will be explored later.

Often issues of timeliness and quality are combined, with tenants asking repeatedly for a problem to be addressed only to receive the most cursory solution. Maintenance not being done correctly came up a lot in discussion around this topic, suggesting this situation is especially distressing, particularly when it means one must advocate repeatedly for action to be taken. Mariana has lived in her home for over four decades, and the building has been owned by the same person for as far back as she can remember. She described the difficulty of getting repairs addressed, and, how when repairs *are* made, the work is a "band-aid solution" that fails to address the root cause of the issue:

> Unless the City comes down and says you have to do something, they won't do it. And then the other part is that when you request work—because they do come in and repair things in your building, like water damage, or leaks or stuff like that, which is great—but it's still, like, you'll make a request, and sometimes it takes a few days to respond or to come into your place or to let you know that they're coming. And even the work that they do in that regard, is like . . . like I could have done that. Like there's no exploring as to the cause of a problem. It's just literally let's, you know, put a band-aid over it and call it a day.

Claire's landlord is similarly unresponsive and also addresses substantial issues with subpar methods:

> He's non-existent. If you call him for something forget it, you know. The guys next door, their toilet leaked and it made a hole into the laundry room below. And he finally had somebody come and fix it but there's a big hole there, and you know, every time the guys in number seven—three guys in number seven—walk, stuff falls down in the laundry room. But he doesn't fix it.

Claire connected this to her landlord/manager's business model. She never had issues with maintenance and repair requests under her previous landlord/manager, who were a mother-daughter team and had owned and managed the building for about forty years. The current landlord bought the building after the mother died with the intention to flip it but was unable to sell it after several attempts. Claire theorized that it is because five of the seven apartments have tenants paying significantly under market rate, "So nobody wants to buy a building that has that many rent control people in it." Claire knows it's preferable to sell a rent-controlled apartment with as few occupied apartments as possible, so the new owner can charge market rents and doesn't have to bother with buyouts to get them.

As in Raquel's situation with the leaking toilet, in many cases, improperly performed maintenance led to recurrences or worsening of the issue. Joyce's building was recently sold, and the new owner hired a manager who "just doesn't know what he's doing." When there was a sewage break in the building, the manager tried to cover the smell with a fragrance, rather than hiring a biohazard company to apply enzymes as Joyce suggested. As a result, the root cause of the issue wasn't addressed, and Joyce and her roommates were experiencing headaches from the methane gas. Eventually, they emailed him again, explaining that they were becoming ill, and he hired a biohazard company to do the work. In Mariana's building, the walkway in the common area has become "spongy," over the years, and unsafe for some of the older tenants. Mariana and her neighbors got together to discuss the safety issue and collectively asked the owner to address it. When the repairs were finally made, after months of waiting, they were minimal, and now the issue has resurfaced:

> This is like a safety hazard, we have to push back and get them to come and repair this. So after months of requesting this repair, they finally did come out. And they only repaired the areas that were literally like a sponge. And that repair lasted maybe a couple years right? Because now it's the same issue there. And we're like going "this is not okay," because the entire walkway actually would probably need to be redone. And they would never do that. That would be like "oh, that's a cost that—you know, I can't afford to do that." Yeah, but legally, I think he should.

To this point, almost half of participants feel that their landlord or manager tries to save money by doing the bare minimum to address an issue. Karli and her partner have the shortest tenure in the study, at three years, and are paying close to market rates. This is significant because cost-savings behavior makes the most sense when the tenant is paying well below market rents. Her impression of her landlord was positive overall, and she appreciated his responsiveness when the plumbing backed up and the sink overflowed into the kitchen while they were out of town. At the same time, she felt frustrated that the incident has since recurred and likely would not have, were he not trying to save money:

> He did act quickly and get a plumber out and get the cleaning service out. So really grateful for that. . . . But in the end, I kind of felt like

he should have done it properly. So what he did was kind of like get the plumber to do like short term measures rather than actually do a big like, inspection or whatever they do, so it wouldn't happen again. So that was obviously frustrating, but I feel like that's because he wanted to save money somehow.

However, not all had an entirely negative opinion of their landlord/manager based on the perception that saving money was a primary concern. Daphne weighed the pros and cons of having a landlord who both is frugal about maintenance *and* allows tenants to have a certain level of autonomy.

He's cheap, which is like most Santa Monica landlords. For the most part he's actually a pretty decent guy. . . . He's temporarily living in the building, but he doesn't come knocking on the door for rent, we have to mail our rent to a PO box. He never just shows up on the doorstep and wants to do a walk through. If you want to paint your walls, you know psychedelic purple, go ahead. When I rented this place, I rented it as-is so I pretty much within reason do whatever I want.

In conclusion, the breadth of landlord and property manager behavior reflects a combination of individual personality and business model, which is likely informed by the culture and ideology of the multifamily housing industry and property ownership more broadly. It illustrates that owners and managers of rent-controlled housing conduct themselves in a variety of ways, generally sharing a common approach of doing the bare minimum of maintenance required, rather than investing in renovations or improvements they will not be able to recoup in the near future by increasing rents. In this sense, the residential experience and the volume of residential alienation conditions present are heavily informed by the behavior of the landlord/manager. However, elements of residential alienation may still be present for tenants with positive impressions of their landlords and managers due to the two other major factors outlined here.

The Role of Policy, Infrastructure, and Resources

The policy landscape that governs the landlord-tenant relationship—along with the infrastructure and resources available to tenants to learn about and enforce their rights—is the third element that shapes the residential experience and informs feelings of security or insecurity. This policy landscape is directly connected to the sociopolitical ideology about renters and their place in the community outlined in Chapter 2.

To understand the relationship between knowledge of tenant protections and these experiences, participants were asked to share what they know about renters' rights in Santa Monica. Some expressed that they know they are protected but do not have specific knowledge about various policies. Several shared the view that the law favors the tenant, while no one expressed the opinion that the opposite was true. According to Joyce, "It's always on the side of the renter and not for the owner," which means if there's a health issue the tenant can follow-up with the city to fix it. Mariana, who has one of the longest tenancies in the study, feels that it's very difficult to evict longtime residents due to various protections around age and other aspects. Daphne compared Santa Monica's "much stricter" rent control law with Los Angeles's policy, which is "a little bit more relaxed." Unlike Los Angeles:

> Santa Monica has the reputation, if you have a problem with your landlord then you go to the Rent [Control] Board and they're always there to help you, and they will fight for you, and they will give you advice. And so they have this reputation that they do protect the tenants, not so much the landlord.

Knowledge about the regulations that govern rent increases was most common, with two-thirds of participants accurately citing that as a key feature of the policy even if they didn't know the exact formula. This is not surprising, given that residents of rent-controlled housing receive two newsletters a year from the RCO, one of which has the next year's maximum allowable rent for their residence printed on it. About one-third of participants mentioned "just cause" eviction policy, and another (sometimes overlapping) third identified the existence of habitability standards. Raquel mentioned the practice of "repair and deduct," which allows tenants in some situations to address an issue if the landlord is effectively refusing to and take the cost off their rent: "A couple of times I've had to tell the landlord, 'if you don't take care of this I'll just do it myself and take it off the rent,' and they come right away."

Not surprisingly, people who had experienced issues were more knowledgeable due to their own research and/or interactions with city staff and other entities. Those who had not experienced significant issues had a vaguer awareness of tenant protections, but many were able to identify resources for information should it be needed. This suggests that even with the somewhat surprisingly low levels of awareness of tenant protections, knowledge of how to access that information would facilitate support if needed.

The majority of participants have engaged with one or more city entities that offer support to renters—whether to address a specific conflict or to seek advice. Nearly two-thirds reported having a conflict with a landlord or manager in Santa Monica at some point in time. Most of the conflicts were resolved, with about half of these involving city resources and half being addressed through some other means (e.g., private attorney). Of the roughly one in four conflicts that were *not* resolved, only a few involved engagement with a city entity. These positive outcomes suggest that city resources provide meaningful support for tenants of Santa Monica's rent-controlled housing.

Only a few participants have been in contact with the city attorney's office to enforce their rights. Early on during the pandemic Vanessa was threatened with eviction because her partner—who was not on the lease but had lived in the home for years—paid the rent instead of her. The city attorney informed her about her rights and offered to send a letter to the manager, advising him of the relevant tenant protections during the pandemic: "You know they could only do so much, but they were definitely supportive and listened and gave me good advice." Years ago, Estelle contacted them when she was experiencing harassment from her property manager. The city attorney wanted to bring a harassment case against her landlord under the new law, but she decided not to pursue it.

Several participants have interacted with the RCB. When Heather's property manager tried to increase her rent by $200 a month after rebuilding a rotting deck, she appealed the sum and the RCB settled on $50 a month. Daphne received a rent reduction from the RCB in a past residence for a ceiling that had been damaged in the Northridge earthquake, and she later leveraged the threat of filing a petition for reduction at her current home to persuade the owner to repair a heater. According to Diane, the RCB is "very tough on landlords." She feels the board is instrumental in protecting tenants, whereas the city council does not seem to be very "pro-renter." Notably, Diane was a longtime SMRR supporter until recently when she became disillusioned with the organization's political leadership. She stopped attending their events about five years ago.

Participants engaged with the RCO more frequently than any other city resource. Vanessa contacted the RCO when a property manager she was in conflict with took away her carport space, to retrieve the necessary documents to prove that she was legally entitled to the space. Raquel called them when the front lawn of her building had not been tended to in months, and the owner addressed it shortly thereafter. Christina reported improperly repaired bathroom plumbing to the RCO, and they required the owner to fix it to the standards of city code. Joyce called them about a collapsed ceiling and mold, and they sent thirteen people to address the problem. She had to move out of her apartment for seven months while the work was being completed, during which time she received relocation assistance as stipulated by city law.

Ramona characterized the RCO as "very supportive." Though she tries not to contact them unless there is a "dire need," they have been helpful in assisting her when she has reached out. In one instance, they proactively reached out to inform her that the owner of her home had applied and been granted permission to remove it from rent control.* On another occasion, they helped resolve a situation in which the landlord was charging more than the MAR, which resulted in Ramona receiving a sizable refund. In a previous home, Code Enforcement came out (ostensibly at the RCO's behest) and intervened when her landlord was nonresponsive to a request to fix a hole in the floor. She concluded the interview by encouraging other Santa Monica renters to reach out to the RCO with their issues:

> You know, I've lived in the rent-controlled units for a long time. I would like to share to the people that are not too aware of rent control and they're more hesitant because they're nervous and scared or that they'll get you know . . . they'll get called out or whatnot, not to be afraid to go and seek help at the rent control because they're there to help you.

Even though Ramona understands that her landlord is legally allowed to remove her family from their home under the owner-occupant clause of the rent control law, she feels supported by the RCO. Furthermore, she urges other renters who may feel vulnerable to retaliation to assert their rights with the support of the office. Ramona lives in a low-income household with severely constrained housing options within Santa Monica and has a strong attachment to her home environment. With a lot on the line and thus a disincentive to rock the boat, her willingness to do so reflects a powerful modification of the landlord-tenant power dynamic. Though she may have lost this particular battle, Ramona believes Santa Monica tenants are still well positioned to advocate for themselves in landlord-tenant disputes.

The majority of participants who have interacted with the city's tenant resources echoed Ramona's perception that tenants are well protected. This illustrates how the city's tenant protections help create and maintain stability, despite the stress of interacting with landlords or managers who have difficult personalities and/or a desire to increase their profits by removing the tenant from their home. This modulation of the landlord-tenant rela-

---

* This is allowable if an owner with an at least 50% interest in the property moves in to a duplex or triplex.

tionship fundamentally alters the power imbalance between the two parties, tipping the scales toward the tenant. This is not to say power is equally held; the property owner will always have more power in a culture that prioritizes property rights to the extent that it does in the United States, but the city's policies and resources make a real difference in the lives of Santa Monica renters.

De Facto and Perceptual Security and Insecurity

As Madden and Marcuse write, "Residential alienation above all manifests as insecurity. As such, it aggravates struggles in other areas of life."[4] These feelings of insecurity may relate to any or all of the three factors discussed in the previous section. Participants mentioned feelings of stability/security or a lack thereof in several sections of the interview, mainly when discussing their relationship with their landlord/manager, speculating about a potential or actually occurring sale, describing whether they feel at home or not at home, or describing what they like or don't like about their apartment. The term "ontological security" is useful for understanding the importance of these feelings and perceptions. The sociologist Anthony Giddens introduced the concept of ontological security in his book *Modernity and Self-Identity*.[5] He defines it as "the confidence that most human beings have in the continuity of their self-identity and in the constancy of their social and material environments. Basic to a feeling of ontological security is a sense of the reliability of persons and things." Ontological security is trust in one's understanding of their world: a sense of constancy and predictability that supports daily life. In Gidden's conceptualization, the inverse of ontological security is "existential anxiety," which concerns perceived threats to the integrity of the individual's security system and to the reliability of people and things. In the context of housing, existential anxiety maps onto the precarity experienced in conditions of residential alienation, which makes it difficult to impossible to feel at home.[6] Ontological security* is fundamental to well-

---

* When ontological security is considered in the context of the home, it shares some key characteristics with dwelling. However, they are not the *same*. Instead, one could say the two have a mutually reinforcing relationship. For one, ontological security is a broad concept that encompasses trust and confidence in the world as a whole. As a holistic concept, it's informed by many elements, including health, relationships, finances, career, and housing. When applied specifically to the residence, ontological security describes a cognitive state that is produced by the realization of supportive material conditions like control and autonomy (Dupuis & Thorns, 1998), living in a "good" neighborhood (Hiscock et al., 2000), and the financial stability and sustainability of the housing arrangement (Saegert et al., 2015). Likewise, having "bad" neighbors was found to undermine ontological security (ibid.; Cheshire, Easthope & Have, 2021). Dwelling is not informed by conscious aspects like trust, confidence, and decision-making. It describes the preconscious conditions of the individual's relation-

being and the lack thereof can lead to a decline in mental and physical health, in addition to other negative outcomes.

Housing researchers Kath Hulse and Vivienne Milligan's use of a tripartite model of security of tenure is helpful for understanding the different types of security and insecurity simultaneously experienced by renters. It differentiates between legal policy, lived experience and material conditions, and perception:

- *De jure security*—As codified by law: Informed by property rights and the legal rules that underpin a lease arrangement.
- *De facto security*—As experienced: Informed by aspects like the ability to afford rent, the motivations and behaviors of the landlord/manager, and rental housing management practices.
- *Perceptual security*—As interpreted: Subjective perception informed by housing experiences and personal biography, knowledge of the housing market, and other factors. This could differ substantially from the other two, with de jure and de facto security in place but a low level of perceptual security.[7]

By examining how housing security can exist in different forms and arise from the factors explored earlier, we can understand how each tenant household may experience multiple kinds of security and insecurity simultaneously. A tenant may have a decent relationship with their building manager and know they're protected by the city's policies and resources but still feel a gnawing sense of insecurity due to their awareness of the housing market. Or, they may have a great relationship with their landlord and know very little about tenant protections because that knowledge is unnecessary given the de facto security provided by that relationship. The degree to which these elements inform their overall ontological security will be different in each case and include other factors like income, job security, physical and mental health, and relationship status.

Direct Threats

Just over one-third of participants have experienced a threat to their housing or heard about their neighbors experiencing one. Rent checks that were either sent to the wrong address, written by an occupant not on the lease,

---

ship with and experience of their lifeworld (Saegert, 1986), as constructed and reified by the emotions, cognitions, and behaviors of attachment (Altman & Low, 1992). In this sense, ontological security can enhance the experience of dwelling and at homeness by providing a sense of stability.

lost in the mail, received late, or altered by the landlord were a common scenario. When asked if she ever feels that the owner would like the building's long-term tenants to leave, Claire explained:

> Oh yes, oh yes. He started a campaign to get me out. . . . He called me on the fifteenth of the month and said he didn't receive my check. And of course I had mailed it for it to get there on the first. And when he done that three times I said, you know that's three months in a row he didn't get my check, he can put me out. So I was at the bank, and I was telling the bank manager, I said "I don't know what I'm gonna do he's going to put me out." He said, "Oh no, you're going to set up automatic payments." So he did, so it's automatically paid, so I haven't heard from him since.

Patrick recalled a similar incident with a previous landlord:

> The surfer boy dude, he was starting to run out of money near the end of his tenure. I could tell that. So he wanted me out so he could raise the rent, and he took one of my checks and altered the date on it, so it made it look like I paid late, and sued me and put an eviction notice on my door—a three day pay or quit.

Patrick hired a Legal Aid attorney and successfully fought the eviction suit, discovering in the process that the landlord had been overcharging him for rent each month. In addition to prevailing against the fraudulent eviction, the landlord was also ordered to pay him the back rent that was due. According to Consumer Specialist Andrea Cavanaugh at the PRD, these rent check scenarios are one of the most common bad faith landlord behaviors the office hears about from tenants.

Building sales are a common source of anxiety for residents of Santa Monica's rent-controlled housing, and with good reason. Ramona and her family had been living in a duplex for eleven years when the building was sold to a new owner who moved into the other apartment and filed a petition to remove the building from rent control. After her petition was granted, the new owner informed Ramona that she wanted her to move out, and, if she didn't, that her husband planned to raise the rent by an unspecified amount. In the meantime, the owner engaged in extensive and disruptive renovations. Ramona speculated that "they just want us out—plain and simple" and that they may be planning on flipping the property.

Raquel felt stable in her home for decades. But, when her building was sold recently, the new owner told some of her neighbors their goal was to "get everybody out by summer," and they started approaching households with cash for keys* offers. Raquel researched her rights and discovered several legal discrepancies in the information the owner provided to her neighbors. She has tried to informally organize her neighbors to know their rights and expressed interest in connecting with LATU when the opportunity was extended in our interview. Additionally, she feels that the new owner is making a minimal effort to maintain the property and "purposely" didn't mow the lawn—which was quickly remedied when she reached out to the city. Given these tactics, she is uncertain about the future of her tenancy:

> I mean I do feel, you know, protected. But I just feel inside, a little shaky, I mean I don't know—I don't know if it's just insecurity that I have, or we just don't know when the next shoe's going to fall, you know?

Tenant Protections and Mitigating Insecurity

Almost two-thirds of the study participants expressed positive sentiments about tenant protections at some point in the interview. Notably, detailed knowledge about how they work was not a prerequisite for these feelings. These opinions came up organically in the conversation, and many of these included expressions of gratitude for the stability that rent control confers. Heather, who is semiretired and has lived in her home for forty-three years, "literally could not be here without rent control, as many of us [longtime tenants] could not." Selena, another longtime resident, compares it to winning the lottery. She is thankful to both the city and the RCB. Despite—or perhaps because of—Vanessa's struggles over the years with her property manager, rent control has been "that security in your home when you know that you can live there from year-to-year without some unexpected increase that would price you out of your home."

Diane feels lucky to still be in her home after decades and feels protected by the RCB in the possible instance that her building is sold. For Katya, the policy is "designed to allow folks to live with a sense of dignity and be able to have a sense of self in their own space," due to its stabilizing effects. Selena describes the peace of mind that rent control provides as more than financial, consisting additionally of an "emotional factor for many of

---

* Landlords who want tenants to move out often use cash for keys offers to apply pressure, sometimes rising to the level of harassment. In expensive housing markets, the compensation that landlords offer is rarely enough to offset the difference between the current rents under rent control and the market rate rent needed to acquire another dwelling. For low-income households, especially, accepting a cash for keys offer likely means leaving the area. See https://www.latimes.com/california/story/2024-01-16/rent-control-cash-for-keys-los-angeles.

us [seniors]." Some participants took a broader social view of the benefits of Santa Monica's tenant protections to the community. As Ramona explained:

> Without rent control the majority of the people who are of a different color, they'll end up leaving. They'll be pushed out because of the high rent and the only ones that'll be able to afford it would be you know, the people who mainly want to be here because of the businesses, because you know, their jobs, or because of the ocean—the Silicon Beach.

Rena agrees, crediting rent control with strengthening socioeconomic diversity and enabling seniors and artists to remain in the city. Stability and diversity increase community engagement, and, in this sense, rent control has "uplifted this community in a way that it would not be this community by any means without it."

Participants were also asked if their knowledge of and experience (when applicable) with tenant protections has had an impact on feelings of stability in their homes. Two-thirds responded affirmatively and pointed to rent control specifically. These participants have had a range of experiences with their landlords/managers, from repeated conflict to no issues over the course of decades in the same home. Diane described her living situation as "stress free" due to the city's tenant protections and a proactive RCB. For Patrick, tenant protections give him a "sense of security . . . knowing that there are things that help me and protect me for my own good, and the good of other tenants." Georgia, who is retired and lives on a fixed income, explained how tenant protections impact how stable she feels in her home:

> 1000% couldn't do it without it. Without that I would be toast. You know, I started my career later and just never had a chance to save up enough to buy a house. I was always that much behind. . . . Yes, I feel very, very blessed in that sense.

Georgia went on to share how she continued to pay $700 a month rent on her apartment even when she was living with the "love of [her] life" in Oklahoma, just in case it didn't work out. When the "just in case" happened, she was able to move back home.

Despite a relatively short tenancy, upward mobility, one of the highest incomes in the study, and a rent close to market rates, thirty-year-old Karli reported that knowing her rent can only increase by a fixed amount is a "big factor" in her feelings of stability. She has friends who have received rent increases large enough that they decided to move out and find an apartment with rent control to move into.

I feel like if I were to kind of like, go back a few years and be in the same situation where I was looking for an apartment, I would tell myself, "definitely find one that has rent control," because it is a big factor. Because the rent could increase by a huge amount if you aren't in those rent-controlled apartments.

Rent control and other protections has given Nate and his family peace of mind through the financial vicissitudes of being a freelance worker in the entertainment industry. "You have good times and fallow periods and through all that we've . . . never had any instability with housing at all," he explained, "and not even any question about whether we can pay rent or anything like that." Knowing that his family's housing costs were predictable means he "never had to worry that we'd have to move or find something or downsize." He's also comforted by the knowledge that the landlord cannot simply force them out to raise the rent. This security factor is part of what makes his apartment feel like home. In the early days of the pandemic, when film and television production stopped, Nate and his partner were both out of work, but they never seriously worried that they would lose their housing. Instead, he felt confident that the city and state would protect renters.

Katya has a prior history of living in rent-controlled housing in the Bay Area. When she was a child, in the 1990s, her family immigrated to the United States from Eastern Europe with a few hundred dollars. Their rent-controlled apartment provided essential security in the midst of rapidly escalating rents and enabled them to save money to eventually buy their own home. According to Katya, a rent-controlled apartment is a resource. "Having a home is important to be able to really work on yourself and become the person you think you want to be," she explained. For Katya, who is in her early thirties, her home provides her with the stability to envision the realization of "possible selves"* and invest her time in her community. After moving from Eastern Europe to the Bay Area and then to another Northern California town for college, she has lived in her current apartment longer than anywhere else and considers Santa Monica to be her "adopted home." Knowing that she has these protections makes her feel empowered to handle

---

* The concept of "possible selves" is useful for understanding how certain conditions and tenure arrangements might enable or restrict the realization of one's goals and aspirations. Markus and Nurius' original conceptualization encompasses an individual's idea of what they might become, what they would like to become, and what they are afraid of becoming. It serves as a "cognitive bridge" between past, present, and future and illuminates how individuals may change from what they are now to what they will become. According to Markus and Nurius, the study of possible selves is also the study of how individuals interpret and make meaning of their conditions and position in the world. See Markus, H., & Nurius, P. (1986). Possible Selves. *American Psychologist, 41*(9), 954–969.

potential conflicts: if she or her friends experience issues with their rent-controlled Santa Monica apartments, she knows how to access helpful resources. These feelings contrast with the disempowerment intrinsic to residential alienation.

The overwhelming majority of participants experience some sense of stability and security connected to tenant protections. Additionally, some individuals listed other elements that cultivate those feelings. Several people feel stable in their homes primarily because of their relationship with their landlord/manager. Not surprisingly, none of them have ever experienced a conflict or significant issue with their landlord/manager. A positive relationship with one's landlord may preclude engagement with the protections to the extent that there would be little basis for some individuals to evaluate their role in feelings of stability. Additionally, a few participants connected feelings of stability to a consistent income, two of whom also feel supported by tenant protections.

Perceptual Insecurity and the Limitations of Tenant Protections

At the same time, a number of individuals expressed concern about remaining in their homes despite possessing, in most cases at least, a basic knowledge of tenant protections (de jure security). Even for those who have not experienced a direct threat of displacement (de facto insecurity), knowledge of the housing market, stories from friends and neighbors, and media coverage create an atmosphere of latent precarity, or perceptual insecurity. Overall, half of all participants—with tenancies ranging from nine to forty-seven years—expressed concern about displacement at some point in the interview.

Though Sharon is well educated about her rights, she does not feel protected. She worries that "ultimately if they really wanted to, they would find a way to make my life miserable," pointing to a recent noise complaint she received that stoked deep anxieties. She is concerned that even this minor issue could jeopardize her ability to remain in her home of over three decades. When asked if she thought the management wanted her to leave, she said, "Yes," but added:

> They've never done anything that I could cite as being an example of that. I think it may be very justified but it's really my own fear about it. It's probably a justifiable concern that the unit downstairs from me—it is cooler but it's darker and noisier—you know, is renting for at least double what I pay.

In this case the destabilizing element is the knowledge of the substantial rent gap between her apartment and market rate, rather than an especially contentious relationship with the landlord or manager. For this reason, she tries to remain "invisible" by requesting only the bare minimum of repairs and investing her own money on needed maintenance.

Loopholes like the Ellis Act or an owner move-in—combined with knowledge of the rent gap and industry practices like upscaling (renovating a property to attract tenants with higher incomes)—are another major factor undermining perceptions of stability and protection. Several participants cited tangible threats to this effect, such as a building sale. Lisa has lived in her home for twenty-five years. Up until recently, she had an uneventful relationship with her property manager and landlord. She found out about the sale when the management company notified her they were planning to send someone to assess her apartment, She looked online and found a listing for the building. The management company put up a "for sale" sign shortly thereafter and didn't communicate with the residents about their plans. Though the new owners have not given the residents any reason to suspect that they plan to remove them from their homes, Lisa has a "looming dread" that they will try to convert the building to condominiums or something similar. To assuage her fears, Lisa contacted the RCO when she learned her building was for sale. The perspective she received as a low-income tenant was sobering:

> Yeah he literally said "just face it, you're not gonna be able to live [in Santa Monica] anymore." . . . I think he was probably sympathetic in certain ways, but trying to give me that truth, that like "you know you gotta, have to face certain facts. That it's just not viable. You know what most of the rent is here and it's pretty sad."

For others, the fear of a sale is present in the back of their minds. Selena has a close relationship with her on-site landlord family but realizes that one day they could sell the building. There was a time when she "literally used to have nightmares that I would lose my apartment, because that's how important financially and emotionally this apartment has been to me. It was the thing that scared me almost the most." As she approaches retirement age, she has made peace with that possibility, and with the knowledge that she would not be able to stay in Santa Monica.*

Mariana described similar fears shared by longtime residents of her building. She reasoned that there is so much deferred maintenance, a new

---

* About nine months after the interview, Selena shared the unfortunate news that the owners were, indeed, selling the building. By that point she had an opportunity to read some of my data analysis and using one of the main theoretical constructs, wrote that her "onto logical security [was] shaken."

owner would likely demolish or otherwise renovate the building. Though that would require offering the tenants a buyout offer, it would not be enough for the longtime tenants to afford another home in Santa Monica. This has prevented them from reporting some of the more serious habitability concerns to the city: "I think the fear that everyone has is that reporting the owner would mean that if he were to sell, right, if he said 'screw you guys, I'm going to sell the building,' then we would all be homeless." Nate shared the same fear, speculating that, if tenants push the landlord too hard to make repairs, they will sell the building. This notion is "not based on any real fear other than just hearing stories of people being Ellis Act'd (evicted) and you know, that exact thing happening to other people in other parts of the city." In this sense, the knowledge of policy loopholes and industry business practices creates perceptions of precarity among renters.

Last, participants who have contentious relationships with their landlords/managers must strategically manage their interactions in anticipation of potential threats. Amy is hypervigilant about documenting all interactions with her landlord, based on the knowledge of his fraudulent eviction tactics. Even though she has had positive interactions seeking support from the city attorney's office, this process of self-advocacy is "exhausting." Vanessa feels protected by the city's policies and resources but realizes that she is still at the mercy of the property manager and HOA, due to the integral role they play in her housing stability and tranquility. While she has thus far navigated several conflicts and resolved them mostly in her favor with the HOA's support, she fears that the situation could worsen with a personnel change. When asked if her knowledge of tenant protections makes her feel more secure in her home, she explained:

> I think there's a benefit because you know they're there. And I know I have more protections here, but it's omnipresent . . . it's just always that unknown, what could come up next, and you don't know what it is and if you're protected. The baseline is, I know I'm more protected, I'm pretty protected, but I'm also—you never know what they're going to try and pull.

This ambiguity around possible landlord tactics combined with the limits of tenant protections and self-advocacy and the pressures of the housing market is a source of anxiety and fatigue for Amy and Vanessa. Though the city has tried to address the ever-evolving landlord tactics through its various policies and resources, there remains behavior that is just beyond the reach of protections like the anti-harassment ordinance, which require proof of "bad faith" intention on the part of the landlord. Moreover, the burden of proof is on the tenant, who meanwhile must try to make a home in a hostile environment.

Coping Strategies

"Constructive coping" describes how people make conscious choices about how to best achieve well-being and stability in challenging situations. Hulse, Morris, and Pawson use this framework to understand renter households' decisions about renting, but it can be applied to explain behaviors around maintenance and other aspects of the residential experience as well. In their study, they found renters "use a form of constructive coping, such as they are able to make a home and belong to a neighborhood" despite the inability to access homeownership.[8] In this sense, constructive coping is a proactive method to reach the level of ontological security needed to experience dwelling in the home environment.

Confronted with the challenges outlined earlier, participants described several coping strategies for navigating the landlord/manager relationship. The most common approach was avoidance. Eight people expressed a hesitancy to ask for anything beyond essential basic maintenance due to a fear of negative consequences.* For Sharon, the knowledge that she would have to leave Santa Monica if she was displaced from her home means the stakes are high for maintaining a conflict-free relationship with the manager. She has the second-longest tenancy in the building, which means she has a high level of vulnerability in terms of the rent gap. After receiving an $80 bill the last several times she reported a plumbing issue in her kitchen, she decided that, given the money she is able to save with a lower rent, "not rocking the boat" and "being invisible" is more important than fighting an unfair charge. She also explained that it feels like a trade-off to spend her own money to address deferred maintenance, because it's still less of an expense than "having to spend like twice as much on rent for the rest of my life" if she were to lose her home.

Vanessa, another participant with decades of residency in her home, feels similarly that it's best to have as little contact with her building manager as possible—especially given a history of conflict. When maintenance needs to be performed in her apartment, she's faced with the decision to handle it herself or ask the manager. Ultimately, she decided that "staying under the radar was way more important to me than the money," given the omnipresent threat of harassment. Because Vanessa's skill set enables her to address many maintenance issues herself, she is in a unique position among

---

* As a renter with below market rent, I share this approach.

study participants. After weighing her options and considering what is at stake, Vanessa prefers to do what work she can on her apartment:

> When I asked for things, what I've found to be true is they will do whatever is minimally required by law. And if I really wanted new carpet I probably could have asked for it. But my M.O. has always been I would deal with them as little as possible and ask for as little as possible. I'd rather do it myself so that they can't come after me for anything.

Dave also prefers to do his own maintenance when possible because his skill set enables him to exceed the quality of work his landlord performs. While he's not concerned about displacement per se, many of his neighbors prefer to avoid contact with the landlord and ask him to help instead. He theorized that "they don't really want to get in trouble, or they don't want to cause too much attention upon themselves." Similarly, many of Christina's neighbors in her building are monolingual Spanish speakers with a mix of immigration documentation statuses. While Christina feels comfortable pursuing habitability issues with the landlord or the Code Enforcement Division, most of her neighbors prefer to make repairs themselves. Many of them are longtime tenants who have raised children in the complex and, like most of the participants, depend on retaining their current housing to remain in Santa Monica. As such, they live in a state of perpetual insecurity: "They just kind of go about their business, but I don't think they're comfortable . . . like any little thing wrong . . . they could be kicked out I guess is their fear."

Gina and most of her neighbors also prefer not to ask the manager for repairs or improvements unless absolutely necessary, out of fear of "being a bother." She related a lengthy story about a neighbor who lived below her when she first moved in and had eventually been evicted after asking for many repairs. Though she was unclear on the details and unsure of who was ultimately in the wrong, the incident served as a cautionary tale. She prefers to do what work she can, which has included installing her own thermostat and unclogging pipes. Though she asked for new carpet at the behest of a past roommate, that was an exception: "It's part of that anxiety. I don't want to be a bother because the more I request from them, the more they want me out." Notably, Gina has never had a problem with her landlord and even described them as "pretty reasonable."

Three participants have adopted a "strength in numbers" strategy. In some cases, this means making sure that multiple neighbors report the same incident, so the participant isn't labeled as a troublesome tenant. After being told that "it's always you," Luis first checks with his neighbors to determine if an issue is building-wide. If the problem is within his apartment alone, he will try to fix it, if possible, and will only call the manager as a last resort:

> I try not to deal with him if I can help it. I'll check with my neighbors. If there's like an issue regarding the entire building I'll check with them first and have them report it and then I'll report it. So it's not just like there's one of us reporting an issue, it's coming from multiple people. And so we can all back each other up . . . so he can't deny or throw his hands up when it's the whole building complaining. As for smaller issues within my apartment, if I can fix it myself, I'll fix it myself . . . if I need to call him I'll call him, I just don't particularly like to.

Though Joyce has taken on the role of advocate in the past, she also prefers to report a problem as a group, explaining, "I've found that it's better in numbers so that I'm not the squeaky wheel, I'm not the complainer, I'm not the troublemaker. Because a lot of times the one that takes the lead is the troublemaker." Similarly, Mariana and her neighbors discussed how to get the landlord to make essential repairs to a dangerous walkway and decided to approach him as a group. Raquel, who speculated that her new landlord wants to remove all current tenants, is reading up on her rights and talking to her neighbors preemptively:

> We pretty much have decided that, until we get the papers that they're either going to knock it down or Ellis it or take it off the market—and yeah we have no choice and at that point—we'll leave. But you know, cash for keys we don't have to say yes.

A few participants were hesitant to report issues due to experiences with previous landlords and managers, rather than based on the circumstances of their current living arrangement. Bonnie has one of the shortest tenancies in the study, at five years, and is paying relatively close to market rent. She has no reason to fear her landlord would want her to move out and has a generally positive rapport with him. Still, she prefers not to ask for repairs unless necessary:

> I mean, I think it's just hesitance and like, not wanting to be a bother. I've had a lot of crappy landlords in the past. And it always felt like . . . a confrontation, to ask for something. And it became an unpleasant experience and relationship as though I'd done something wrong. So I think it's just sort of fear-based from historical experience.

In contrast, Patrick and Rena are both longtime tenants who have found strategies to assert themselves in interactions with their landlord/managers when needed, without fear of reprisal. Patrick has a contentious relationship with his landlord and simply dismisses communications that are not to his liking. This confidence in the face of a perceived intent to remove him from his home may be due to past successes in conflicts with the landlord: "He's always trying to come up with stupid excuses to get me out of here . . . so, he's alright, he's just, you know, I do what I want. And he says something, I tell him 'forget it.' We move along in life." Rena has a generally positive relationship with her landlord/manager. She describes him as an ethical person who also takes a long time to complete needed work and will usually only do the bare minimum to address an issue. She theorized that he trusts her and her partner due to their length of tenancy and listens to them when the importance of something is emphatically stated: "He knows I'm not bullshitting when something's gone awry, because I don't complain a lot." Her strategies are to choose her battles, follow-up repeatedly, and, when necessary, use words that convey possible outcomes he may want to avoid:

> Sometimes there's about four or five of us who can get better service because we've been here the longest [and] we know how to talk to them. And when we have to, we know the special words to say. Like "you don't want a liability here," "you don't want a lien," "you don't want the health department to come out." You know? But that's taken a long time to kind of negotiate and learn about and not use inappropriately or as a threat—just to remind him. Maybe I use it once every four or five years.

After decades of living in their building, Rena and her partner have developed an understanding of how to engage with their landlord/manager to get the desired results without putting themselves at risk. However, as illustrated earlier, the dynamic is fraught with tension and difficult decisions for many tenants. Even when the law is on one's side, the possibility remains that the landlord/manager will make life so unpleasant that continuing to reside in the home is untenable, whether that's the landlord/manager's desired outcome or not. Ultimately, these feelings and experiences illustrate how security and insecurity can exist simultaneously, ebbing and flowing in a fluid state around flare-ups with the landlord, building sales, and other factors. Even in the best of circumstances—which Santa Monica's tenant protection programs have arguably created—to rent in America is to live with a certain level of precarity.

How These Experiences Relate to Behavior and Decisions

The experiences outlined earlier inform tenants' behavior and decisions—both consciously and unconsciously—in and around many areas of their lives. Participants described how their housing arrangements connect positively to outcomes like more discretionary income, increased capacity, expanded career opportunities, community engagement and participation, and investing in maintaining or improving their home.

Most participants have a rent/income ratio that is sustainable long term. Two weren't able to answer this question due to an evolving financial situation, two didn't know, and one isn't able to continue paying their current rent in the long term on their retirement income. For many, having predictable housing costs has had a tangible impact on their financial well-being and, by extension, their greater well-being. In Bonnie's case, even a $100 monthly rent increase would have been impactful. Now, with a slightly higher-paying job than her previous one and fixed housing costs, she is able to save for the future. Karli and her partner prioritize their rent first, then bills and other expenses, and whatever is left enables them to "splurge" a little and save as well. Christina has money to spend on her children that she would not have if the rent was higher. Daphne can travel overseas to her home country to visit family with the money that she saves. Several participants have been saving or have saved money to buy property outside the Los Angeles area. Rent control has enabled some of the older participants to save for retirement and contribute to Roth IRA accounts.

For others, the rent/income ratio provides a cushion for life's vicissitudes. Daphne was able to afford a 20% pay cut during the early days of the pandemic, and after her salary was restored, she now saves that portion of her paycheck for retirement. Heather was able to pay for substantial medical bills when she had lymphoma, while retaining her housing and avoiding debt.

The stability and longevity facilitated by Santa Monica's tenant protections impacts residents' personal capacity and well-being and, by extension, life decisions like career changes and retirement. This is the case for participants across the age and tenure length spectrum. Planning for the future is one aspect. When she first moved into her apartment in the mid-1990s, Georgia was excited to be protected by rent control because the fixed housing costs meant she would have a chance to retire. Without it, she feared she would have to work for her entire life. Instead, she was able to retire at age sixty-five. Raquel will also be able to retire soon, if she is able to stay in her apartment and does not face the possible Ellis Act eviction she fears after the sale of her building. For Vanessa, knowing that the rent doesn't take up a substantial portion of their income allows her and her partner more flexibility with what they plan for the future. Katya is also able to plan more long term due to her housing stability.

Increased capacity is another outcome. Rena and her partner have lived in their home for over four decades and are highly active members of the community. Between paying low rent and having generally low overhead, they were both able to retire early. With their increased capacity, they commit the time they were spending at work to volunteering in the community. Her partner was also able to take care of his father when he was ill, in a way he would not have been otherwise. "It's recognizing that if your energy and your income and all of your productivity has to go to a lump sum for housing it totally limits either physical time or psychological energy or talent, resources, and assets that you can give back," she explained.

Amy echoed this sentiment about increased capacity to realize possible selves. She had previously lived in a more expensive apartment in the Westwood neighborhood of Los Angeles. When she got a large rent increase she started looking for a rent-controlled apartment in Santa Monica and moved into her current home in 1994. At the time, she was searching for a living arrangement with less overhead so she could pursue being an artist and comedian. She has been able to achieve that goal and save money in the process as a result of living in a rent-controlled home.

Tenant protections are also a consideration in major life decisions. During the pandemic, Sarah decided she needed a change from her current job, which was creating unsustainable stress. She credits her stabilized rent and positive relationship with her landlord with supporting that decision by enabling her to take on a lower-paying position without worrying about a large rent increase. Luis has also enjoyed the flexibility to make life choices that best suit his needs because his rent is predictable and affordable. In the past fifteen years that he has lived in his home, he has been able to leave his job to pursue other opportunities on several occasions:

> Because my rent is affordable I feel like I have the leeway to change jobs or start new projects, or start a new business or take some time off and travel. . . . I have a lot of flexibility there, because I'm not always worrying about coming up with rent the next month, so I'm secure financially.

Several participants with long-term tenancies reflected on some of the ways their housing has provided a supportive foundation for their life choices in the past. Claire was able to stay in a low-paying job that she loved at a local church for nineteen years due to her affordable rent and stable housing. Vanessa changed careers and attended graduate school, both of which she attributes to knowing that her housing costs were predictable. When Estelle first moved into her apartment in the early 1980s, she had no family support, but her rent-controlled apartment opened opportunities for her:

> [My rent-controlled apartment] enabled me at the time to work and to go to school, which is what I did. So I put all my time and effort into working and going to school, trying to build a career and also trying to be a good member of the community.

Several years ago, Mariana was able to leave a six-figure job and open a private practice, cutting her hours in half. She explained:

> [Stability through rent control] allows me to make decisions—like not only do I feel stable, I don't have to work a 40 hour week . . . and I can afford to pay my bills and I can afford to save, and I can afford many things, and I don't have to work extra . . . I work less than twenty hours.

For Mariana, who grew up in her home and raised her (now adult) son there as well, stable housing through Santa Monica's tenant protections have increased her capacity to realize possible selves. She is also able to continue living in her hometown and her community in the Pico Neighborhood, to which she is deeply attached. Having stable housing costs—combined with less responsibility than a homeowner—has also increased her quality of life:

> That's one of the benefits of living in rent control. And I appreciate that, probably more than most. Because when I compare my livelihood to others of my age, who are, you know, paying mortgages and like maybe they have a really nice home, but they're also working really hard to keep up their homes and pay their mortgages and send their kids to college. And I'm able to do that and not have that stress that goes along with all that.

For some, housing has played an *unconscious* role in their decision-making process. Bonnie started her own freelance business three years ago, a few years after moving into her apartment. While her housing was not an active part of that decision, talking through it in the interview, she reflected, "Knowing that I had a generally stable housing situation probably made it easier for me to make a move towards starting my own business." Similarly, for Gina, who recently accepted a much-lower-paying job that she enjoys more than her previous one, her housing "did not play as direct a role as it could have, but it played an indirect role because it's something that I didn't worry about."

A number of other participants identified housing stability and expected longevity of tenure, facilitated by tenant protections, as an active component in their capacity to build community and their decision to participate in various volunteer activities. Knowing that she will be able to afford her home in the foreseeable future makes Ramona feel able to commit to working with local organizations long term. Nate connected his family's housing stability with his increasing investment in the community, including following local politics and volunteering at his son's school and youth sports. He also appreciates that his son can cultivate friendships without having to worry about moving and losing his friends. Katya participates in an astonishing number of organizations and other volunteer activities. She connected housing stability—through both tenant protections and her current income—with her capacity and decision to dedicate more of her time to these endeavors.

Vanessa is another highly active member of her community. She's almost thirty years older than Katya but shared very similar sentiments. The security she experiences through tenant protections confers a sense of ownership and investment in the community she has called home for four decades. "I'm invested in the community," she said, "and part of that, yes, is because I know that I can live here." Rena feels similarly. "We have our community . . . we believe really deeply in that," she explained. Rent control "enables us to give a lot back to the community."

One-third of the participants connected their decision to invest time and resources in maintaining or upgrading their home with the housing stability and affordability conferred by tenant protections. Several others reported that they would probably do the work either way because they want their home to be in good condition and the landlord doesn't maintain it to their desired level of quality. Diane has felt comfortable paying for painting and carpet replacement over the years, based on the knowledge that she will be able to remain in her home long term. Rena and Mariana are similarly willing to invest financially in their longtime homes.

Mariana sees home improvements as "a good investment because I'm not going anywhere. If I want my home to look nice, it's going to be because I make it look nice." Over the years, she has redone the floors and cabinets, bought her own appliances, and painted many times. Patrick also pays for periodic maintenance like painting and flooring. For him, "stability has a lot to do with it . . . because I treat this like it's my home." Selena's decision to invest in upgrading her apartment, over the years, is connected to her sense of stability and financial sustainability through rent control, her relationship with the family that owns her building, and her attachment to her home:

People said "you're putting money [in] and you don't even own?" . . .
And I said "I've had rent control for thirty years. It's thirty years, I
can do this." It's not only "can," I want to. . . . She (the owner) let
me choose the tile I wanted. I put stainless steel counters in my
kitchen. . . . What apartment's gonna let you put in a stainless-steel
counter?

For Nate and his family, the knowledge that they can stay in their home for
the foreseeable future is a factor in how much money they allocate for upgrades. In turn, he surmises that the more improvements they make, the
more the space will feel like a permanent home. However, because he and
his partner are relatively young and upwardly mobile, they are not sure
exactly how long they will stay in their home. For this reason, they have held
back on some larger investments like replacing kitchen cabinets for the time
being.

Economists who study rent control and its impacts have—to my knowledge—never considered the policy's impacts on any of these aspects. These
findings illustrate how tenant protections support many areas of renter
households' lives, with benefits that stretch well beyond simply keeping
people in place. These personal benefits have a spillover effect, as many renters who feel stable and can put down roots are inspired to contribute and
engage in their communities.

Conclusion

Elements of residential alienation *do* exist in Santa Monica's renter households. Eliminating them would require radically reconfiguring our housing
system. However, despite the challenges of navigating landlord-tenant power dynamics, frugal landlords who only do the bare minimum, and living
in one of the most expensive housing markets in the region—combined with
legal loopholes that incentivize removal of long-term tenants—participants
overwhelmingly feel at home in their residences. Additionally, more participants experience the stabilizing effect of tenant protections than do not.
These conditions of relative ontological security and dwelling contribute
to decisions and behaviors that positively impact not only the individual
but also the community and, in some cases, even the landlord. The next
chapter discusses the implications of these findings, including how the
person-place relationship and the elements of residential alienation and
insecurity coexist, as renters use coping strategies (including tenant protections and resources) to maintain a state of dwelling in their environments.

Ultimately, Santa Monica's protenant culture and the city government's historical and ongoing commitment to supporting renter households—alongside sustained independent advocacy—has created conditions that are a radical departure from the tenant experience across most of the United States. By pushing the limits of what is possible within the confines of America's private property regime, these activists, elected officials, and bureaucrats have indelibly shaped the tenant experience in the People's Republic of Santa Monica. At the same time, the real estate investment industry lobby is indefatigable in its efforts to chisel away at, undermine, and prevent protenant policies that limit profits. This tension between the use and the exchange value of housing is embedded in the landlord-tenant relationship, bringing this battle into renters' homes.

6

At Home in Santa Monica's
Rent-Controlled Housing

Almost all thirty participants in this study feel at home in their residences. Most feel attachment to some scale of their home environment, from apartment to city. Still, they must navigate circumstances connected to a complex web of external factors to maintain a state of dwelling. While economists are interested in how rent control functions as a mechanism to get housing units into the hands of the "right" consumer, human geographers, environmental psychologists, and sociologists who practice the sociology of residence are concerned with how it works to support individual, household, and community well-being.

In that spirit, I offer a conceptual framework (outlined in Figure 6.1) to explain how these many elements function together to inform dwelling and at-homeness. This first group of factors forms security, insecurity, and the residential experience. These four elements play off of each other, informing the extent to which one experiences residential alienation or ontological security in the residence.

Sociopolitical refers to Santa Monica's legacy of tenants' rights activism—both inside and outside city hall—and its indelible imprint on the cultural ideology around renting. Simultaneously, the *Market* dimension remains a driving force shaping the residential experience. In response to this tension, the *Sociolegal* element is the way in which Santa Monica has been a place where the legal arrangements governing a large segment of its privately owned rental housing stock are guided by progressive principles and activist elected officials, and where many tenant protections are implemented by voters. These laws are supported by resources and enforcement infrastructure that are unusually robust, compared to other American cities. *Landlord/manager* addresses the role of individual variation in personality and business model. Though a landlord's or property manager's conduct may be informed by the fundamental American values of capitalism, entrepreneurship, and private property, it may, at the same time, be considered legally and socially deviant within the context of Santa Monica's progressive values. In this sense, operating in this setting are two layers of sociocultural norms and beliefs about renting, and the landlord may relate more to one than to the other.

In identifying and connecting these factors, I was inspired by and drew from Australian housing researchers Kath Hulse, Vivienne Milligan, and Hazel Easthope's conceptual framework of "secure occupancy." They used this framework to understand the experiences of tenants living in the PRS housing in Australia—which has a housing system similar to the one in the United States. This framework is useful for looking at the quality of the residential experience and how external factors inform it. They define the study of secure occupancy as "the nature of occupancy . . . and the extent to which households can make a home and stay there for reasonable periods of time if they wish to do so, provided that they meet their tenancy obligations."[1] This includes elements like the degree to which households can participate in rental markets, access and remain in affordable housing that meets their needs, and receive financial and nonfinancial support from governments or other agencies. In a report funded by the Australian government, the researchers explain that research about secure occupancy is important for understanding how it affects the residential experience of housing and home, which is an important foundation for human well-being. They identify four key factors that inform secure occupancy: market, legal, social policy, and sociocultural norms and beliefs around renting. I modified their framework based on my findings and the unique case of Santa Monica.

The second group of factors in my conceptual framework pertains to the person-place relationship and consists of *environmental features* (e.g., nature, climate, amenities), *sociocultural/socioeconomic character, political climate and citywide issues, social fabric,* and *physical characteristics of the residence.* Together these inform the holistic experience of place, which can be understood with constructs like place attachment, place alienation, and sense of community. These inform both one's desire and determination to remain in their home environment and one's decision to relocate.

These thirty Santa Monica renters expressed attachment to their homes, neighborhoods, city, and region using affective language like "love," "attached," "blessed," and "rooted" to describe their relationship to place. This attachment is illustrated by their desire to remain in their home environ-

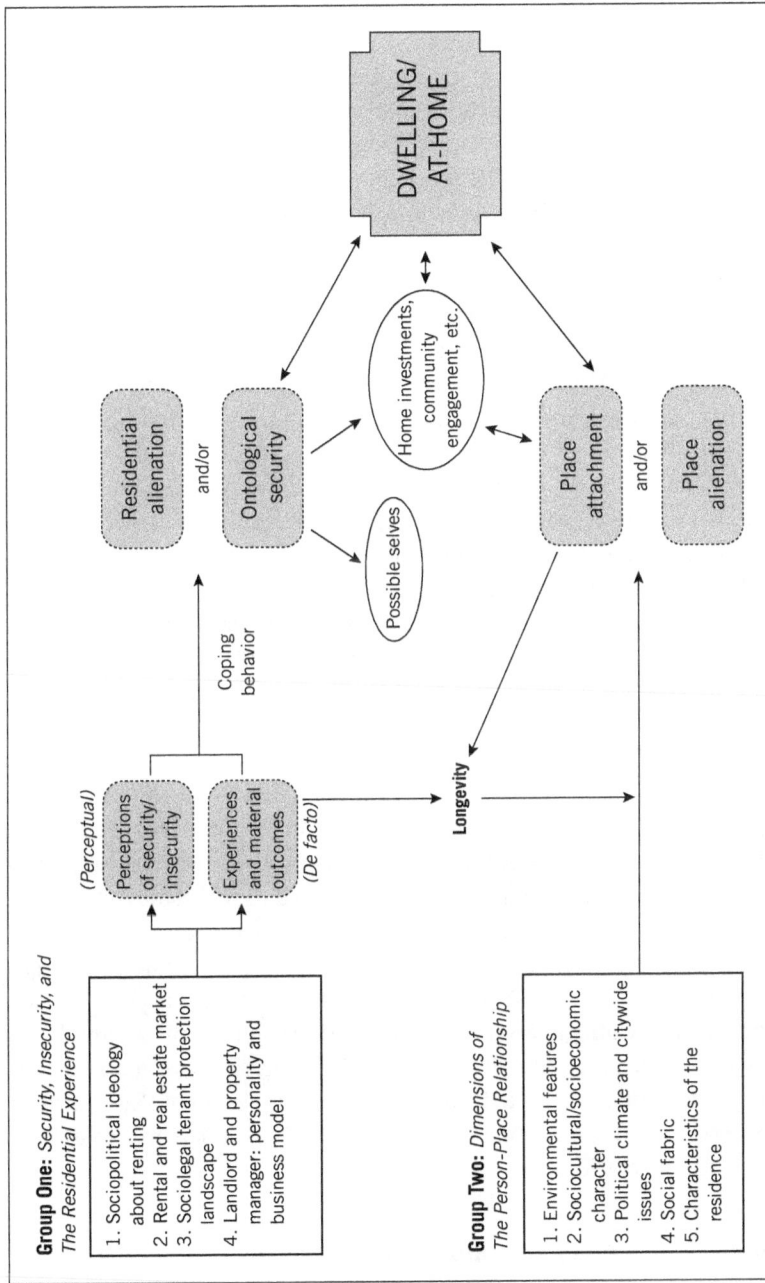

Group One: *Security, Insecurity, and The Residential Experience*

1. Sociopolitical ideology about renting
2. Rental and real estate market
3. Sociolegal tenant protection landscape
4. Landlord and property manager: personality and business model

(Perceptual)

Perceptions of security/insecurity

Experiences and material outcomes

(De facto)

Coping behavior

Residential alienation

and/or

Ontological security

Home investments, community engagement, etc.

Possible selves

DWELLING/AT-HOME

Place attachment

and/or

Place alienation

Longevity

Group Two: *Dimensions of The Person-Place Relationship*

1. Environmental features
2. Sociocultural/socioeconomic character
3. Political climate and citywide issues
4. Social fabric
5. Characteristics of the residence

Figure 6.1 An operationalization of dwelling/at-homeness and the factors that inform it in Santa Monica's rent-controlled housing.

ment: the majority hope to stay in their homes for the foreseeable future, at least, and over one-third plan to remain as long as possible. The emotions and cognitions about place in Group Two combine with the perceptions, experiences, and material outcomes in the residence that arise from Group One factors to inform one's sense of at-homeness, general well-being, and subsequent behaviors. These behaviors may include the decision to remain in the home or to move, to invest in home improvements, and/or to participate in community groups. A sense of ontological security or stability in the home can also factor in to decisions like changing careers, returning to school, or retiring early.

A holistic view of the person-place relationship concerns different scales of the home environment and expands our understanding of "home" as an existential state that extends beyond the residence itself. As environmental psychologist Lynne Manzo wrote in a call for more multifaceted exploration of the topic, the person-place relationship is "an ever-changing, dynamic phenomenon" that exists within a wider political context that shapes it.[2] The determination to remain in place based on attachment—even in the face of conditions that are less than ideal—aligns with housing researcher Easthope's assertion that "people often make economic decisions not purely as rational actors, but rather based on their ideas about the nature of different 'places.'"[3] In other words, the relationships people have with their home environments frequently operate on a deeper level than what is traditionally considered in the cost/benefit framework of the economic lens.

When the Political Is Personal

Sociopolitical and sociolegal factors are inextricably intertwined and exist at multiple scales, which are sometimes in tension. They are informed by the rental housing market, which is in turn connected to real estate investment and speculation more broadly, with its increasingly globalized and financialized nature. These three elements have an iterative and dynamic relationship with landlord business models and approaches. Property owners respond to the sociolegal and market conditions shaped by sociopolitical forces with various business decisions and behaviors. These factors are, in turn, impacted and respond to trends in property investment (e.g., purchasing property to rent on Airbnb). In this way, activity at the macrolevel informs the microscale of individual lives.

Fortunate People in a Fortunate Land

Santa Monica is exceptional among American cities for the protenant ideology behind the policies and enforcement infrastructure that govern the landlord-tenant relationship and rental housing. This has real effects on the residential experience for tenants in rent-controlled housing and in particular, on security of tenure, both perceived and actual. Most study participants feel unequivocally at home, and they have generally positive opinions of their apartments. A recent study on the experience of living in market rental housing in Sydney and Melbourne has a framing and focus similar to my study, and the researchers asked many of the same interview questions about the residential experience. However, a significantly smaller percentage of participants in their study reported feeling completely at home in their residences.[4] The most salient conditions informing the degree to which their respondents experienced a sense of home were the physical condition, maintenance, ability to personalize the space, relationship with the landlord or manager, and quality of the neighborhood. Many of my participants have experienced issues with one or more of these aspects but still feel at home. The discrepancy between these findings among renters in two "homeowner societies" suggests a mediating variable between the two contexts. Those variables are the sociolegal and sociopolitical landscape in Santa Monica, which mitigate, though do not and cannot eliminate, the impacts of market actors and rent-seeking behaviors.

There is a strong connection between tenant protections and stability and the resulting experience of at-homeness, due to the longevity of tenure that rent control enables. This has created a situation where a quarter* of the city's pre-1979 multifamily housing is occupied by people who have lived there since before 1999. Half of the participants in my study fall into this category. The high level of place commitment and attachment exhibited by participants—even in the face of difficulty or disillusionment—illustrates the importance of the residential stability this policy has created. This defies common experiences with private market renting in homeowner societies like the United States, where the tenure is usually characterized by high levels of mobility, insecurity, and other negative outcomes, compared with owning. For example, housing researchers Kim McKee, Adriana Soaita, and Jennifer Hoolachan's study on the experience of low-income tenants in the United Kingdom found that the lack of stability and critical levels of uncertainty about the future of one's living situation undermined participants' ability to create a home and feel a positive connection to where they lived.[5] rban planning researcher Richard Waldron's study on private market tenants in Dublin, Ireland revealed similar conditions, where "participants reflected on the temporary nature of renting which mitigated against their efforts to establish permanent homes where they could settle down and start

---

* This was true at the time the interviews were conducted but has diminished in recent years.

families."[6] Due to this perpetual uncertainty, fifteen participants didn't view renting as a long-term option. This contrasts dramatically with the tenant experience in Santa Monica.

The relative stability afforded by Santa Monica's tenant protections enables renters to put down roots and fully engage in their communities. This has a range of potential positive outcomes. Participants described longevity of tenure as a benefit not only to the individual household but also in the context of creating social stability in the apartment building and neighborhood. Many participants identified having good neighbors and a positive social atmosphere in the building as being important to feeling at home. Almost two-thirds have exchanged favors with neighbors, two-thirds described neighbors as friendly or considerate, and two-thirds mentioned their longevity of tenure. This aligns with research on neighbors, ontological security, and the role of constancy in the environment.[7] The importance of longevity of neighbor tenure and positive neighbor relationships illustrates how the material outcomes of rent control have a direct and positive effect on ontological security and at-homeness. This is likely mutually true of the neighbors the participants describe, suggesting that the effects of rent control on individual well-being are amplified through the social fabric of rent-controlled buildings.

Many participants shared aspects of their residences and apartment buildings that meet their needs in some way. Whether attributed to amenities, physical characteristics, location, or feelings of safety and well-being, the psychosocial and material benefits of their residential environment generally outweigh the stressors and annoyances, like deferred and improperly performed maintenance, more often than not. It's also true that limited housing choices for most participants means some households endure less-than-ideal conditions in their residences in order to remain in their home environment. Still, the use of affective language, attachment language, and expressions of gratitude toward both their apartment and rent control policy—along with reporting that they feel at home—suggest an overall residential satisfaction, ontological security, and holistic state of dwelling that for most participants transcends the aspects of residential alienation discussed later.

Almost all participants experienced de facto security, meaning there are no current threats to their housing situations. There were two exceptions: Manuel and his family are planning to move out of state soon because their income/rent ratio are not sustainable, and Ramona's family is being displaced so the new owner's daughter can move in. Significantly, Ramona has a high opinion of rent control and the city's tenant resources despite her situation. Just over one-third of the participants have experienced some kind of direct threat to their continued tenancy or heard about a neighbor experiencing one. Issues with the landlord or manager receiving rent payment (e.g., lost in the mail, claimed "not received") were the most common. A few people have been asked to take a "buyout" and leave in the past, and one was recently threatened with eviction after the end of the COVID-19 eviction moratorium. Just over one-third of the participants (some of whom were other individuals) articulated a fear of displacement on some level, ranging from abstract scenario to imminent possibility. These fears are based on contemporary or previous experiences with the landlord or manager, knowledge of the rental housing market, and/or policy loopholes.

Five individuals experience perceptual insecurity that the knowledge of tenant protections cannot completely overcome. These feelings and beliefs are attributed to knowledge of the rental housing market, policy loopholes and landlord/manager behavior, the importance of which varies with the individual. One newer and relatively young tenant explained that the protections are effective in *theory*, but she wonders how difficult it would be to deploy them in practice. This stemmed from her experience trying to manage a neighbor who was smoking in the common areas. Another participant is concerned that the new owner of her apartment building might evict the tenants. This was apropos of nothing in particular, other than her situational knowledge of landlord practices, illustrating the role of information sharing among Santa Monica renters in shaping security and insecurity.

However, instead of living in a state of perpetual insecurity that undermines at-homeness, many participants deployed coping strategies to manage the risks and establish ontological security. This is to say not that the challenges of these circumstances were negated but that participants were motivated by their desire to remain in the home environment and found ways to feel at home in spite of them. About two-thirds of participants reported using some kind of coping strategy. In addition to avoiding the landlord/manager (the most common strategy) due to fear of displacement or conflict, a few participants described how they interpreted the precarity of their situation and made a contingency plan. Georgia, who is retired and worries the relationship between her rent and retirement income will not be sustainable over time, simply tries not to think about this upsetting prospect. When she does, she hopes that some of her wealthy friends will be able to help her if needed or that she will qualify for the Preserving Our Diversity* subsidy program. Raquel, whose building was just sold and has several

* According to the website, the program "provides cash-based assistance to low-income, long-term Santa Monica residents in rent-controlled apartments in Santa Monica to help achieve a minimum monthly after-rent income of $747 for a one-person household or $1,306 for a two-person household." Participants must be sixty-five years or older and have lived in

neighbors who have received cash for keys offers, feels confident she will be able to access Community Corporation (subsidized) housing if needed, due to the City's policy to move residents who have been displaced by Ellis Act evictions to the top of the waiting list. In these cases, Santa Monica renters look to other City programs to put their mind at ease in the face of a possible threat to their housing.

The efficacy of these coping behaviors shows how most renters in the study are able to manage potential insecurity to the extent that thoughts of precarity are at the back of one's mind and not a significant concern. This contrasts with renters for whom concern about insecurity is so prevalent that feelings of at-homeness are critically undermined by it.[8] There was no one in my study who fit this latter profile, as the one person who doesn't feel at home did not actually feel insecure. This suggests that tenant protections in Santa Monica are mitigating the impact of these residential alienation elements to a significant extent. Just over two-thirds of the participants experience perceptual security that they specifically connect to tenant protections and to rent control in particular. These participants have had a breadth of experiences with their landlords/managers, ranging from prolonged conflict to no issues whatsoever. Fear of the building being sold was present even among some participants who feel stable due to tenant protections, for the most part, though it was often in the back of one's mind rather than an omnipresent concern. Several experience perceptual security primarily due to de facto elements of the relationship with their landlord/manager or their income and secondarily because of policy.

Perceptions of the sociopolitical dimension were mixed. Some participants expressed positive views of the city government and its commitment to support renters, while others felt its priority is development interests and/or attracting high-income renters to the city. Some long-term tenants shared an analysis that the strong strand of protenant leadership in the early days of the tenant movement has been watered down in recent years. "I got here in '82 and rent control had just gotten underway, and you had Santa Monica renters' rights," Patrick explained, "Danny Zane, Judy Abdo, Kevin McKeown—who I think still sits on the Council—you had those people that genuinely cared about renters you know? And they would fight for them. But they're all gone now." Or as Rita put it, "Rent control is slowly evaporating and I don't think that's part of what they're working on right now." As a counterpoint, Heather believes elected officials still have renter interests at heart, and the fact that Kevin McKeown is a renter on City Council illus-

---

their homes since before January 2000. City of Santa Monica. (n.d.). Santa Monica Housing Office—Preserving Our Diversity (POD). Available at https://www.santamonica.gov/housing -pod.

trates that. Similarly, Gina has a practice of voting for candidates who are renters and articulate a commitment to renter issues. As Sharon explained, "There has always been a segment of the council that is pro-renter and pro-rent control. And I think renters have made sure to vote for those people. I don't know about this new council."

Participants who expressed the view that elected officials don't act in the interest of renters didn't feel this sea change threatened their stability but noted that the emphasis on rent control seemed to be contracting as leaders focus on other priorities. Housing development was often discussed in conjunction with tenant rights and resources. For some younger renters, increasing density and housing stock is an important part of supporting tenants, while older tenants tend to view that priority in competition with or opposition to support for existing tenants and quality of life in the city more broadly. Individual politics and political analyses, not surprisingly, played a role in these interpretations.

Participants often differentiated between resources like the city attorney's office and the RCB and those like the city council, with a consistently positive view of the former and mixed feelings about the latter. Some pointed to these resources as evidence the City cares about renters. As Joyce explained, "The fact you can go to City Hall and get free advice all the time on situations I think is really good. I mean, it shows me they care." Diane articulated this distinction, "I think that [elected officials'] priority is more gentrification and making deals with real estate developers. I mean they pay lip-service to renters but it's really the Santa Monica Rent Board that protects us." These public agencies, their structures, and their budgets were put in place by previous city councils. Major changes would require voters' approval, but small changes are possible by city council action. How Santa Monica continues to evolve politically and the impact of these changes on renters remains to be seen, but for now, almost all participants feel protected by and satisfied with these public agencies. The policy landscape shaped by the sociopolitical realm over the past four decades has indisputably resulted in real protections and resources for tenants. In this sense, even if one does not perceive the city government to be prorenter, the laws and resources for enforcement support ontological security and the perception of stakeholder status beyond what renters in America typically experience.

Undermining Local Control

Santa Monica's leaders and residents are limited in their ability to enact policies that create stability—both perceived and actual—for renters. Hundreds of thousands of renter households in California live under the shadow of the Ellis Act, the real estate investment industry's most successful maneuver to supersede local control. In Santa Monica alone, 3,340* homes have been withdrawn from the city's rent-controlled housing stock since the policy began in 1986. Between media coverage, personal experience, and conversations with friends, neighbors, and coworkers, likely all but the newest Santa Monica renters are aware of the Ellis Act and its devastating effects.† This echoes housing researchers Lynda Cheshire, Hazel Easthope, and Charlotte Have's conclusion in their research on the role of neighborliness in informing "at-homeness," where they argue that housing "remains embedded within wider social, political and economic relations that stretch beyond it and influence how it is understood and experienced."⁹

Raquel's anxieties about a possible Ellis Act eviction were triggered when she heard about the new owner approaching a few of her neighbors with cash for keys offers.‡ She's lived in her home with her family for twenty-five years and describes herself as what they call a "low-payer" due to the significant gap between her rent and a market rent. She theorizes the new owner will "knock it down to make condos or take it off the market, so they could upgrade and rent it at a higher rent." Raquel did some research on her rights using the city's tenant resources and decided with her neighbors that none of them will accept the buyout offers. Instead, they will wait until the day when (if) the Ellis paperwork is delivered. In the meantime, she's plan-

---

* Of these 3,340 rental homes that were withdrawn, 1,016 were returned by their owners to the rental market for various reasons and recontrolled. An additional 258 apartments were built on the site of multifamily housing that was torn down using the Ellis Act—in less than five years after the former tenants were evicted—and are thus also under rent control. These reversals of withdrawal leave the city with a net loss of 2,066 rent-controlled apartments. While city law regarding Ellis Act evictions stipulates the previous tenant's right to return within a specific time frame, to do so they must complete paperwork indicating that intention when moving out and then uproot their lives to move back when their old apartment is available. This is not a common scenario. See City of Santa Monica. (2023). *Santa Monica Rent Control Board Annual Report.*

† I first became aware of the Ellis Act when over three hundred renter households in the rent-stabilized (Los Angeles uses that term instead of "rent control") Lincoln Place Garden Apartments—a few blocks from the house where I grew up in Venice—received mass lease terminations under the act. Residents were given ninety days to leave. After a prolonged battle and some creative legal maneuvering from the owner's legal team, the Ellis Act evictions went forward for fifty-four households. They were forcibly removed from their homes by the sheriff right before Christmas, in what may have been the largest lockout eviction action in Los Angeles history. Some former tenants set up tents and camped on the median in protest. The apartments sat mostly empty for years, save some senior and disabled households who were allowed to remain a little longer. Eventually, a group of former tenants prevailed in a lawsuit against the company and were allowed to move back in at stabilized rents adjusted for the time that had passed. Hundreds of households had their homes ripped away, in one of the most quietly violent events in Los Angeles tenant history.

‡ This concern was so top of mind, Raquel shared this story at the beginning of the interview when I asked her to tell me about where she lives.

ning to retire at the end of the year and is crossing her fingers she'll still be able to remain in her longtime home, located just a few blocks away from where she grew up. The inhumanity of the Ellis Act—with its dubious rationale of enabling rental property owners to exit the business*—is truly striking in the midst of a national housing crisis that has attracted bipartisan attention.

Participants often connected housing-related stresses like high turnover in their buildings with external factors like the rental market and policy loopholes. This aligns with cultural geographer Kathy Burrell's findings on the negative impact of the housing market and resulting high turnover in her study of how external contextual factors relate to homemaking practices in an urban neighborhood in the United Kingdom. Burrell's respondents "appeared most unsettled by . . . the feeling that a culture of shallow roots has developed in the area."[10] In Santa Monica, participant impressions of transient tenants were divided between two main groups: students or other young people living with roommates, and people who have money and housing choices. In both cases, their participants connected their short tenures to the housing market. Several participants theorized their landlords deliberately rent to tenants that won't stay long with the intention of capitalizing on the vacancy decontrol provision of Costa-Hawkins. Without vacancy decontrol there would be no incentive to rent to tenants who don't intend to stay long.

Likewise, long-term tenants with rents far below market rates are aware of the lost profit in the gap between their rent and the market rent for their home. While the Ellis Act isn't the best method for closing this rent gap due to the restriction on rerenting the apartment within a certain time frame, buyout offers, harassment, and other landlord tactics are well known among Santa Monica renters. Longtime tenants often compared their rent to their knowledge of what a similar apartment in their building currently goes for when vacant—sometimes framed in gratitude and other times with trepidation. Patrick's landlord periodically comes up with things to "bother" him. After his attorney cousin sent the landlord a letter in response to a conflict between them, the following year there was another issue. "He tries things every so often," he explained, "and then they go away and he forgets about it. It's like a little cat mouse game is what it is. The last couple of landlords tried to come up with things too. Because my rent is so low."

---

* Bills in the state legislature that would have required ownership of a property for at least five years before using the Ellis Act to remove tenants were introduced and failed in 2015, 2019, 2020, 2021, and 2022. In other words, the Ellis Act is not actually designed for its ostensible purpose.

While Patrick doesn't let this experience and knowledge ruffle his onto-logical security, Sharon's anxiety about displacement is triggered by the fact that the apartment downstairs from hers rents for at least double what she pays. This lends gravity to any interaction with the management company, including a recent noise complaint. She's aware of some of the legal or qua-si-legal tactics landlords and managers use to remove long-term residents, such as extensive renovations where "they make it really difficult for you to get moved back in." As the tenant with the second-longest tenancy in the building, she tries to remain invisible to management as much as possible. As both of these cases illustrate, Costa-Hawkins has not only enabled rents in vacant rent-controlled housing to skyrocket way beyond affordability for new tenants, significantly undermining the intended effect of rent control; it also contributes to stress and residential alienation for long-term tenants.

Power and the Landlord-Tenant Relationship

Like the relationship between worker and employer, the landlord-tenant relationship is characterized by power and, in particular, an imbalance in power between the two parties. The tenant, manager, and owner each have different things at stake, with the tenant standing to lose the most. How-ever, policy debates often frame these competing interests as though the two parties have an equal stake. In homeowner societies like the United States, the United Kingdom, and Australia, the landlord (and, by exten-sion, manager) unambiguously holds most of the cards. There are a few basic protections on a federal level in the United States. The implied war-ranty of habitability, established by *Javins v. First National Realty Corp.* in 1970, applies to rental properties in jurisdictions across the nation. This means there are certain physical standards that must be observed (at least in theory) or the tenant isn't obligated to uphold their rental contract by paying rent.[11] Theory and practice may be very far apart, as a law's efficacy depends on how the jurisdiction invests in enforcement infrastructure and resources. Other parts of landlord-tenant law typically govern things like how long of a notice period each party must give the other to terminate the lease and what method of communication is permitted to do so. In most parts of the United States, a tenant can be removed from their home at the landlord's whim, with thirty days to vacate.

Because the stakes are high, interpersonal dynamics between landlord/managers and tenants can impact the residential experience significantly. In this vein, housing researchers Michael Byrne and Rachel McArdle's study on the landlord-tenant relationship in Ireland found that insecurity and the power dynamic between landlord and tenant are deeply intertwined. Though tenant rights had recently improved with the passage of new legislation, their participants reported great difficulty asserting their rights due to both the lack of implementation and enforcement resources and the fear of losing their homes due to a tight rental market.* Receiving a retaliatory eviction in response to tenant advocacy was a common concern. This deficit preserved the deeply skewed power imbalance, creating conditions of residential alienation. Cultural norms about the residence as the landlord's property over the tenant's home also played a role in the residential experience.[12]

The housing researchers Elinor Chisholm, Philipa Howden-Chapman, and Geoff Fougere's work on the role of power in the landlord-tenant relationship offers a useful framework for exploring these experiences. They draw on the "secure occupancy" framework and on Lukes' conceptualization of power dynamics within interpersonal relationships to identify three dimensions of power:

- First dimension: *Visible power*—People are dissatisfied with conditions and attempt to change them. Conflicts of interest are clearly observable.
- Second dimension: *Hidden power*—People are dissatisfied with conditions, but there is no visible conflict. Conflicts of interest are hidden.
- Third dimension: *Invisible power*—People appear satisfied with conditions that are objectively dissatisfactory. Conflicts of interest are invisible.

In their review of qualitative research on how tenants experience housing quality issues in the United States, Australia, New Zealand, and England, Chisholm, Howden-Chapman, and Fougere found a pattern of tenants experiencing stress around reporting issues to the landlord, with repairs taking a long time to be completed, if they're completed at all. Retaliatory eviction or worsening relations with the landlord/manager were an outcome for some respondents.[13]

Santa Monica tenants are undoubtedly in a stronger position than tenants in uncontrolled private market housing, from both a sociolegal and a sociopolitical standpoint. But even some participants who feel very secure due to tenant protections and have successfully advocated for their rights

---

* For example, though landlords are only allowed to increase rents in certain areas 4% a year (including between tenancies), there's no way for a prospective tenant to check the MAR for an apartment. Absent that resource, the landlord is free to set it at whatever they wish. Oregon renters experience a similar lack of access to vital data. In contrast, any member of the public may look up the MAR for a specific rent-controlled apartment in Santa Monica.

must continue to navigate contentious situations with difficult landlords and managers. The primary variable that determined whether a participant had a positive, negative, or mixed opinion about their landlord or property manager was their responsiveness to maintenance and repair issues. Of those who discussed these problems, one-third of the participants reported that maintenance and repairs were not performed in a reasonable time frame, almost two-thirds described conditions of deferred maintenance, and one-third felt that needed repairs were executed inadequately, due to the landlord or manager's desire to save money. The landlord/manager's personality and the tenor of their interactions are also a factor for several participants. For example, Patrick described being able to "talk to, and you know, have a conversation with" a previous landlord/manager, whereas his relationship with the current one is contentious and "just ends up in a shouting match."

Coping strategies, combined with knowledge and deployment of tenant protections, mitigate the perceptual insecurity created through these conditions. A number of individuals have accepted that deferred/inadequate maintenance or these difficult relationships are essentially the "price of admission" for remaining in their home environment—and the cost is worth it. This constructive coping approach means individuals interpret the trade-off between affordable/stable housing and minimal maintenance as a reasonable one.* For some, coping strategies may be evidence of the "invisible power" of the landlord. In these situations, the resident appears to be satisfied with conditions that may be objectively evaluated as unsatisfactory. For others, coping strategies point to the hidden power of the landlord/manager. This is evident by situations where participants modify their behavior to avoid conflict and its unknown potential negative outcomes. As Rent Control Commissioner Anastasia Foster explained, "People are really afraid to raise their head up because they think if they're a nuisance to the landlord the landlord might be more inclined to Ellis, and it's used as a cudgel—it's used as a weapon."

This evidence of "hidden power" aligns with Byrne and McArdle's finding that tenants seek to avoid conflict, both for the possible consequences and associated stress and uncertainty. Potential conflict disrupts home as haven and may lead to conditions of insecure tenure—whether actual or perceived. Accordingly, participants in my study mitigated displacement risk and potential conflict with strategies like taking care of their own maintenance or simply accepting deferred maintenance conditions to remain

---

* Most participants reported that their landlord/manager makes essential repairs, so these conditions are generally more in the aesthetic realm (e.g., floor coverings, fixtures) or general infrastructure (e.g., electric wiring).

"invisible" and avoid being a "bother." Several participants also reported problems as a group to avoid unwanted attention. That this is the case, even in a context with exceptionally strong tenant protections and resources, speaks volumes about both the nature of private market housing and the limitations of policy interventions.

The reluctance to be perceived as a "difficult tenant" in the face of the landlord's hidden power aligns with Morris et al.'s findings about use of the avoidance strategy.[14] As in the Australian context, this is strongly connected to Santa Monica's highly valorized rental housing market, where the stakes are exceptionally high for low-income households and significant for many middle-income households. Some participants managed their fear of displacement with this avoidance strategy. These coping behaviors helped these individuals achieve some level of ontological security in the face of perceived challenges to their continued tenure or general unpleasantness in interactions with the landlord/manager. Coping strategies don't necessarily eliminate anxiety. Three participants who have lived in their homes for decades worry that the landlord/manager can find a way to remove them or "make my life miserable" if they really want to, due to the rent gap. These three are well versed in their rights, and two have successfully advocated for themselves in the past with the assistance of city resources. Additionally, two of the three have lengthy histories of conflict with their landlords/managers. For one of these participants, the conditions around the relationship with the landlord/manager have resulted in mixed feelings about at-homeness.

Whether or not they result in perceptual security, experiences of successfully resolving conflicts or disputes with landlords/managers by deploying tenant protections support de facto housing stability and may also mitigate elements of residential alienation like habitation issues. Roughly three-quarters of the forty-four conflicts participants experienced were resolved, with half of those involving a city entity. Other tactics include consulting with an attorney or researching their rights and self-advocating. Of those that were not resolved, only three involved a City entity. These conflicts include wrongful eviction, dangerous living conditions, and unlawful rent increases. This finding illustrates that to a certain extent "visible power"—which can be observed by examining who is victorious in a dispute—lies more with the tenant than the landlord/manager. Santa Monica tenants' experience challenging their landlords/managers through a variety of methods contrasts sharply with Byrne and McArdle's findings that tenants were overwhelmingly reluctant to advocate for themselves for fear of displacement (legal or extralegal).[15]

This visible power of tenant over landlord is also evident in media coverage of lawsuits filed by the city attorney against landlords who harass or fraudulently evict their tenants, which is routinely covered in the free periodical, the *Santa Monica Daily Press*. The city attorney's office even has a guest column in the paper called "Consumer Corner," which focuses on a variety of topics including the latest updates on tenant rights. The leadership at the city attorney's office considers this to be a part of their proactive public outreach practice, educating both tenants and landlords about the law. Last, "visible power" of tenant interests over landlords is evident in the many lawsuits brought by trade industry groups, against which the City successfully defended local policy.

Toward a Fuller Understanding of Rent Control

The combination of financial sustainability and housing stability created by Santa Monica's tenant protections has had a significant impact on many participants' capacity and well-being and, by extension, on their decisions and behaviors. In addition to the obvious material benefit for low- and moderate-income households who are able to remain in this highly desirable location for decades despite escalating rents, this study also revealed some benefits that have received less attention in debates around this policy.

Caretaking and Maintenance

Public debates about whether rent control "works" often include the claim that it leads to the deterioration of the housing stock. To that end, economist David Sims references a 1990 survey that found over 90% of economists believe rent control reduces the quality of rental housing. In his own quantitative analysis of rental housing data in Massachusetts, he concludes this is the case.[16] A recent quantitative analysis by a group of data scientists, using housing stock data in New York City, compared the condition of controlled and noncontrolled housing and found that rent control was associated with higher "damage rates."[17] While I don't debate the validity of these works, I argue that they miss important context about housing markets and investment practices.

Most landlords—from mom and pops to large corporations—are investors who have purchased rental property to make money. While business models, financial arrangements, and timelines for return on investment vary, owners generally put resources into improving or maintaining their properties proportionate to financial returns. Depending on the owner, this may or may not include meeting legal minimum standards per the local housing code if they make the calculation that they can evade them. For this reason, conditions of deterioration and deferred maintenance are also found in older housing in noncontrolled markets. In low-vacancy markets where demand is high, there is little incentive to make upgrades and nonessential capital improvements unless the landlord plans to raise rents significantly to recapture their investment, which often means displacing residents.* Similarly, when rents are low due to high vacancy, investment activity would logically vary based on the quality and age of housing stock. Again, if the landlord invests in significant improvements they will accordingly seek higher rents.

Because almost all rent-controlled housing in Santa Monica was built over four decades ago, at minimum, it mostly consists of Class C properties. In real estate parlance, Class C describes older housing stock that hasn't undergone significant renovation. A real estate investment firm called Feldman Equities defines Class C as properties that are typically older than thirty years (other sources say twenty), in "fair to poor" condition, and may be in a less desirable location.[18] Though they're considered "the 'riskiest' investment," they also "offer some of the best potential cash-on-cash returns." This is because of the "value-add" and "upscale potential," which means that extensive renovations can reposition the property to Class B or in select cases Class A. This holds true in localities with and without rent control. Thus it may be expected that in any market, Class C properties have some level of deterioration. Class C multifamily housing is also sometimes known as "naturally occurring affordable housing," or NOAH.

According to the latest rental housing report from the Joint Center for Housing Studies at Harvard, 3.9 million rental homes across the United States fail to meet basic standards of quality. This includes 13% of rental homes built before 1940. The report identified an urgent need to invest in maintaining the nation's rental housing stock. In Santa Monica, tenants can reach out to the Code Enforcement Division if their landlord isn't responding to requests for repairs. The Code Enforcement Division also works in conjunction with the city attorney's office to identify deferred maintenance that might be part of a pattern of harassment behavior. Los Angeles has a proactive code enforcement program where apartments are inspected on a regular basis. In both jurisdictions, there are administrative bodies that determine when a tenant may withhold a portion of rent in a situation of

---

* I experienced this talking to hundreds of renters on the Renters Rights Hotline in Portland, Oregon, between 2015 and 2016. The rental market was quickly heating up, and there was simply no incentive, beyond potential fines from Code Enforcement, for landlords who owned Class C properties. Because these properties are older they are typically the most affordable housing option, and in low-vacancy markets, tend to have the most demand as they're the only homes a significant segment of the populace can afford. In contrast to a newer property, where the tenant is paying rent at the top of the market and thus has more leverage to advocate for repairs, the landlord has the upper hand over these low-income tenants.

significant deterioration, until the owner remedies the issue. Conversely, tenants in the multitude of Irish, British, and Australian studies, referenced earlier, also described conditions of deterioration and deferred maintenance. Unlike Santa Monica tenants, they had little recourse to resolve these issues and high anxiety about rocking the boat. Though Santa Monica tenants share some of these concerns around being perceived by the landlord/manager as a "difficult tenant," they also tend to have a trade-off analysis, in which some deterioration is acceptable in light of their sustainable rent and other protections.

In conclusion, though there may be a correlation between deterioration and rent control, conditions of deterioration and deferred maintenance are not unique to jurisdictions with rent control. Moreover, tenants in jurisdictions with more robust tenant protections have greater recourse to remedy these issues, along with the added element of perceiving some deterioration as a reasonable trade-off for the continued access to their home environment—especially if they're longtime tenants paying rents that are well below market rates. To that point, the majority of participants reported considering housing stability and rental value—either consciously or unconsciously in retrospective analysis—in making decisions around caretaking their homes. While residents are not able to improve infrastructure or perform other major tasks (e.g., replacing a roof), there are some who have engaged in extensive upgrades to their home's interior. Overall, one-third directly connected their decision to invest their time and resources in maintaining or upgrading the home with tenant protections. The majority of these decisions were connected to upgrades, such as buying new appliances or installing cabinets and countertops. In some cases, this work brings significant added value to the interior of the dwelling, which is a benefit to the landlord when they show the residence to the next prospective tenants. In other cases, the improvements are small—perhaps a nicer faucet or sink—but still ultimately add value.

In addition to these scenarios, there were many other participants who engaged in various caretaking practices like painting and replacing flooring. While participants don't always consciously connect these decisions to policy, they are related to the longevity of tenure it supports: Longtime tenants are much more likely to engage in these practices than tenants who have lived in their homes for twenty years or less. As outlined, these decisions are a mix of different types of coping behaviors, which vary by participant. Some people would rather do their own work, either because they have the skills and it's easier, or even enjoyable, or to avoid unwanted attention from the landlord. There were several participants who caretake the residence out of necessity because the landlord has proven to be unresponsive or incompetent. A few others appreciate the autonomy from the landlord's supervision and surveillance and did their own maintenance or upgrades to preserve that dynamic.

Tenants who help with maintenance and repairs save money and time for their landlords/managers, but research on rent control and its impacts has never examined the value that residents add through their own labor and financial resources. My findings on tenant maintenance, repairs, and improvements as a common practice complicate the often repeated belief that rent control causes deterioration in housing quality. Additionally, there are a range of business models and approaches in evidence here, from landlords of longtime tenants who diligently keep up with maintenance to landlords of participants with shorter tenancies who do the bare minimum and sometimes don't do it correctly. The variation points to a need for in-depth comparative research across jurisdictions with different housing policies to understand how landlords make decisions about maintenance and their business models more broadly. Additionally, a quantitative analysis of the full value tenants contribute through their labor and purchase of materials—in both controlled and noncontrolled jurisdictions—would add further nuances to our understanding of the policy's impact on housing quality.

Benefit to the Community

My findings also suggest rent control confers benefits on the community as a whole (building, block, neighborhood, city), not just on individual households. While there are certainly many elements of this policy for economists to continue exploring, there are, as this research shows, significant benefits that are beyond the frame of economic analysis. Expanding the scope of benefit analysis complicates the claim that rent control confers inequitable welfare benefits to some fortunate households at the expense of others.[19] Furthermore, scholars who adopt the misallocation argument don't consider that "long-stayers" and the "wrong consumers" have many reasons for remaining in their homes long term, and this commitment to place may have positive spillover effects for other residents of the area.

Findings on the importance of constancy in cultivating ontological security[20] dovetail with community attachment theory[21] and are exemplified here in my findings on the importance of long-term neighbors and social fabric. This is to say that the longevity supported by the tenant protections produces conditions of constancy that may benefit neighbors, friends, schools, and coworkers, in addition to the household. Renter investment of time, knowledge, finances, and other resources in community-based organizations and other volunteer endeavors has an unknown value to the community as a whole. This is facilitated by both longevity/stability of tenure and increased temporal capacity.

Some studies connect community engagement among renters to a desire to improve conditions in the building or neighborhood or to prevent displacement.[22] Notably, none of the participants in my study volunteer their time with a tenant union, housing justice organization, or neighborhood watch. However, community engagement and participation were common, with over two-thirds of participants reporting some regular volunteer activity. In addition, over one-third belong to a citywide group, and a number are active in neighborhood or Los Angeles–area groups. Some participants are hyperinvolved, dedicating their time to multiple organizations on a regular basis, as board members or in other integral roles. That they have the capacity to engage in these activities and don't need to invest time in a tenant union or safety-based organization suggests these needs are mostly met, leaving them with the resources to participate more expansively. A number of participants connected their decision to invest their time in the community over the years to both the stability they have experienced in their homes and the knowledge that they can participate in the long term if they wish. They represent a range of ages and tenure lengths. In addition to these individuals, other longtime tenants who did not make this explicit connection have been able to participate in various groups over the years due to their longevity of tenure.

Turning to more quantifiable community benefits, a mixed-methods study on the economic behavior of tenants in rent-controlled housing would be valuable for understanding possible positive economic externalities, especially as pertains to the local economy and charitable organizations. This would answer Manual Pastor, Vanessa Carter, and Maya Abood's call for more research that looks at rent control's net impact on business activity—specifically on local small businesses—in their report on the impacts of rent control/stabilization.[23]

Possible Selves

Many participants connected tenant protections and the resulting stability with the ability to better plan their lives and make major decisions. This goes beyond meeting material needs for safety and stability toward supporting self-actualization, the top of Maslow's hierarchy of needs. For older long-term tenants, retirement was a common thread. Several have already been able to retire or work less due to their housing situation, while another hopes to retire soon assuming her housing situation remains stable. Other participants described how having a secure foundation in their housing stability has played a role or continues to play a role in helping them plan for the future. It has also enabled some to change careers, take a fulfilling but low-paying job, start a small business, or attend graduate school. A few participants explained that their housing was not a consideration at the time the decision was made, but, on reflection, they identified it as a significant subconscious factor. These findings support the conclusion that tenant protections—when supported and enforced—can cultivate ontological security and facilitate the conceptualization and realization of possible selves.

An individual's life stage also has a bearing on possible selves. The array of positive possible selves becomes more realistic and concrete with age, and the feared possible selves for older people tend to focus more on physical and lifestyle aspects than career or relationship.[24] Many of the older participants hope to stay in their homes for the rest of their lives, or for some, at least until they can purchase property outside of the metro area or make other arrangements. By enabling early or even timely retirement, their housing serves as a stable base for living a dignified life during these later stages. For the younger participants, housing security, facilitated by tenant protections, enables them to maintain an expansive view of the future and their possible selves, where housing remains a constant rather than an unpredictable variable. This is especially significant given the depth of our national housing crisis and the decreasing accessibility of homeownership for younger generations. None of my participants under fifty expressed a desire to live in their homes forever, but they were appreciative of the material stability and access to their preferred locale for the foreseeable future. Even the participant with the shortest tenure (three years) expressed this sentiment.

Place Alienation and the Politics of Place

Regardless of how robust tenant protections are, when the person-place relationship is flooded with more negative than positive impressions, even renters with the best deals in town may choose to leave their longtime homes. These shifts represent a different kind of threat to residential and community stability. Conditions of place alienation at the city level reinforce environmental psychologist Lynn Manzo's argument that the politics of place are essential to a holistic understanding of the person-place relationship. In this sense, place alienation can be understood as an outcome of the ways in which "the places to which we have access, or to which we are denied access, are dictated by a larger political reality."[25]

All participants in the study expressed some level of attachment to their neighborhood and/or city, even if it was accompanied by critique, frustration, or disillusionment. There was no correlation between length of tenure and appreciation for any of the positive aspects of the neighborhood or city. Participants across the tenure length spectrum felt concern about common issues like homelessness, overdevelopment, and high housing costs. However, sentiments about how the city has changed were both overwhelmingly negative and primarily expressed by longtime residents with tenures of over twenty years. Likewise, negative attitudes about the city were exclusively expressed by longtime residents and primarily relate to changes in its physical, sociocultural, and socioeconomic character. The area's recent emergence as a center for the tech industry and its identity as Silicon Beach, the influx of wealthy tech workers, demolition of beloved local institutions, and large new developments, were all identified as interconnected factors. In this sense, many longtime residents feel alienated from the Santa Monica they once knew. Moreover, they feel these changes are to some extent consciously supported by decision-makers who prioritize tourists and new residents with money.

Witnessing one's home place change—especially in a direction perceived to prioritize wealthy outsiders—can evoke feelings of loss as connections with the past are gradually eroded.* This finding aligns with sociologist Steven Tuttle's research on gentrification in Chicago's predominantly Latino Pilsen neighborhood. While some residents felt decreasing alienation due to reduced crime and increased services, for others, witnessing sociocultural and socioeconomic change led to a declining sense of ownership and belonging, along with an implied threat of displacement for their own households and other community members. Tuttle connects this anxiety to the "social production of space" as theorized by philosopher and sociologist Henri Lefebvre, which describes how users shape "space" into "place" by giving it meaning through repeated interactions, or what Lefebvre calls "spatial practice."[26] As Tuttle explains, "If place is a product of action, the conditions by which place is produced and variations in one's sense of control over it can affect relations to it."[27] In other words, a perceived loss of belonging and informal ownership can lead to feelings of alienation. Similarly, geographer Minji Kim's research on tourism-induced neighborhood change and its impact on long-term residents in a neighborhood in Seoul illustrates how place attachment is dynamic and fluid, evolving over time in response to changing conditions. In this case, resident attachments are attenuated by proximity to tourism hot spots and related conditions like congestion, noise, and littering.[28]

Santa Monica's tenant protections directly grant thousands of households continued access to the city by securing their housing. At the same time, socioeconomic and sociocultural change transforms the built and social environment over time, and elected leaders may fail to adequately respond to the negative impacts of these changes, especially on longtime residents. The impact of this on the person-place relationship and residents'

---

* I almost cried when one participant mentioned the recently shuttered Wildflower Pizza on Main Street. These feelings of loss hit at a gut level.

decisions to remain are beyond the scope of tenant protections. They are, however, within the scope of SMRR's original progressive vision. The city's future remains to be seen, but the people of Santa Monica have an active role to play in shaping it.

Subverting the American Private Property Paradigm

For over four decades, Santa Monica's commitment to tenants' rights has directly confronted the conflict between private property rights—which are sacrosanct to American ideology around individuality and freedom—and the well-being of the city's many tenant residents. This commitment has been shared by city bureaucrats, elected officials, and most important, voters, as illustrated by an extensive history of policymaking in response to landlord behavior and the landlord lobby's legal threats. This unapologetically protenant and procommunity stance has ensured that landlord trade organizations still call the city "socialist" forty-five years after voters passed rent control. They aren't wrong: Santa Monica's sociopolitical landscape *does* in some ways resemble European nations and cities with socialist policies and leadership.

Yet, despite these commendable efforts, some tenants in Santa Monica still experience housing instability and stress related to landlord/manager behavior, the rental and real estate market, and policy loopholes. This reveals the limitations of a progressive local government's ability to implement redistributive housing policy when actors at the state level have the power to undermine it with legislation like Costa-Hawkins and the Ellis Act. The rhetoric of unfairness, battle, and burden that pervades the real estate investment industry's discourse about tenant protections illustrates that resistance to these policies exists today at similar levels to the late 1970s when the initial activism occurred. Certainly, there are landlords who accept rent control as a reality of doing business in Santa Monica and are able to work within its confines and remain financially viable while treating their tenants with dignity.* But, the relentless legal, legislative, and discursive attacks signal that the industry as a whole has not accepted these regulations.†

---

* A landlord whose family owns and lives on a small property in Santa Monica reached out to me when I was recruiting interview participants, enthusiastic about this research. She explained that she supports rent control and doesn't have any problems operating within its parameters. There are likely other landlords who feel this way, and this perspective provides an important counterpoint to the narrative that rent control hurts mom-and-pop landlords.

† On their membership page, Santa Monica landlord trade group ACTION Apartment Association urges landlords to join so they can "fight Santa Monica's war on owners." In another document on their website, titled "10 Great Things to Do as a Housing Provider,"

Viewed through the framework of secure occupancy, these mixed outcomes are still a significant improvement to the experience of renting in the PRS. As Hulse et al. point out in their analysis of housing systems, "The size, structure and composition of the rental market, which defines the place of renting in a system of housing provision, has many consequential ramifications for secure occupancy."[29] They identify four types of housing systems:

- A dominant and strongly regulated public housing rental sector that provides secure occupancy for residents (Austria and the Netherlands)
- A substantial and strongly regulated public housing sector that provides secure occupancy, and a smaller and less regulated PRS which does not (Ireland and Scotland)
- A dominant and lightly regulated PRS with limited ability to support secure occupancy, and a smaller and less regulated public housing sector that provides greater security (United States and Australia)
- A dominant and strongly regulated PRS that provides secure occupancy over all or most rental housing (Germany).

In countries like Germany, the Netherlands, and Austria, cultural norms, institutional settings, and legal provisions are designed to support long-term renting (both PRS and social) with strong consumer protections. In Germany, for example, 60% of households are renters, primarily living in PRS housing, and renting is viewed similarly to owning one's home. In the Netherlands and Austria, tenants find security in the countries' abundant public rental housing. However, in homeowner societies like the United States and Australia, where the PRS is the dominant rental sector and is *lightly* regulated, policy is "designed to ensure maximum flexibility for landlords in entry and exit, and in managing their asset unencumbered by tenant conditions that provide secure occupancy for tenants."[30] Meanwhile, public housing is typically heavily stigmatized, underinvested, and available only for the lowest-income households. Though the PRS tenant in a homeowner society has some rights as a consumer of a commodity good (e.g., implied warranty of habitability), the property owner's rights to conduct commerce are heavily prioritized.

Santa Monica's rental landscape is a hybrid of the United States and German models. The majority of its rental housing falls under what by U.S. national standards would be considered extreme regulation. Rental housing

---

author Rosario Perry proclaims, "For the last 100 years no investment has done better than SM apartments."

built after 1978 and fifteen years earlier than the current year is not under the city's rent control law but *is* protected under the state's much more modest rent increase cap of 5% plus the CPI. There is also a very small stock of income-based housing provided by a mix of actors, including the Community Corporation and private developers. While the residents of Santa Monica's locally regulated rent-controlled housing enjoy many protections and resources, they are critically weakened by the aforementioned factors of policy loopholes at the state level (primarily, with a few exceptions), and the resulting market dynamics, landlord/manager behavior, and business practices. Though overturning these harmful policy loopholes would bring increased stability to current residents, it would unfortunately not restore housing affordability that has been permanently lost for thousands of residences.

In light of this, I propose Santa Monica represents a fifth category in Hulse et al.'s housing system typologies. Tenants in my study had significantly higher rates of feeling at home than the Australian renters in Morris, Hulse, and Pawson's study. At the same time, they experienced some of the same problems and used some of the same coping mechanisms as renters in Sydney and Melbourne. Tenant protections clearly play a role in mediating those effects, and the local government's commitment to renter households remains exceptional in the American context.

This research also illuminates the role tenant protections play in supporting ontological security and possible selves. Hackett et al. found that community land trust (CLT) homeowners experienced ontological security in connection to that form of tenure, which meant they could spend less time and energy "securing the present, and more time enjoying their lives, or planning and pursuing their future."[31] This expansive and forward-looking stance was also present for the vast majority of my participants. Renters—whether in rent-controlled housing or not—have significantly less control over their living environment than homeowners. Additionally, they will never be able to recapture the value of their rent paid over the years or improvements they have made to the property when they move out, even as compared to the limited-equity investment a CLT offers. However, the money some of my study participants have been able to save or allocate to various other expenditures *is* a source of wealth and/or capacity building. Additionally, they have been able to realize life goals, work less, and make other lifestyle choices that suit their needs.

This contrasts with the devastating effects of foreclosure experienced by many homeowners in the subprime mortgage crisis and ensuing foreclosure epidemic of the early twenty-first century. While proponents of homeowner ideology sell the owner-occupied house as a means of stability, status, and wealth accumulation, traditional homeownership can put an economically vulnerable household in a more precarious situation than if it continued renting. As real estate scholar Morris A. Davis argues, "The costs and risks of homeownership are almost never discussed by public agencies and the benefits of homeownership as widely articulated are either hard to measure or quickly refuted."[32] Because one of the main benefits of ownership is building equity, households face considerable pressure to allocate resources toward purchasing property. However, these outcomes can also be thwarted by aspects like predatory lending and depreciating property values, and the rhetoric of ownership doesn't reflect that reality.

Accordingly, researchers in the United Kingdom found that some homeowners in Scotland experience less ontological security than renters in social housing due to the threat of foreclosure.[33] A study on the impacts of the foreclosure crisis on homeowners revealed that even the threat of foreclosure led to depression, fatigue, feelings of helplessness, the end of marriages, loss of appetite, and, in one case, the contemplation of suicide.[34] A number of my participants were cognizant of some of the drawbacks of ownership in their analyses of the trade-off between the two tenures, and some do not wish to own property at all. This aligns with Hulse, Morris, and Pawson's "deviance" typology of tenants, which describes renters who push back against the homeownership norm by making choices that have greater utility for their lives.[35] At the same time, many participants under age fifty expressed the hope of eventually owning a home, while acknowledging that there was no clear path to achieving that goal within the area. For these individuals, renting is a means of constructive coping to access their preferred location.

Conclusion

The state and process of dwelling in one's home environment is an essential part of the human experience. This study shows how housing stability for renters—combined with living arrangements that support dwelling by meeting material, social, and emotional needs—facilitates positive outcomes for individuals, households, and communities. These outcomes include longevity of tenure far beyond what is typical for renter households in homeowner societies, sense of community within apartment buildings, increased capacity and well-being, and feeling rooted and at home. This is directly connected to the city's sociolegal tenant protection landscape, which is a product of the sociopolitical ideology about renting. Simultaneously, this study also illustrates the deleterious effects of the Ellis Act and other loopholes, combined with the power of market forces.

Given that tenants have been in a position of greater precarity and lower social standing than property owners since the earliest days of colonial settlement in the United States, work to improve these outcomes in this locale and others nationwide is considerable and ongoing. Advocates face formidable challenges, including a well-funded real estate investment industry that is willing to expend considerable resources to maintain the profitable status quo. Though this research takes place in a policy context that is uniquely committed to equity for renter households, many of these findings have implications and relevance for other locales in which the one-third of Americans who rent their homes reside. In writing this book, my hope is that tenant activists and housing justice advocates can draw from the findings of this study to bring a new perspective to the debate about rent control and other tenant protections.

While the economic studies are helpful for understanding certain relationships and phenomena, policymakers' and academics' reliance on the economic lens to understand the impact of policies like rent control has resulted in a discussion that is overly centered on the housing itself. This limited perspective critically fails to consider the experiences of the *people* who make their homes in said housing. As the seminal economist John Maynard Keynes wrote, "The ideas of economists and political philosophers, both when they are right and when they are wrong, are more powerful than is commonly understood. Indeed, the world is ruled by little else."[36] Applying sociologist Jim Kemeny's "sociology of residence" lens, I center tenant voices to uncover additional benefits of this policy beyond what can be quantified in an economic analysis. I also show how the residential experience is part of the holistic person-place relationship, which is shaped by external factors like the housing market and the local sociopolitical landscape, in addition to individual life circumstances. Ultimately, dwelling/at-homeness is a holistic state of being that is greater than the quantifiable sum of its parts. More occupant-centered research on the residential experience in different types of housing tenures and policy settings is critical to the project of building a housing system that works. A better world *is* possible.

Conclusion

Onward!

Santa Monica's tenant protections have had positive and significant impacts on the lives of the renters who participated in this study. Yet, despite four decades of proactive prorenter policymaking at the local level, the area's high land values—combined with legal loopholes at the state level—partially undermine their efficacy. This informs individual landlord and property manager behavior, which can set tenants on edge with worry about displacement or create other conditions that detract from their ability to make a home. These negative impacts on the residential experience cannot be eliminated by local policy alone: they are indicative of the limitations of rent control in both America and other nations that prioritize property rights and favor homeowners. Rent control and other tenant protections are still essential and should be in place for renter households across the nation on the federal level. Still, while protenant policy can meaningfully mitigate conditions of residential alienation endemic to private market rental housing, the conflict of interest between "use value" and "exchange value" is, ultimately, irreconcilable.

The logic of the YIMBY (Yes in My Backyard) movement holds that the market can fix this housing crisis if jurisdictions simply remove restrictions and let developers build.* In this fantasy, if we let the invisible hand do its

---

* This is an incredibly controversial topic within the housing field, with many people willing to die on either side of the proverbial hill. While it's beyond the scope of this book to dive into that debate, see Will Parker's February 6, 2024, article in the *Wall Street Journal*—"Rent Comes Down for the Wealthy, While Rising for the Rest: Surplus of New Housing Is Driving

work, we'll reach a Pareto optimal situation in which all housing "consumers" will live in stable affordable housing, in their location of choice. Where demand exists, so follows supply. This aligns with the overarching logic of neoliberalism and laissez-faire. However, our national housing affordability and homelessness crisis is *not* a market failure or aberration but the market working exactly as it should for the privileged few who benefit from it. As such, the only way to truly address this conflict of interest between home and commodity good is by creating housing that exists *outside* of the market. This shift would require a massive public investment in the European social housing model. This approach to housing production centers on human beings and their fundamental need to make a home over developers' and investors' desire to make a profit.

In the 1986 classic, *Critical Perspectives on Housing*, Peter Marcuse and urban planner Emily Achtenberg articulated a vision for the decommodification of housing through what they describe as "social ownership." In its purest form, this would necessitate removing the production, ownership, and financing of housing from the private sector. Their vision of social ownership is as follows:

> Control the speculative private ownership of housing and expand the amount of housing under public, collective, community, or resident ownership that is operated solely for resident benefit and subject to resident control, with resale for profit prohibited.[1]

In the short term this would take the form of traditional interventions like rent control, policy to curb the effects of speculative property investment activity, and preservation of existing public housing stock along with a change in how that housing is managed—shifting toward more resident control. Though the authors don't evoke Marcuse's concept of residential alienation, this is implicitly addressed in the importance of resident control. In the long term, social ownership would require programs and funding to support the conversion of private market housing into socially owned housing on a massive scale. Ownership would include

---

Down Prices at the Top of the Market"—for a helpful analysis of how building market rate rental housing doesn't make a significant impact on the middle- and lower-end of the rental market. New rental housing is also exempt from essential tenant protections like rent control and just-cause eviction policy in even the most progressive jurisdictions. This means that, even if rents actually do increase minimally or not at all for some period of years due to a significant increase in supply, as the YIMBY movement claims, the residents of these buildings will still live in precarity absent meaningful protections. An overview of the YIMBY movement and research around the supply-side approach is available at https://www.planeti zen.com/definition/yimbys.

a mix of government, nonprofits, individual resident households, and resident collectives.

This shift away from reliance on the housing market and speculative investment for the provision of housing is already happening in other countries. For example, Paris is in the midst of an ambitious initiative to convert the city's private market rental housing into social housing. In 2024, over a quarter of the city's residents live in housing owned by the government, and the city reserves the first right of refusal on most residential buildings. The city has an annual budget of 625 million euros to make these purchases, with an ultimate goal of reserving 30% of the city's housing stock as social housing for low-income residents and 10% for middle-income residents by 2035. Support for the program is bipartisan; policymakers with conservative views mostly align with policymakers who are members of the Communist Party on the necessity of social housing to preserve the city's vibrancy and culture. It's common sense in an expensive and desirable city like Paris, where the currents of real estate investment run the risk of decimating not only character and sense of place but the ability of residents who provide essential services to live in their communities.[2]

In contrast, the United States has a very small amount of social housing proportionate to the need. Public housing that is funded by the federal government and owned by local housing authorities provides homes for 1.2 million households, or about 1% of the total population.[3] Its quantity is limited by the Faircloth Amendment, which restricts the number of federally funded public housing residences in existence to the number local housing authorities owned in 1999. However, due to underfunding for public housing, the number of allowable residences for each housing authority is often higher than the quantity they actually own and operate.[4] Public housing in the United States is exclusively the purview of low-income households, in contrast with European nations such as Austria, where the government creates housing for households with a range of incomes.[5] This approach both addresses the reality that housing affordability is a challenge for households at multiple income tiers and through its normalization, avoids the stigmatization around public housing that persists in the United States.*

CLTs are another model of decommodified housing that exists in the United States on an extremely limited basis. In this model of "shared equity

---

* I continue to see comments on social media and on news platforms disparaging contemporary public housing programs as creating "ghettos," "eye sores," and other stereotypes. My assumption is these views arise from instances where large public housing projects like Chicago's Cabrini-Green gradually deteriorated socially and physically, due to lack of investment from the federal government, combined with other social issues. *The Candyman* (1992), directed by Bernard Rose, is a powerful example of how public housing is represented in popular culture.

housing," a nonprofit organization owns and leases land to the resident, and the resident owns the house and other structures. Typically, these are single-family homes, and the ground lease is transferable to the resident's heirs. When the resident decides to sell their home, they get the funds they applied to the mortgage, plus a modest return to account for inflation. The intention is to assure that the housing remains affordable in perpetuity.[6] Research on this model and how it supports well-being and stability—including lower mortgage delinquency rates[7]—for low-income households suggests this tenure is a promising alternative to renting and traditional homeownership.[8] Despite that, and the increasing inaccessibility of the American dream of traditional homeownership, the CLT model tends to receive little government funding or attention, especially at the federal level. According to a 2022 inventory, only about fifteen thousand shared equity homes exist nationwide.[9]

The limited equity cooperative (LECs) is a promising model of decommodified housing that proliferated in the United States—especially New York City—in the 1960s, 1970s, and 1980s but has failed to scale up nationally on a meaningful level, due to a combined lack of funding and awareness.[10] Housing researcher John Emmeus Davis defines the LEC model as (1) housing operated by a state-chartered corporation composed of the building's residents, (2) ownership rights secured by a proprietary lease between the owner and the corporation, making each resident a shareholder, member, and leaseholder, and (3) transactions governed by a resale formula that determines the amount of profit the residents make at the time of sale. This ranges from limited- to zero-equity. Each resident makes small monthly payments over the course of their tenure, and when they move, receive what they paid plus a small increase, according to a predetermined formula. LEC housing is typically affordable to households with lower incomes than CLTs.[11]

Washington, DC, is notable for its support of tenant-led LECs, primarily through the Tenant Opportunity to Purchase Act (TOPA), which is supported by a dedicated (though limited) city fund. This policy contains a critical mechanism for transferring ownership to the residents, requiring the property owner to offer the tenants the right to make the first offer when their building is for sale. As a result of this 1980 legislation, the city contains forty-four hundred LEC homes in ninety-nine buildings. According to housing researcher Amanda Huron's comprehensive study on LECs in D.C., monthly housing costs tend to be about half the rate of market rent in the same area. What's more, residents receive a payout when they sell their share and move. Having a policy like TOPA in place not only creates affordable housing and equity; it also prevents displacement—especially in gentrifying neighborhoods.[12] Inspired by the success of the housing model and policy mechanism, similar policies are gaining traction in other jurisdictions. San

Francisco has the Community Opportunity to Purchase Act (COPA), which gives certain nonprofit community development corporations the right of first refusal. Chicago, Philadelphia, Baltimore, and several other Maryland cities also have some version of TOPA.[13]

This paradigm shift will require federal and state policymakers to adjust how welfare benefits are allocated. For example, the mortgage interest tax deduction should be based on income rather than be available to all homeowners as an entitlement and should not include second homes. Because the deduction can only be taken if the taxpayer is itemizing their deductions—which is less common for households making under $200,000—the policy in its current form disproportionately benefits high-earning households and, by extension, white households. The annual cost of this wasteful policy totals about $30 billion.[14] The additional tax revenue generated by eliminating this benefit for higher-earning property owners and vacation properties could be directly funneled into social housing programs. On the state level, repealing or significantly revising Proposition 13—which confers tax benefits on property owners that aren't directly available to renters nor are they required to be passed on to renters—would generate billions of dollars in revenue that could be used for housing, education, and other investments that would increase the quality of life for California residents. Some of this money could be used to create shared-equity ownership opportunities, expanding ownership to Californians who aren't able to afford the cost of the state's $800,000 median home price.[15]

Instead of relying on the LIHTC program to create the majority of the nation's new affordable rental housing stock, federal lawmakers could repeal the Faircloth Limit and use those same funds to build more public housing. Decades of social science research and resident-led reform movements have provided housing authorities with best practices to create social housing that doesn't go the way of Cabrini-Green. Public housing has the added benefit of affordability in perpetuity, in contrast to LIHTC housing, which has a minimum affordability period of only thirty years, creating a disastrous affordability cliff for residents when the end of that time approaches. Reforming the way public housing is managed, including the need for tenant councils in each apartment community, is also critical to the residential experience. Management practices with a carceral flavor have the potential to create conditions of extreme residential alienation. At the same time, buildings that have residents with high-acuity needs require skilled staff with training in mental health, conflict de-escalation, and other aspects of social services. Too often buildings with these residents are managed by companies that are not equipped to support their needs.

In addition to changes on the federal level in how the government invests in and supports the creation of housing, local legislation plays a key role in reform. First, local and state governments should implement policies that discourage speculative investment in land and housing, such as a vacancy tax on empty parcels and housing and a house flipping tax. The primary objective of these vacancy taxes is to deter the practice of investors "storing wealth" in housing they have no intention of offering for rent,* activating unused rental housing by pushing owners to rent vacant properties or sell them to someone who will. In Vancouver, BC, the number of vacant properties decreased by 54% in the first six years of the tax, which is promising.[16] However, the remaining vacant properties suggest the tax is low enough to be considered part of the cost of doing business for some investors. Experimenting with a higher tax and including vacant lots would hopefully produce even better results, with more housing back in circulation and fewer vacant lots languishing for years and in some cases decades.

Second, jurisdictions with escalating housing costs and low vacancy rates should aggressively regulate Airbnb and other vacation rental platforms and their hosts. Santa Monica and New York City both have strict policies that only permit residential rentals for less than thirty days in the owner or renter's residence, when the resident is present. These policies aim to eliminate the practice of an owner or leaseholder converting an entire house or apartment into a year-round Airbnb. This incredibly popular business model takes housing off the market at the time when it's needed most. It also creates conditions of residential alienation for neighbors, who must deal with a parade of strangers in a best-case scenario and parties or other disruptions in the worst case. Last, local and state governments should establish local TOPA and COPA policies, paired with generous local and federal funding, so tenants, nonprofits, and government agencies can purchase multifamily and single-family housing when it's offered for sale, and permanently remove it from the private market.

While deeply held ideology about private property rights and the superiority of traditional homeownership may not change for generations, these housing programs would enable millions of American households to put down roots and make their homes in safe, stable, and affordable housing in the shorter term. This paradigm shift would bring untold benefits to individual lives and communities. It would mean people would have more time to spend on what they enjoy doing, with family and friends, developing skills and planning for the future, and realizing possible selves. Workers would be able to live closer to their jobs with more affordable housing options, and kids wouldn't have to switch schools every time the rent went up. Future residents could participate in designing the kind of housing communities they'd like to live in and then participate in their management, which

---

* Remember David Harvey's second circuit of capital? This is it!

would diminish the likelihood of experiencing conditions of residential alienation.

In the Meantime . . .

There are several policy changes that could make a positive difference in the lives of renters in Santa Monica and California more broadly. First and foremost, as should now be abundantly clear, the Ellis Act and the Costa-Hawkins Rental Housing Act are detrimental to the efficacy of local rent control programs. They work together: Costa-Hawkins creates the potential for a property owner to make more profit by evicting longtime tenants and closing the rent gap, which in turn inflates the price of multifamily housing. If a longtime tenant refuses buyout offers, an Ellis eviction looms as the likely next step, tipping the scales decisively in the landlord's favor. Over time, these policies contribute to a slow bleed of rent-controlled housing stock and create conditions of precarity, stress, and residential alienation among renter households. Thanks to Costa-Hawkins and vacancy decontrol, an annual income of $115,000 is required to afford a rent-controlled studio apartment in Santa Monica at a market rent without being cost burdened.[17] The single most impactful policy intervention to support the stability of California renters living in rent-controlled housing is to repeal both of these laws. Best of all, it doesn't cost anything but the ire of the real estate investment industry.

While Santa Monica city leaders and tenant advocates have created an impressive landscape of tenant protections and resources, there is still room for improvement on the local level. First, the city should close the rent control exemption for duplexes and triplexes with one owner residing on the premises. While it is commendable that the city has a program to monitor exempt properties and return housing to rent control when the owner no longer lives there, the exemption has contributed significantly to the loss of rent-controlled housing. As of 2022, there were 1,162 rental homes that were exempt due to owner occupancy on the property.[18]

This is the situation that Ramona and her multigenerational household were facing at the time we conducted her interview. After over a decade in her home—in the neighborhood where she grew up—the property changed hands. The new owner moved into one of the two residences in the duplex, informing Ramona and her family they intend to raise the rent to market rates once pandemic restrictions expire.* The owners later told her that they actually wanted her home for their daughter. Either way, "they just want us

---

* Legal Aid staff informed Ramona that the owner can only raise the rent by the increment allowable under state law, which is 5% plus CPI with a limit of 10%. The new owner was not

out, plain and simple." Now Ramona's entire household will be displaced, possibly from the city entirely. Even though she feels that the rent control law is beneficial and the RCO is a good resource, and she has had several positive experiences with asserting her rights, at the end of the day, she feels that having to move is concrete evidence that property rights still matter more than renters. The City of Santa Monica should follow through on its commitment to renters and amend the law to eliminate this harmful exemption.*

The city should also consider a pilot program that provides funding and other support for helping residents form tenant associations. Several participants described employing a strategy of collaboration with their neighbors to resolve issues with their landlord/manager. They identified the benefits as creating increased pressure to resolve an issue, while insulating any one individual from retaliation. A city pilot program could include training tenants on how to form tenant unions in their buildings and negotiate with their landlords or managers. This would empower renters while strengthening building communities and protecting the most vulnerable residents from retaliatory behavior. On a similar note, the city should establish a rotating council of Santa Monicans who live in rent-controlled housing to advise on policy. Data collection from the RCO and PRD, public comment, and the RCB already provide a wealth of information about what Santa Monica renters experience. A formal tenant advisory body would add an extra layer to renters' involvement in shaping policy that impacts them.

Last, update city code to include life expectancies for items like flooring and paint. This would resolve the ambiguity around some of the most common maintenance issues. West Hollywood already has a list of maintenance standards that prescribe specific landlord actions relative to the age of the item.[19] For example, landlords are required to replace floor and window coverings every seven years and paint every four years in both apartments and common areas. It is somewhat surprising that Santa Monica does not already have these standards. At the same time, there should be some level of flexibility so this is not used as a harassment technique in situations where the tenant would have great difficulty removing their items from the home.

Epilogue

It seems like everywhere you turn these days, whether it's an article in the *New York Times* or a conversation in a coffee shop, people are talking about

---

aware of that, and Ramona strategically decided not to inform her, possibly for fear that knowledge would lead to a different tactic.

  * The one triplex listed for sale in the multifamily sale snapshot in Chapter 3 included this language: "Great owner user opportunity—rent control exempt if owner occupied." This suggests the exemption may also contribute to higher sale prices.

the housing crisis. As conditions worsen, the struggle continues. In California, activists and advocates organized once again to qualify a measure for the November 2024 ballot to repeal the Costa-Hawkins Rental Housing Act of 1995. The measure was not successful, but if it had been local governments would have been able to enact much more expansive rent control laws that could include single-family homes and properties built after 1995. As with previous efforts, the measure was opposed solely by real estate investment PACs. A January 2024 poll showed the measure losing by two percentage points with 20% of voters undecided, while a summer 2024 poll had it winning by six points with 26% of voters undecided.[20] After further vicissitudes in polling, the measure lost by a 20% margin. Fluctuating public opinion about this issue illustrates the impact narratives about rent control—which are underpinned by academic research and classical economic theory—have on the lives of millions of renter households. The opposition outspent the measure's supporters by more than double, raising over $125 million to defeat the measure.[21] Every campaign to repeal this law is more costly than the previous one.

Meanwhile, Santa Monica continues to make national headlines with its protenant policymaking. In August 2023, SMRR sent out a call to members urging them to contact the city council and tell them to expand tenant protections as proposed by Council Member Caroline Torosis.[22] In response, the city council drafted an ordinance and voted to adopt it in January 2024. Mayor Phil Brock explained, "Renters make up the majority of our Santa Monica community, and many have called this city home for years. . . . It is critically important that families who make up the fabric of our city have the ability to stay here."* [23] The ordinance included new protections for residents of noncontrolled housing, an expanded list of what constitutes tenant harassment, and adding housing status as a "protected class" in Santa Monica. This means a landlord or property manager reviewing a prospective tenant's application cannot deny the application based on a history of homelessness, current homelessness, or residence in transitional housing or shelter. Santa Monica is the first city in the state with this kind of policy.[24]

---

* It's worth noting that Mayor Brock and several other members of the city council were members of the 2020 "Change Slate" of city council candidates, which was not endorsed by SMRR and caused concern at the time over the possibility of eroding tenant rights. That this council *and* SMRR both supported these policies illustrates how strong support for tenant rights remains among Santa Monicans.

Notes

PREFACE

1. Kemeny, J. (1992). *Housing and Social Theory*. New York: Routledge, xviii.

INTRODUCTION

1. Buttimer, A. (1980). Home, Reach and the Sense of Place. In A. Buttimer & D. Seamon (Eds.), *The Human Experience of Space and Place*. New York: St. Martin's. 20.

2. Yin, R. (2003). *Case Study Research: Design and Methods* (3rd & 4th eds.). Newbury Park, CA: Sage.

3. Saldaña, J. (2009). *The Coding Manual for Qualitative Researchers*. New York; Sage.

4. Booth, W. C., Colomb, G. G., & Williams, J. M. (1995). *The Craft of Research*. Chicago: University of Chicago Press, 54.

5. Desmond, M. (2016). *Evicted: Poverty and Profit in the American City*. Milwaukee, WI: Crown Books, 254.

6. See Gilderbloom, J., & Ye, L. (2008). Pros and Cons of Rent Control. In J. Gilderbloom (Ed.), *Invisible City: Poverty, Housing and New Urbanism*. Austin: University of Texas Press.

7. Remarks at the Housing California conference, March 2024.

8. DeSanctis, A. (2024, March 29). *MBA Opposes Biden Administration's Rent Control on LIHTC-Financed Multifamily Properties*. Mortgage Bankers Association.

9. Galbraith, J. K. (1958). *The Affluent Society*. New York: Houghton Mifflin, 9.

10. Appelbaum, R. P., & Gilderbloom, J. I. (1986). Supply-Side Economics and Rents: Are Rental Housing Markets Truly Competitive? In R. G. Bratt, C. Hartman, & A. Meyerson (Eds.), *Critical Perspectives on Housing*. Philadelphia: Temple University Press, 172.

11. Sturtevant, L. (2018). *The Impacts of Rent Control: A Research Review and Synthesis*. National Multifamily Housing Council Research Foundation.

12. Glaeser, E. L. (1996). The Social Costs of Rent Control Revisited. NBER Working Papers 5441, National Bureau of Economic Research, 2.

13. Glaeser, E., & Luttmer, E. (2003). The Misallocation of Housing under Rent Control. *American Economic Review, 93*(4), 1044.

14. Skak, M., & Bloze, G. (2013). Rent Control and Misallocation. *Urban Studies, 50*(10), 1988–2005.

15. Diamond, R., McQuade, T., & Qian, F. (2018). *The Effects of Rent Control Expansion on Tenants, Landlords, and Inequality: Evidence from San Francisco*. Stanford, CA: Stanford University.

16. Here & Now Anytime. (2023, May 2). Research Finds Rent Control Reduces Affordability in Long Run; Supreme Court Reform. *Here & Now Anytime*. National Public Radio.

17. Preston, D., & Singh, S. (2018). *Rent Control Works: A Response to Business School Professors' Misguided Attack on Rent Control*. Tenants Together, 2.

18. Asquith, B. J. (2019). *Do Rent Increases Reduce the Housing Supply under Rent Control? Evidence from Evictions in San Francisco*. W. E. Upjohn Institute, 42.

19. Ibid., 4.

20. Gilderbloom & Ye (2008), 67, 68.

21. Kemeny, J. (1988). Defining Housing Reality: Ideological Hegemony and Power in Housing Research. *Housing Studies, 3*(4), 205–218.

22. Kemeny, J. (1992). *Housing and Social Theory*. New York: Routledge, 34.

23. Ibid., xvi.

24. Ibid., xvii.

25. Ibid., 10.

26. Rosenthal, T. J. (2019). 101 Notes on the LA Tenants Union (You Can't Do Politics Alone). *Housing Justice in Unequal Cities*, 51.

CHAPTER 1

1. Botros, A., Berger, C., & Lake, S. (2024, March 16). Homeowners Are Red, Renters Are Blue: The Broken Housing Market Is Merging with America's Polarized Political Culture. *Fortune*. https://fortune.com/2024/03/16/homeowners-red-renters-blue-broken-housing-market-polarized-political-culture/.

2. Shlay, A. B. (2015). Life and Liberty in the Pursuit of Housing: Rethinking Renting and Owning in Post-Crisis America. *Housing Studies, 30*(4), 561.

3. Gowan, P., & Cooper, R. (2018). *Social Housing in the United States*. People's Policy Project.

4. Neeson, J. M. (1993). *Commoners: Common Right, Enclosure and Social Change in England, 1700–1820*. Cambridge: Cambridge University Press, 177.

5. Blomley, N. (2003). Law, Property, and the Geography of Violence: The Frontier, the Survey, and the Grid. *Annals of the Association of American Geographers, 93*(1), 126.

6. Polanyi, C. (1944). *The Great Transformation: The Political and Economic Origins of Our Time*. Boston: Beacon, 37.

7. Neeson (1993), 133.

8. Ibid.

9. Marx, as cited in Huron, A. (2018). *Carving Out the Commons: Tenant Organizing and Housing Cooperatives in Washington, D.C.* Minneapolis: University of Minnesota Press.

10. U.K. Parliament. (2023). *Enclosing the Land.* Available at https://www.parliament .uk/about/living-heritage/transformingsociety/towncountry/landscape/overview /enclosingland/.

11. Vale, L. (2000). *From the Puritans to the Projects: Public Housing and Public Neighbors.* Cambridge, MA: Harvard University Press, 22.

12. Heskin, A. D. (1983). *Tenants and the American Dream: Ideology and the Tenant Movement.* New York: Praeger. Heskin's book is one of the only studies about the tenant movement in Santa Monica.

13. Vale (2000), 96.

14. Wright, G. (1981). *Building the Dream: A Social History of Housing in America.* Cambridge: MA: MIT Press.

15. Heskin (1983).

16. Hutchison, J. (2000). Shaping Housing and Enhancing Consumption: Hoover's Interwar Housing Policy. In J. Bauman, R. Biles, & K. Szylvian (Eds.), *From Tenements to the Taylor Homes: In Search of an Urban Housing Policy in Twentieth-Century America.* University Park: Pennsylvania State University Press.

17. Garb, M. (2005). *City of American Dreams: A History of Home Ownership and Housing Reform in Chicago, 1871–1919.* Chicago: University of Chicago Press.

18. Vale (2000), 119.

19. Garb (2005).

20. Vale (2000).

21. Stone, M. (1986). Housing and the Dynamics of Capitalism. In R. G. Bratt, C. Hartman, & A. Meyerson (Eds.), *Critical Perspectives on Housing.* Philadelphia: Temple University Press, 53.

22. See Stone (1986); Ronald, R. (2008). *The Ideology of Home Ownership: Homeowner Societies and the Role of Housing.* London: Palgrave Macmillan.

23. Hanchett, T. W. (2000). The Other "Subsidized Housing": Federal Aid to Suburbanization, 1940s–1960s. In J. Bauman, R. Biles, & K. Szylvian (Eds.), *From Tenements to the Taylor Homes: In Search of an Urban Housing Policy in Twentieth-Century America.* University Park: Pennsylvania State University Press.

24. Davis, M. (2012). *Questioning Homeownership as a Public Policy Goal.* Policy Analysis, 696.

25. Oregon Center for Public Policy. (2024). Property Tax Freeze for Seniors Erodes Funding for Local Services and Worsens Inequities.

26. Kemeny, J. (1986). A Critique of Homeownership. In R. G. Bratt, C. Hartman, & A. Meyerson (Eds.), *Critical Perspectives on Housing.* Philadelphia: Temple University Press.

27. Joint Center for Housing Studies of Harvard University. (2023). *The State of the Nation's Housing 2023.* Available at https://www.jchs.harvard.edu/state-nations-hous ing-2023.

28. Ehlenz, M. (2014). *Community Land Trusts and Limited Equity Cooperatives: A Marriage of Affordable Homeownership Models?* Lincoln Institute of Land Policy, Working Paper 4.

29. See Saegert, S., Fields, D., & Libman, K. (2009). Deflating the Dream: Radical Risk and the Neoliberalization of Homeownership. *Journal of Urban Affairs, 31*(3), 297–317.

30. See Davis (2012); Cox, K. (1982). Housing Tenure and Neighborhood Activism. *Urban Affairs Quarterly, 18*(1), 107–129.

31. Rohe, W., McCarthy, G., & Van Zandt, S. (2000). *The Social Benefits and Costs of Homeownership: A Critical Assessment of the Research.* Research Institute for Housing America.

32. Goetz, E., & Sidney, M. (1994). Revenge of the Property Owners: Community Development and the Politics of Property. *Center for Urban & Regional Affairs, 16*(4), 319–334.

33. U.S. Department of Housing and Urban Development. (1995). Urban Policy Brief, No. 2.

34. Ronald (2008), 34.

35. Carson, A., Chappell, N., & Dujela, K. (2010). Power Dynamics and Perceptions of Neighborhood Attachment and Involvement: Effects of Length of Residency versus Home Ownership. *Housing, Theory and Society, 27*(2), 162–177.

36. Hooper, M., & Cadstedt, J. (2014). Moving beyond "Community" Participation: Perceptions of Renting and the Dynamics of Participation around Urban Development in Dar es Salaam, Tanzania. *International Planning Studies, 19*(1), 25–44.

37. Portney, K. E., & Berry, J. M. (1997). Mobilizing Minority Communities: Social Capital and Participation in Urban Neighborhoods. *American Behavioral Scientist, 40*(5), 632–644.

38. Joselit, J. W. (1986). The Landlord as Czar Pre–World War I. In R. Lawson (Ed.), *The Tenant Movement in New York City, 1904–1984* (39–50). New Brunswick, NJ: Rutgers University Press.

39. Spencer, J. (1986). New York City Tenant Organization and the Post–World War I Housing Crisis. In R. Lawson (Ed.), *The Tenant Movement in New York City, 1904–1984* (51–93). New Brunswick, NJ: Rutgers University Press.

40. Naison, M. (1986). From Eviction Resistance to Rent Control: Tenant Activism in the Great Depression. In R. Lawson (Ed.), *The Tenant Movement in New York City, 1904–1984* (94–133). New Brunswick, NJ: Rutgers University Press.

41. Pastor, M., Carter, V., & Abood, M. (2018). *Rent Matters: What Are the Impacts of Rent Stabilization Measures?* USC Dornsife Program for Environmental and Regional Equity.

42. Ambrosius, J., Gilderbloom, J., William, S., Meares, W., & Keating, D. (2015). Forty Years of Rent Control: Reexamining New Jersey's Moderate Local Policies after the Great Recession. *Cities, 49*.

43. Keating, D., & Kahn, M. (2002). Rent Control in the New Millennium. *Race, Poverty & the Environment, 9*(1), 30–33.

44. More information about this historic act is available at https://housingjusticeforall.org/housing-stability-and-tenant-protection-act-of-2019/.

45. Fairbanks, R. B. (2000). From Better Dwellings to Better Neighborhoods: The Rise and Fall of the First National Housing Movement. In J. Bauman, R. Biles, & K. Szylvian (Eds.), *From Tenements to the Taylor Homes: In Search of an Urban Housing Policy in Twentieth-Century America* (21–42). University Park: Pennsylvania State University Press; Veiller, L. (1910). *Housing Reform: A Hand-Book for Practical Use in American Cities.* New York, NY. Russell Sage Foundation.

46. Karolak, Eric J. (2000). "No Idea of Doing Anything Wonderful": The Labor-Crisis Origins of National Housing Policy and the Reconstruction of the Working-Class Community, 1917-1919. In J. Bauman, R. Biles, & K. Szylvian (Eds.), *From Tenements to the Taylor Homes: In Search of an Urban Housing Policy in Twentieth-Century America* (60–80). University Park: Pennsylvania State University Press.

47. Quoted in Ibid., 62.

48. Hutchison (2000), 81–101.

49. Radford, G. (2000). The Federal Government and Housing in the Great Depression. In J. Bauman, R. Biles, & K. Szylvian (Eds.), *From Tenements to the Taylor Homes:*

In Search of an Urban Housing Policy in Twentieth-Century America (102–120). University Park: Pennsylvania State University Press.

50. Ibid., 110.

51. Marcuse, P., & Keating, W. D. (2006). The Permanent Housing Crisis: The Failures of Conservatism and the Limitations of Liberalism. In R. Bratt, M. Stone, & C. Hartman (Eds.) *A Right to Housing: Foundation for a New Social Agenda* (139–162). Philadelphia: Temple University Press.

52. Radford (2000), 117.

53. Harvey, D. (2005). *A Brief History of Neoliberalism.* Oxford: Oxford University Press.

54. Gowan & Cooper (2018).

55. Carter, Z. D. (2020). *The Price of Peace: Money, Democracy, and the Life of John Maynard Keynes.* New York: Random House.

56. Harvey (2005).

57. Marcuse & Keating (2006).

58. Swanstrom, T. (1989). No Room at the Inn: Housing Policy and the Homeless. *Washington University Journal of Urban and Contemporary Law, 081.*

59. Scally, C., Gold, A., & DuBois, N. (2018.). *The Low Income Housing Tax Credit: How It Works and Who It Serves.* Urban Institute.

60. U.S. Office of Policy Development and Research. (n.d.) Low-Income Housing Tax Credit (LIHTC). Available at https://www.huduser.gov/portal/datasets/lihtc.html.

61. Dawkins, C. (2013). The Spatial Pattern of Low Income Housing Tax Credit Properties: Implications for Fair Housing and Poverty Deconcentration Policies. *Journal of the American Planning Association, 79*(3), 222–234.

62. Aurand, A., & Stater, K. (2018). *BALANCING Preservation and Neighborhood Opportunity in the PRIORITIES: Low-Income Housing Tax Credit Program beyond Year 30.* National Low Income Housing Coalition and Public and Affordable Housing Research Corporation.

63. Scally, Gold, & DuBois (2018).

64. Harvey (2005).

65. Harvey, D. (1983). The Urban Process under Capitalism: A Framework for Analysis. In Robert W. Lake (Ed.), *Readings in Urban Analysis: Perspectives on Urban Form and Structure.* Transaction, 116–124.

66. Harvey, D. (2001). Globalization and the "Spatial Fix." *Geographische Revue, 2,* 24.

67. Dardin, J. T., Hill, R. C., Thomas, J., & Thomas, R. (1987) *Detroit: Race and Uneven Development.* Philadelphia: Temple University Press, 11.

68. See Gibson, K. (2007). Bleeding Albina: A History of Community Disinvestment, 1940–2000. *Transforming Anthropology, 15*(1), 3–25.

69. Wyly, E., Ponder, C. S., Nettling, P., Ho, B., & Fung, E. (2012). New Racial Meanings of Housing in America. *American Quarterly, 64*(3), 571–604.

70. Yardi Matrix. (2022, July). *Build-to-Rent Fuels Growth in Institutional Single-Family Rental Market.* Yardi Matrix.

71. Fields, D., & Uffer, S. (2016). The Financialization of Rental Housing: A Comparative Analysis of New York City and Berlin. *Urban Studies, 53*(7), 1486–1502.

72. Wyly, E. (2013). Why (Not a Right to) Housing? *Housing Policy Debate, 23*(1). 29–34.

73. Fields & Uffer (2016), 5.

74. Coalition for Economic Survival & Anti-Eviction Mapping Project. (2024). *Map of Ellis Act Evictions in Los Angeles.* Coalition for Economic Survival.

75. Baxter, D. (2017). *Assessing Risk and Security in the Housing Market: A Mixed-Methods Exploration of Involuntary Mobility.* Doctoral Dissertation, University of York, 2.

76. Morris, A., Hulse, K., & Pawson, H. (2017). Long-Term Private Renters: Perceptions of Security and Insecurity. *Journal of Sociology, 53*(3), 653–669.

77. Desmond, M., Gershenson, C., & Kiviat, B. (2015). Forced Relocation and Residential Instability among Urban Renters. *Social Service Review, 89*(2), 227–262.

78. Desmond, M. (2016). *Evicted: Poverty and Profit in the American City.* Milwaukee, WI: Crown Books.

79. Cox, R., Wenzel, S. C., & Rice, E. (2016). Roadmap to a Unified Measure of Housing Insecurity. CESR-Schaeffer Working Paper No. 2016-013. https://papers.ssrn.com/sol3/papers.cfm?abstract_id=2817626#.

80. Pollack, C. E., Griffin, B. A., & Lynch, J. (2010). Housing Affordability and Health among Homeowners and Renters. *American Journal of Preventive Medicine, 39*(6), 515–521.

81. Suglia, S. F., Duarte, C. S., & Sandel, M. T. (2011). Housing Quality, Housing Instability, and Maternal Mental Health. *Journal of Urban Health, 88*(6), 1105–1116.

82. Mason, K. E., Baker, E., Blakely, T., & Bentley, R. J. (2013). Housing Affordability and Mental Health: Does the Relationship Differ for Renters and Home Purchasers? *Social Science & Medicine, 94*, 91.

83. Greene, D., Tehranifar, P., Hernandez-Cordero, L. J., & Fullilove, M. T. (2011). I Used to Cry Every Day: A Model of the Family Process of Managing Displacement. *Journal of Urban Health, 88*(3), 404.

84. Skobba, K., & Goetz, E. (2013). Mobility Decisions of Very Low-Income Households. *Cityscape, 15*(2), 155–171.

85. Manzo, L., Kleit, R., & Couch, D. (2008). "Moving Three Times Is Like Having Your House on Fire Once": The Experience of Place and Impending Displacement among Public Housing Residents. *Urban Studies, 45*(9), 1855.

86. Joint Center for Housing Studies of Harvard University. (2025). *The State of the Nation's Housing 2025.* https://www.jchs.harvard.edu/state-nations-housing-2025.

87. Colburn, G., & Allen, R. (2018). Rent Burden and the Great Recession in the USA. *Urban Studies, 55*(1), 226.

88. Harvey (2005).

CHAPTER 2

1. Rose, S. (n.d.). Tenants Victimized by Gouging Landlords. *Santa Monica Evening Outlook.*

2. Kroft, S. (2013). Catching Whitey Bulger; Mob Hitman; An FBI Agent and the Mafia. *60 Minutes.*

3. See Čapek, S. M., & Gilderbloom, J. I. (1992). *Community versus Commodity: Tenants and the American City.* Albany: State University of New York Press.

4. McWilliams, C. (1946). *Southern California Country: An Island on the Land.* Duell, Sloan, & Pearce.

5. Santa Monica History Museum. (n.d.). Santa Monica History. Available at https://santamonicahistory.org/santa-monica-history/.

6. Roderick, K., & Lynxwiler J. E. (2005). *Wilshire Boulevard: The Grand Concourse of Los Angeles.* Angel City Press.

7. Pacific Pier: Santa Monica Pier. (2018, September 21). *History of the Santa Monica Pier.* Pacific Park Santa Monica Pier. Available at https://pacpark.com/history-of-the-santa-monica-pier/.

8. McCoy, H. (1935). *They Shoot Horses, Don't They?* Simon & Schuster.

9. Santa Monica Municipal Airport. (n.d.). *Santa Monica Airport (SMO) History.* City of Santa Monica. Available at https://www.smgov.net/departments/airport/history.aspx.

10. Santa Monica Travel and Tourism. (n.d.). *Santa Monica Tourism.* Santa Monica Travel and Tourism. Available at https://www.santamonica.com/economic-value-of -tourism/.

11. U.S. Census Bureau. (2021). QuickFacts. U.S. Census Bureau. Available at https:// www.census.gov/quickfacts/fact/table/US/PST045224.

12. Chen, C. (2021). *Los Angeles Metro Report.* Zumper. Available at https://www .zumper.com/apartments-for-rent/los-angeles-ca#rent-report. Note: though this report is periodically updated, Santa Monica remained the most expensive area in 2024.

13. Santa Monica Rent Control Board. (2020). *2020 Annual Report Santa Monica Rent Control Board.* City of Santa Monica.

14. Ibid., 22.

15. AAGLA. (n.d.). History. Available at https://aagla.org/history/.

16. Belinkoff Katz, A. (2018). *People Are Simply Unable to Pay the Rent: What History Tells Us about Rent Control in Los Angeles.* UCLA Luskin Center for History and Policy.

17. Heskin, A. D. (1983). *Tenants and the American Dream: Ideology and the Tenant Movement.* New York: Praeger, 39. Unless otherwise noted, Heskin's book is the source for all historical information in this section.

18. Čapek & Gilderbloom (1992).

19. Brennenman, D. (1977, September 28). *Santa Monica Rent Control Fight Brews.* Evening Outlook. From personal collection.

20. Čapek & Gilderbloom (1992), 67.

21. Jim Conn, personal interview, 2021.

22. Los Angeles County Assessor. (2024). *Proposition 13.* Los Angeles County. Available at https://assessor.lacounty.gov/real-estate-toolkit/proposition-13.

23. Picker, L. (2005, April 1). *The Lock-In Effect of California's Proposition 13.* National Bureau of Economic Research. Available at https://www.nber.org/digest/apr05/lock -effect-californias-proposition-13.

24. Bock, A. (1979, April 11). 54.3 % back Prop. A. *Evening Outlook.* In personal collection.

25. Ibid.

26. Goldman, J. (1987, February 26). High Court's Action Kills Challenge to Rent Control Goldman. *Los Angeles Times.*

27. City of Santa Monica. (1979, November 6). Sample Ballot & Voter Information Pamphlet, Special Municipal Election; Stavnezer, M. (1979, December). *Free Venice Beachhead,* 120.

28. Gross, L. (2009, November 25). *West Hollywood: City Built on Rent Control Celebrates 25th Anniversary.* Tenants Together.

29. Čapek & Gilderbloom (1992), 94.

30. Greenstein, personal interview, 2018.

31. Conn (2021).

32. Elena Popp, personal interview, 2021.

33. Heskin (1983), 56.

34. Čapek & Gilderbloom (1992), 136.

35. Abrams, G. (1992, April 26). Wealth Possessed: Love, Money and Property Don't Always Mix—Just Ask Hannah Nash and Her Estranged Sons. *Los Angeles Times.* https:// www.latimes.com/archives/la-xpm-1992-04-26-vw-1120-story.html.

36. Ryon, R. (1986, October 5). Ellis Act Faces an Uncertain Future: Legislation That Gave Landlords a Non-Rental Option May Backfire. *Los Angeles Times*.

37. Larsen, D. (1986, June 22). The Ellis Act: Going-Out-of-Business Bill for Santa Monica Landlords? *Los Angeles Times*.

38. Keyser Marston Associates. (2017). *The Ellis Act and Its Effects on Rent-Stabilized Housing in Santa Monica: A Study of Factors Leading to Withdrawal and Possible Mitigation Strategies*. Keyser Marston Associates.

39. Santa Monica Rent Control Board (2020).

40. Goldman, J. (1986, September 14). City Atty. to Pursue Legal Options Santa Monica Calls for Challenge to Ellis Act. *Los Angeles Times*.

41. Wilkinson, T. (1988, August 14). Tests of Ellis Act Put Landlords, Tenants on Hold. *Los Angeles Times*.

42. Moran, J. (1989, August 13). Santa Monica Renters Face Sharp Rise in Evictions. *Los Angeles Times*.

43. Wilkinson (1988, August 14).

44. Wilkinson, T. (1988, May 19). Landlords Raise Voices in Protest of Rent Control. *Los Angeles Times*.

45. *Los Angeles Times*. (1989, February 25). Local News in Brief: Rent Control Wins Round in U.S. Court. *Los Angeles Times*.

46. Wilkinson, T. (1989, April 29). Death Threats and Long Waiting Lists—Santa Monica: A House Divided by Rent Control. *Los Angeles Times*.

47. Moran, J. (1990, March 1). Report Confirms Rising Rental Unit Withdrawal Rates—Santa Monica: Rent Board Officials Hope to Persuade the Legislature to Change the Ellis Act That Allows Landlords to Pull Out of the Housing Market. *Los Angeles Times*.

48. Hill-Holtzman, N. (1990, July 29). Rent Control at a Crossroads in Santa Monica. *Los Angeles Times*.

49. Ibid.

50. Moran, J. (1990, November 2). Santa Monica Voters May Change City's Direction Election: Ballot: Includes Measures Dealing with the Homeless, Rent Control and Development. "There's a Different Wind Blowing," Says a Retiring Councilman. *Los Angeles Times*.

51. Moran, J. (1991, November 8). Evictions Predicted as Landlords Fail in Bid to Ease Rent Control—Santa Monica: Landlord Backed Prop. U Is Defeated. Tenants Rights Advocates' Rival Measure, Prop. W, Will Be Decided by Absentee Ballots. *Los Angeles Times*.

52. *Los Angeles Times*. (1990, November 22). Santa Monica Vote Publication Info. *Los Angeles Times*.

53. Hill-Holtzman, N. (1992, February 1). Santa Monica Softens Its Tough Rent Control Law Housing: A Major Revision Allows for One-Time-Only Increases on Units with Historically Low Fees, but Only if They Are Voluntarily Vacated. *Los Angeles Times*.

54. Santa Monica Rent Control Board. (1994). *Annual Report*. City of Santa Monica.

55. *Los Angeles Times*. (1991, June 5). Appeals Court Upholds Rent Control Law. *Los Angeles Times*.

56. Vanzi, M. (1995, July 25). Legislature Deals Blow to Rent Control. *Los Angeles Times*.

57. Moore, M. (1995, December 27). Era of Strict Rental Controls Comes to a Close Jan. 1 in 5 California Cities; Housing: State Law Means Rents in the Municipalities,

Including Santa Monica and West Hollywood, Can Rise 15% if Tenants Move. Local Officials Say They Can't Stop It. *Los Angeles Times*.

58. Glionna, J. (1997, May 27). Rent Wars Escalate in Santa Monica. *Los Angeles Times*.

59. *Los Angeles Times*. (1997, August 19). Santa Monica—Suit Accuses Landlord of Trying to Coerce Tenants into Leaving. *Los Angeles Times*.

60. Rhoades, G. (2013, January 3). Untitled press release. Public Rights Division.

61. Howard, B. (1999, May 18). In Rent Control's Wake, Santa Monica Shores Fetches $95 Million. *Los Angeles Times*.

62. Dolan, M. (1999, January 5). California and the West; State's High Court Upholds Cities' Rent Control Laws; Judiciary: Ruling in Santa Monica Case Comes Even as New Law Scales Back Ordinances in Some Locales. The Decision Is Seen as a Broad Victory for Municipalities. *Los Angeles Times*.

63. Santa Monica City Attorney. *Item 9-B, City Council Meeting 01–26–99*. Santa Monica City Attorney.

64. Welch, D. (1999, April 27). Activist Wins Council Seat in Unique Vote. *Los Angeles Times*.

65. City of Santa Monica. (2015, December 18). *Election 2002: Santa Monica Municipal Election Information*.

66. Holland, G. (2007, December 4). California in Brief/Rent Control Challenge Rejected. *Los Angeles Times*.

67. Hanatani, M. (2009, November 3). Landlords Busted by City Task Force. *Santa Monica Daily Press*.

68. *Santa Monica Daily Press*. (2010, March 18). SM Adds to Stock of Rent Controlled Units. *Santa Monica Daily Press*.

69. *Santa Monica Daily Press*. (2010, June 3). Rent Control Board Wants Powers Expanded. *Santa Monica Daily Press*.

70. *Santa Monica Daily Press*. (2010, June 24). Voters to Decide Expanded Tenant Protections. *Santa Monica Daily Press*.

71. Archibald, A. (2012, May 12). Rent Control Changes Game for Landlords. *Santa Monica Daily Press*.

72. *Santa Monica Daily Press*. (2012, June 16). Rents to Rise as Much as $26 a Month, or 1.54%. *Santa Monica Daily Press*.

73. Ballotpedia. (2012, November). City of Santa Monica Rent Control Adjustments, Measure GA. Ballotpedia.

74. *Santa Monica Daily Press*. (2012, May 2). Rent Control Tenants Sue Landlord to Stop Alleged Harassment. *Santa Monica Daily Press*.

75. Archibald, A. (2013, July 18). City Settles Tenant Harassment Complaints. *Santa Monica Daily Press*.

76. Herrera, K. (2014, March 4). City Attorney, Landlord Resolve Harassment Complaints. *Santa Monica Daily Press*.

77. Simpson, D. M. (2014, April 14). Tenant Harassment Claims Rising. *Santa Monica Daily Press*.

78. Simpson, D. M. (2014, July 25). Council Wants Rising Tenant Complaints Addressed. *Santa Monica Daily Press*.

79. Simpson, D. M. (2014, October 1). City Attorney: Stopping Tenant Harassment Takes Muscle. *Santa Monica Daily Press*.

80. Simpson, D. M. (2014, December 23). Council Tightens Tenant Harassment Laws. *Santa Monica Daily Press*.

81. Hall, M. (2016, April 7). Council Asked to Act on Tenant Protections, Pass on New Noise Rules. *Santa Monica Daily Press.*

82. Simpson, D. M. (2015, May 7). Landlord Discrimination against Section 8 Vouchers Outlawed. *Santa Monica Daily Press.*

83. Sanders, S. (2015, May 13). Santa Monica Cracks Down on Airbnb, Bans "Vacation Rentals" under a Month. National Public Radio.

84. *Santa Monica Daily Press.* (2017, March 25). Rent Control Board Supports Bill to Repeal Costa-Hawkins Act. *Santa Monica Daily Press.*

85. *Santa Monica Daily Press.* (2017, April 18). Code Compliance Officers Charged with Increased Responsibility for Tenant Harassment Cases. *Santa Monica Daily Press.*

86. Pauker, M. (2018, December 15). Sultan Begins Reign on Rent Control Board. *Santa Monica Daily Press.*

87. Costello, D. (2018, August 30). Court Declares That Landlords Can't Circumvent Rent Limits by Charging Extra for Water. *Santa Monica Daily Press.*

88. Farrell, C. (2018, May 14). Santa Monica City Council Approves Ordinance to Enhance Tenant Protections for Educators and Students Facing No-Fault Evictions. *Santa Monica Daily Press.*

89. Wachtel, I. (2018, August 15). Santa Monica City Council Unanimously Back Prop 10 to End Skyrocketing Rents. Businesswire.

90. This projection was based on a 2014 study about the housing market after rent control ended in Cambridge, MA. Autor. D., Palmer, C., & Pathak, P. (2014). Housing Market Spillovers: Evidence from the End of Rent Control in Cambridge, Massachusetts. *Journal of Political Economy.* 122(3), 381–384.

91. All donation data from the California secretary of state.

92. Dillon, L. (2018, November 6). Voters Reject Proposition 10, Halting Effort to Expand Rent Control across the State. *Los Angeles Times.*

93. Dillon, L. (2018, October 31). How California Became a National Battleground for Rent Control as Money Flows in from Landlords. *Los Angeles Times.*

94. Pauker, M. (2019, January 10). City Expands Benefits for Evicted Tenants. *Santa Monica Daily Press.*

95. Pauker, M. (2019, September 12). Tenants of Small Buildings Now Qualify for Relocation Benefits. *Santa Monica Daily Press.*

96. Pauker, M. (2019, May 13). Rent Control Board Asking for Restrictions on Renovations. *Santa Monica Daily Press.*

97. Pauker, M. (2019, March 14). Rent Control Report Highlights Value of Long-Term Occupancy. *Santa Monica Daily Press.*

98. Pauker, M. (2019, December 17). Universal Legal Representation for Renters Would Cost up to $1 Million. *Santa Monica Daily Press.*

99. City of Santa Monica. (2021, April 8). City Launches Pilot Right to Counsel Program to Help Santa Monica Tenants Facing Eviction. City of Santa Monica website.

100. *Santa Monica Daily Press.* (2019, April 19). Citywide—City Attorney Files Multiple Criminal Charges in Tenant Harassment Case. *Santa Monica Daily Press.*

101. Pauker, M. (2019, December 2). Landlords Fined for Harassing Tenants. *Santa Monica Daily Press.*

102. Dixson, B. (2020, October 6). New Ordinance Takes Effect Tuesday but Revisions Are Coming. *Santa Monica Daily Press.*

103. Harter, C. (2020, November 16). Re-elected Rent Control Board Talks Shop. *Santa Monica Daily Press.*

104. Ballotpedia. (2020). California Proposition 21, Local Rent Control Initiative. Ballotpedia.

105. Harter (2020, November 16).

106. Santa Monicans for Renters Rights. (2021, April 23). *Rental Assistance and Tenant Protections* (Zoom seminar).

107. *Santa Monica Daily Press.* (2021, February 3). City Sues Santa Monica Landlords for Fraudulently Trying to Evict Rent-Controlled Tenants during COVID-19 Pandemic. *Santa Monica Daily Press.*

108. Harter, C. (2021, October 6). City Sues NMS Properties over Alleged Illegal Evictions and Unlawful Rentals. *Santa Monica Daily Press.*

109. Manzo, L. C. (2003). Beyond House and Haven: Toward a Revisioning of Emotional Relationships with Places. *Journal of Environmental Psychology, 23*(1), 47–61.

CHAPTER 3

1. Reyes, E. A. (2021, April 14). Proposed L.A. Law Banning Landlords from Harassing Renters Clears Key Hurdle. *Los Angeles Times.*

2. Duringer, S. (2019, August). Legal Corner. *Apartment Age,* 84.

3. Yukelson, D. (2020, February). The Former Golden State of California. *Apartment Age,* 51.

4. Vaughan, E. (2020, November). Board President's Message: Advocating for Our Common Good. *Apartment Age,* 13–14.

5. Vaughan, E. (2020, August). Board President's Message. *Apartment Age,* 13.

6. Vaughan, E. (2019, August). Board President's Message. *Apartment Age,* 11.

7. Yukelson, D. (2020, June). Message from AAGLA's Executive Director. *Apartment Age,* 17.

8. Yukelson, D. (2020, November). Message from AAGLA's Executive Director: Waiting for the Next Shoe to Drop. *Apartment Age,* 17.

9. Duringer, S. (2019, August). Legal Corner. *Apartment Age, 46*(8), 84–85.

10. Yukelson, D. (2019, August). Message From AAGLA's Executive Director. *Apartment Age,* 19.

11. Yukelson, D. (2020, March). Message From AAGLA's Executive Director. *Apartment Age,* 19.

12. Yukelson, D. (2020, May). Are Los Angeles Area Renters Better Off Than They Were 40 Years Ago? Definitely Not. *Apartment Age,* 19.

13. Vaughan, E. (2020, April). "A Moratorium on Evictions? No F-ing Way!" *Apartment Age,* 13–14.

14. No author. (2020, May). *Apartment Age,* 59.

15. Greenberg, H. (2020, August). *Apartment Age,* 20.

16. Brook, Y. (2020, October). The Looting of Landlords. *Apartment Age,* 96.

17. Dunford, O. (2021, March). Guest Editorial: San Francisco Cannot Foist the Pandemic's Economic Burden onto Landlords. *Apartment Age,* 13.

18. Vargas, I. (2021, March). Essential Workers: Landlords Are Heroes Too! *Apartment Age,* 43.

19. Greenberg, H. (2021, January). I'm Mad as Hell: I Will Not Take It Any Longer! *Apartment Age,* 73.

20. Stein, J. (2021, February). A Comparison between Artichoke Hearts and Residential Rental Real Estate. *Apartment Age.*

21. Yukelson, D. (2020, September). Sometimes It Can Be the Little Things That Count in Life. *Apartment Age*, 17.

22. Yukelson, D. (2020, October). *Apartment Age*, 6.

23. Yukelson, D. (2021, January). Executive Director's Message. *Apartment Age*, 19.

24. Yukelson, D. (2021, February). Executive Director's Message. *Apartment Age*, 19.

25. Crown, D. (2019, August). The Property Manager's Guide to Renter Selection. *Apartment Age*, 80.

26. Negri, K. (2019, November). Ask Kari. *Apartment Age*, 74.

27. Fast Evict Law Group. (2021, February). Learn How to Deal with Dirty Tenants. *Apartment Age*, 101.

28. Fast Eviction Service. (2020, February). Obvious Signs That Should Cause You to Avoid Accepting a Tenant. *Apartment Age*, 95.

29. Swearer, A and Canaparo, G. (2019, November). New York City's Rent Control Laws Erase Property Rights and Worsen Housing Supply. *Apartment Age*, 66.

30. Coupal, J. (2020, February). *Apartment Age*, 17.

31. Shelley, S. (2020, February). California's War on Private Property Rights. *Apartment Age*, 57.

32. Valdez, R. (2020, June). Prediction for 2030: A Government Take Over of Rental Housing. *Apartment Age*, 86; Madden, D., & Marcuse, P. (2016). *In Defense of Housing*. Brooklyn, NY: Verso.

33. Valdez, R. (2020, July). Prediction for 2030: Government Can Help Housing by Doing Less. *Apartment Age*, 84.

34. Negri, K. (2021, February). Ask Kari. *Apartment Age*, 58.

35. No author. (2020, June). Santa Monica Rent Control Board Sets Annual Increase at Just 1.4% with a Likely $32 Monthly "Cap." *Apartment Age*, 49.

36. Valdez, R. (2020, September). Prediction for 2030: Can We Stop the Government Take Over of Rental Housing? *Apartment Age*, 64.

37. Wright, R. (2020, October). Proposition 21 Escalates: "The War on Mom and Pop Rental Property Owners." *Apartment Age*, 57.

38. Stein (2021, February), 92–93.

39. Turner, C. (2021, April). A Message from the President. *Apartment Age*, 13.

40. Block, W. (2021, March). Why Do We So Readily "Kid Glove" Those Who Don't Pay Their Rent? *Apartment Age*, 104.

41. Ibid., 105.

42. Burrus, T., & Spiegelman, S. (2021, April). Are Rent Control Laws Unconstitutional? *Apartment Age*, 89.

43. Yukelson (2020, February), 51.

44. Sherry, D. (2020, December). Rent Control: A Cautionary Tale of the City of Santa Monica. *Apartment Age*, 71.

45. Cox, H. (2021, January). California Voters Reject Economically Illiterate "Rent Control" Ballot Measure. *Apartment Age*, 97.

46. Vaughan, E. (2019, November). Message from the President. *Apartment Age*, 10.

47. Diamond, R., McQuade, T., & Qian, F. (2019). *The Effects of Rent Control Expansion on Tenants, Landlords, and Inequality: Evidence from San Francisco*. Stanford, CA: Stanford University.

48. Millsap, A. (2020, April). More Rent Control in California Will Make Housing Problem Worse. *Apartment Age*.

49. Vaughan, E. (2019, September). Message from AAGLA's President. *Apartment Age*, 10.

50. Weiser, F. (2020, June). Opportunities to Challenge California's Rent Control Ordinances under the Fifth Amendment Takings Clause under the U.S. Constitution. *Apartment Age*, 54–55.

51. Foster, A., personal interview, 2021.

52. See Fields, D., & Uffer, S. (2016); Fields (2017). The Financialization of Rental Housing: A Comparative Analysis of New York City and Berlin. *Urban Studies*, 53(7), 1486–1502; Fields, D. (2017). Unwilling Subjects of Financialization. *International Journal of Urban and Regional Research*, 41(4), 588–603.

53. See George (1879); Barton (2010); Hern (2016). George, H. (1879). Progress and Poverty: An Inquiry Into the Cause of Industrial Depressions and of Increase of Want with Increase of Wealth: The Remedy. D. Appleton and Company; Barton, S. (2010). Land Value, Land Rent and Progressive Housing Policy. *Progressive Planning*, 185, 23–25; Hern, M. (2016). *What a City Is For: Remaking the Politics of Displacement*. Cambridge, MA; MIT Press.

54. Fields & Uffer (2016), 5.

CHAPTER 4

1. Quoted in Seamon, D., & Mugreraur, R. (1985). *Dwelling, Place and Environment: Towards a Phenomenology of Person and World*. Dordrecht: Martinus Nijhoff, 8.

2. Saegert, S. (1986). The Role of Housing in the Experience of Dwelling. In A. Altman & C. Werner (Eds.), *Home Environments*. New York: Plenum, 287–288.

3. Altman, I., & Low, S. (1992). Place Attachment: Human Behavior and Environment. *Advances in Theory and Research*. New York: Plenum.

4. Ibid.

5. Korosec-Serfaty, P. (1986). Experience and Use of the Dwelling. In A. Altman & C. Werner (Eds.), *Home Environments*. New York: Plenum.

6. Werner, C., Altman, I., & Oxley, D. (1986). Temporal Aspects of Homes: A Transactional Perspective. In A. Altman & C. Werner (Eds.), *Home Environments*. New York: Plenum.

7. Ibid.

8. Ross, A., Talmage, C. A., & Searle, M. (2020). The Impact of Neighboring on Changes in Sense of Community over Time: A Latent Transition Analysis. *Social Indicators Research*, 149(1), 327–345.

9. Hiscock, R., Kearns, A., MacIntyre, S., & Ellaway, A. (2001). Ontological Security and Psycho-Social Benefits from the Home: Qualitative Evidence on Issues of Tenure. *Housing, Theory and Society*, 18(1–2), 50–66.

10. Santa Monica Rent Control Board. (2020). *2020 Annual Report: Santa Monica Rent Control Board*. City of Santa Monica.

11. Rozena, S., & Lees, L. (2021). The Everyday Lived Experiences of Airbnbification in London. *Social & Cultural Geography*, 24(2), 264.

12. Korosec-Serfaty (1986), 65.

13. See Seamon, D. (1980). Body-Subject, Time-Space Routines, and Place-Ballets. In A. Buttimer & D. Seamon (Eds.), *The Human Experience of Space and Place*. Routledge. 148–165.

14. Rowles, G. (1990). Place Attachment among the Small Town Elderly. *Journal of Rural Community Psychology*, 11, 103–120; Lewicka, M. (2014). In Search of Roots: Memory as Enabler of Place Attachment. In L. Manzo & P. Devine-Wright (Eds.), *Place Attachment: Advanced in Theory, Methods and Applications*. Routledge.

15. Capek and Gilderbloom (1992).

16. Hummon, D. (1992). Community Attachment: Local Sentiment and Sense of Place. In A. Altman & S. Low (Eds.), *Place Attachment.* New York: Plenum.

17. See Tuttle, S. (2021). Place Attachment and Alienation from Place: Cultural Displacement in Gentrifying Ethnic Enclaves. *Critical Sociology, 48*(3), 1–15, 5.

18. See Manzo, L., & Perkins, D. (2006). Finding Common Ground: The Importance of Place Attachment to Community Participation and Planning. *Journal of Planning Literature, 20*(4), 335–350.

19. See Goetz & Sidney (1994).

20. See Oldenburg, R. (1989). *The Great Good Place.* De Capo Press.

CHAPTER 5

1. Marcuse, P. (1975). Residential Alienation, Home Ownership and the Limits of Shelter Policy. *Journal of Sociology & Social Welfare, 3*(2), 181–203.

2. Madden, D., & Marcuse, P. (2016). *In Defense of Housing.* Brooklyn, NY: Verso, 56, 60.

3. See McKee, K., Soaita, A. M., & Hoolachan, J. (2019). "Generation Rent" and the Emotions of Private Renting: Self-Worth, Status and Insecurity amongst Low-Income Renters. *Housing Studies, 35*(8), 1–20.

4. Madden & Marcuse (2016), 67.

5. Giddens, A. (1991). *Modernity and Self Identity: Self and Society in the Late Modern Age.* Stanford, CA: Stanford University Press, 50.

6. See Dupuis, A., & Thorns, D. C. (1998). Home, Home Ownership and the Search for Ontological Security. *The Sociological Review, 46*(1), 24–47; Hiscock, R., Kearns, A., MacIntyre, S., & Ellaway, A. (2001). Ontological Security and Psycho-Social Benefits from the Home: Qualitative Evidence on Issues of Tenure. *Housing, Theory and Society, 18*(1–2), 50–66; Saegert, A., Greer, A, Thaden, E. & D. Anthony. (2015). Longing for a Better American Dream: Homeowners in Trouble Evaluate Shared Equity Alternatives. *Social Science Quarterly, 96*(2), 297–312; Libman, K., Fields, D. & Saegert, S. (2012). Housing and Health: A Social Ecological Perspective on the US Foreclosure Crisis. *Housing Theory and Society, 29*(1), 1–24; Hackett, K., Saegert, S., Dozier, D. & M. Marinova. (2019). Community land trusts: releasing possible selves through stable affordable housing. *Housing Studies, 34*(1), 24–48, for housing research that explores ontological security among both renters and homeowners.

7. Hulse, K., & Milligan, V. (2014). Secure Occupancy: A New Framework for Analysing Security in Rental Housing. *Housing Studies, 29*(5), 638–656. The authors adapted Van Gelder's (2010) model of the security of tenure for their analysis.

8. Hulse, K., Morris A., & Pawson, H. (2019) Private Renting in a Home-Owning Society: Disaster, Diversity or Deviance? *Housing, Theory and Society, 36*(2), 183.

CHAPTER 6

1. Hulse, K., Milligan, V., Easthope, H., & Australian Housing and Urban Research Institute. (2011). *Secure Occupancy in Rental Housing: Conceptual Foundations and Comparative Perspectives.* Australian Housing and Urban Research Institute, 20.

2. Manzo (2003), 47.

3. Easthope, H. (2014). Making a Rental Property Home. *Housing Studies, 29*(5), 136.

4. Morris, A., Hulse, K., & Pawson, H. (2021). *The Private Rental Sector in Australia: Living with Uncertainty*. Singapore: Springer Singapore.

5. McKee, Soaita, & Hoolachan (2019).

6. Waldron, R. (2023). Experiencing Housing Precarity in the Private Rental Sector during the COVID-19 Pandemic: The Case of Ireland. *Housing Studies*, *38*(1), 101.

7. Hiscock et al. (2001).

8. See Morris, Hulse, & Pawson (2021).

9. Cheshire, L., Easthope, H., & Have, C. (2021). Unneighbourliness and the Unmaking of Home. *Housing, Theory and Society*, *38*(2), 133.

10. Burrell, K. (2014). Spilling over from the Street: Contextualizing Domestic Space in an Inner-City Neighborhood. *Home Cultures*, *11*(2), 150.

11. See Gilmore, B. G. (2020). "Everybody Loves the Landlord": Evictions & the Coming Prevention Revolution. *Mitchell Hamline Law Journal of Public Policy and Practice*, *41*(3), 201–230.

12. Byrne, M., & McArdle, R. (2020). Secure Occupancy, Power and the Landlord-Tenant Relation: A Qualitative Exploration of the Irish Private Rental Sector. *Housing Studies*, *37*(1), 1–19.

13. Chisholm, E., Howden-Chapman, P., & Fougere, G. (2020). Tenants' Responses to Substandard Housing: Hidden and Invisible Power and the Failure of Rental Housing Regulation. *Housing, Theory and Society*, *37*(2), 139–161; Lukes, S. (2004). *Power: A Radical View*. Palgrave Macmillan.

14. Morris, Hulse, & Pawson (2021).

15. Byrne & McCardle (2020).

16. Sims, D. P. (2011). Rent Control Rationing, Community Composition, and Residential Segregation. *The B.E. Journal of Economic Analysis & Policy, De Gruyter*, *11*(1), 1–30.

17. Schweitzer, B. W., Garrett, R. C., Carter, L., Tuiyott, A., Maurer, K., & Fisher, T. J. (2023). An Analysis of the Impact of Rent Control on New York City Housing. *Computational Statistics*, *38*(4), 1643–1656.

18. Feldman Equities. (n.d.). What Is the Difference between Class A, B, and C Properties? Feldman Equities. Available at https://www.feldmanequities.com/education/what-is-the-difference-between-class-a-b-and-c-properties/.

19. See Gross, M. (2020). *The Long-Term Impacts of Rent Control*. Department of Economics, University of Michigan.

20. See Hiscock et al. (2001).

21. See Trentelman, C. (2009). Place Attachment and Community Attachment: A Primer Grounded in the Lived Experience of a Community Sociologist. *Society & Natural Resources*, *22*(3), 191–210; Hummon, D. (1992). Community Attachment: Local Sentiment and Sense of Place. In A. Altman & S. Low (Eds.), *Place Attachment*. New York: Plenum.

22. See Saegert, S., & Winkel, G. (1998). Social Capital and the Revitalization of New York City's Distressed Inner-City Housing. *Housing Policy Debate*, *9*(1), 17–60; Crosby, A. (2020). Financialized Gentrification, Demoviction, and Landlord Tactics to Demobilize Tenant Organizing. *Geoforum*, *108*, 184–193; Glass, M. R., Woldoff, R. A., & Morrison, L. M. (2019). Saving the Neighbourhood: Understanding Tenant Activism in Middle-Class Manhattan. *Housing Studies*, *35*(9), 1–18.

23. Pastor, Carter, & Abood (2018).

24. Cross, S., & Markus, H. (1991). Possible Selves across the Life Span. *Human Development*, *34*, 230–255.

25. Manzo (2003), 55.

26. Lefebvre, H. (1991). *The Production of Space*. Oxford: Blackwell.

27. Tuttle, S. (2021). Place Attachment and Alienation from Place: Cultural Displacement in Gentrifying Ethnic Enclaves. *Critical Sociology, 48*(3), 5.

28. Kim, M. (2021). Plural and Fluid Place Attachment amid Tourism-Induced Neighborhood Change in a Disadvantaged Neighborhood in South Korea. *Geoforum, 121*, 129–137.

29. Hulse et al. (2011), 5.

30. Ibid., 6.

31. Hackett, K., Saegert, S., Dozier, D. & M. Marinova. (2019). Community Land Trusts: Releasing Possible Selves through Stable Affordable Housing. *Housing Studies, 34*(1), 42.

32. Davis, M. (2012), 1.

33. Hiscock et al. (2001).

34. Saegert, Fields, & Libman (2009).

35. Hulse, Morris, & Pawson (2019).

36. Keynes, J. M. (1936/1997). *The General Theory of Employment, Interest and Money*. Reprint, New York: Prometheus, 383.

CONCLUSION

1. Achtenberg, E. P., & Marcuse, P. (1986). Toward the Decommodification of Housing. In R. G. Bratt, C. Hartman, & A. Meyerson (Eds.), *Critical Perspectives on Housing*. Philadelphia: Temple University Press, 477.

2. Fuller, T. (2024, March 19). How Does Paris Stay Paris? By Pouring Billions into Public Housing. *New York Times*.

3. U.S. Department of Housing and Urban Development. (n.d.). Public Housing. Available at https://www.hud.gov/program_offices/public_indian_housing/programs/ph.

4. Brey, J. (2021, February 9). What Is the Faircloth Amendment? *Next City*.

5. See Mari, F. (2023, May 23). Imagine a Renters' Utopia. *New York Times Magazine*.

6. See Ehlenz, M. (2014). Community Land Trusts and Limited Equity Cooperatives: A Marriage of Affordable Homeownership Models? Lincoln Institute of Land Policy, Working Paper 4.

7. See Thaden, E. (2011). *Stable Home Ownership in a Turbulent Economy: Delinquencies and Foreclosures Remain Low in Community Land Trusts*. Lincoln Institute of Land Policy; Temkin, K., Theodos, B., & Price, D. (2010, October). *Balancing Affordability and Opportunity: An Evaluation of Affordable Homeownership Programs with Long-Term Affordability Controls*. Urban Institute.

8. See Hackett et al. (2019).

9. Wang, R., Wandio, C., Bennett, A., Spicer, J., Corugedo, S., & Thaden, E. (2022, June). *The 2022 Census of Community Land Trusts and Shared Equity Entities in the United States: Prevalence, Practice and Impact*. Lincoln Institute of Land Policy.

10. See Ortiz, L. (2017, April 25). Will Limited-Equity Cooperatives Make a Comeback? *Shelterforce*.

11. Davis, J. E. (2006). *Shared Equity Homeownership: The Changing Landscape of Resale-Restricted, Owner-Occupied Housing*. National Housing Institute.

12. Huron (2018).

13. PolicyLink. (n.d.). Tenant and Community Opportunity to Purchase Policies Are Gaining Traction. PolicyLink. Available at https://www.policylink.org/topa-copa-map.

14. Waters, E., Minott, O., & Lautz, A. (2023, November 2). Is It Time for Congress to Reconsider the Mortgage Interest Deduction? Bipartisan Policy Center.

15. McMillin, D. (2024, January 3). Median Home Prices in Every State. Bankrate. Available at https://www.bankrate.com/real-estate/median-home-price/#how-much.

16. City of Vancouver & Housing Vancouver. (2023). *Empty Homes Tax Annual Report: 2022 Vacancy Reference Year.* City of Vancouver.

17. City of Santa Monica. (2023, April 20). *Santa Monica Rent Control Releases Annual Report.* City of Santa Monica.

18. City of Santa Monica. (2022). *2022 Annual Report: Santa Monica Rent Control Board.* City of Santa Monica.

19. City of West Hollywood. (n.d.). *Required Maintenance and Housing Services.* City of West Hollywood.

20. Ballotpedia. (2024). California Proposition 33, Prohibit State Limitations on Local Rent Control Initiative. Ballotpedia. Available at https://ballotpedia.org/California_Proposition_33,_Prohibit_State_Limitations_on_Local_Rent_Control_Initiative_(2024)#Polls.

21. Ballotpedia. (2024). California Proposition 33, Prohibit State Limitations on Local Rent Control Initiative. Ballotpedia. Available at https://ballotpedia.org/California_Proposition_33,_Prohibit_State_Limitations_on_Local_Rent_Control_Initiative_(2024)#Campaign_finance.

22. SMRR (2024, January 23). *You Did It! Council Voted to Formally Adopt Expanded Renter Protections.* Santa Monicans for Renters Rights.

23. Snowden, S. (2024, February 9). Council Approves DEI Study and Authorizes Added Renter Protections. *Santa Monica Daily Press.*

24. National Low Income Housing Coalition. *New Renter Protections to Take Effect in Santa Monica, Including Rent Stabilization and Anti-Retaliation Measures.* National Low Income Housing Coalition.

Index

Lauren E. M. Everett is an independent scholar, artist, writer, community organizer, and public servant. Her work has appeared in the journal *Metropolitics* as well as other publications.

Also in the series *Urban Life, Landscape, and Policy*:

www.ingramcontent.com/pod-product-compliance
Lightning Source LLC
Chambersburg PA
CBHW030646270326
41929CB00007B/227